THE
EVERYTHING®
GUIDE TO
NEW YORK CITY

Hotels, restaurants, shopping, major attractions and the best-kept secret spots in the Big Apple

Rich Mintzer

Adams Media Corporation
Holbrook, Massachusetts

An Everything® Series Book.
Everything® is a registered trademark of Adams Media Corporation.

Published by Adams Media Corporation
260 Center Street, Holbrook, MA 02343. U.S.A.

ISBN: 1-58062-314-X

Printed in the United States of America.

J I H G F E D C B

Library of Congress Cataloging-in-Publication Data
Mintzer, Richard.
The everything guide to New York City / Rich Mintzer.
p.   cm.
Includes index
ISBN 1-58062-314-X
1. New York (N.Y.)—Guidebooks. I. Title.
F128.18 M56   2000
917.47'10443—dc21   99-055412
CIP

This publication is designed to provide accurate and authoritative information with regard to the subject matter covered. It is sold with the understanding that the publisher is not engaged in rendering legal, accounting, or other professional advice. If legal advice or other expert assistance is required, the services of a competent professional person should be sought.
— From a *Declaration of Principles* jointly adopted by a Committee of the American Bar Association and a Committee of Publishers and Associations

City maps by Jeffrey L. Ward
Illustrations by Barry Littmann
Subway map ©Metropolitan Transportation Authority and
New York City Transit Authority. Reprinted with permission.

*This book is available at quantity discounts for bulk purchases.
For information, call 1-800-872-5627.*

Visit our home page at www.adamsmedia.com

Contents

Acknowledgments ix
Introduction xi

Chapter 1: New York City, A Brief History 1

How It All Began 2
Stuyvesant 3
The 1700s and Growth! 4
An Inauspicious Start to Better Times Ahead 6
A Disastrous Decade and a Fun Decade 8
Tough Times and Big Buildings 9
A Couple of Jackies and a Lot of Baby Boomers 12
And Then Came the '60s! 13
From Bad to Worse 15
The Late '70s, a Slow Comeback, Despite Disco 16
New York Comes Back, Again! 17

Chapter 2: When to Go, How to Get There, and Where to Stay 21

When to Go 22
How to Get There 23
   By Car 23
   By Plane 26
   By Bus 30
   By Train 31
Travel Agents 32
Packing for Your Trip 32
Where to Stay 34
   New York Hotels 34

Hotel List 36
   Midtown (East Side)—42nd Street to 59th Street 39
   Midtown (West Side)—42nd to 59th Streets 48
   Downtown—below 42nd Street 59
   Uptown—above 59th Street 64

Chapter 3: Getting Around, Tours, and Dining 69

Getting Around 70
   Car Rentals and Car Services 72
   Mass Transit 74
   The Subway System 75
   Walking 76
   Taxis 76
Getting Around the City, for People with Disabilities 80
Tours 81
   Bus Tours 82
   Boat Tours 83
   Helicopter Tours 85
   Walking Tours 85
   Other Tours 86
Dining 87
   Finding Restaurants! 88
   101 Places to Eat! 90
Map of Greater New York City 103
Map of Manhattan: 96th to 14th Street. 105
Map of Greenwich Village and Lower Manhattan 107

Chapter 4: "Can't Miss" Sights 109

   The Apollo Theater 111
   Carnegie Hall 112
   Ellis Island National Monument 113
   The Empire State Building 115
   F.A.O. Schwarz 116

CONTENTS

Lincoln Center for the Performing Arts 117
New York Public Library 119
New York Stock Exchange 121
Radio City Music Hall 122
Rockefeller Center 123
Saint Patrick's Cathedral 126
South Street Seaport 126
Statue of Liberty 129
The United Nations 130
The World Financial Center 132
The World Trade Center 134
Shopping in NYC 135
Barney's in New York 135
Bloomingdale's 135
Macy's-Herald Square 136
Saks Fifth Avenue 136
Henri Bendel 137
Tiffany & Company 137
Cross-Cultural Department 137

Chapter 5: Marvelous Museums of the City .. 139

Abigail Adams Smith House Museum 142
American Museum of Natural History 143
Children's Museum of Manhattan 145
The Cloisters Museum 146
Cooper-Hewitt National Design Museum 147
The Frick Collection 148
The Guggenheim Museum 149
Intrepid Sea-Air-Space Museum 150
Jewish Museum 152
Lower East Side Tenement Museum 153
Metropolitan Museum of Art 154
The Museum of Modern Art 156
Museum of Television and Radio 158
The Museum of the City of New York 159
The New York City Fire Museum 160

New-York Historical Society 162
The Studio Museum in Harlem 163
Whitney Museum of American Art 164

Chapter 6: Central Park 165

Activities and Family Things To Do 166
The Central Park Wildlife Center 167
Wollman Memorial Rink 168
Playgrounds 170
The Carousel 170
The Charles A. Dana Discovery Center 171
The Swedish Cottage Marionette Theater 171
The Loeb Boathouse and the Lake 171
Tennis, Anyone? 171
Other Activities 172
Sights in the Park 172
The Arsenal 172
Bethesda Terrace 173
The Dairy 173
The Harlem Meer 173
Belvedere Castle 174
The Reservoir 174
Lawns, Gardens, and Wide-Open Spaces 175
Yes, You Can Picnic in Manhattan 175
Fine Dining 177
Other Manhattan Parks 178
Battery Park 178
Fort Tryon Park 179
Riverside Park 179
Carl Schurz Park 179
Union Square Park 180
Washington Square Park 180
Map of Central Park/North 181
Map of Central Park/South 181

CONTENTS

Chapter 7: The Neighborhoods of Manhattan ... 183

The Lower East Side 185
Chinatown and Little Italy 187
Greenwich Village 189
Times Square and 42nd Street 193
Harlem 197

Chapter 8: The Boroughs and Long Island ... 201

Brooklyn 203
   The New York City Transit Museum 204
   The New York Aquarium 205
   Coney Island 206
   The Brooklyn Botanic Gardens 208
   Brooklyn Museum of Art 209
Queens 211
   American Museum of the Moving Image 212
   Hall Of Science 213
   Queens Museum of Art 214
The Bronx 214
   The New York Botanical Garden 215
   The Bronx Zoo 216
   City Island 218
   Yankee Stadium 219
Staten Island 220
   Historic Richmond Town 221
   Fort Wadsworth 222
   Snug Harbor Cultural Center 222
Long Island 224
   Old Bethpage Village Restoration 226
   The Nassau County Museum of Art 227
   Old Westbury Gardens 227
   Sands Point Preserve 228

Chapter 9: A Year-Round Calendar of Events . . . 231

Annual New York Events 232
Madison Square Garden 235
Broadway: The Great White Way 237
Television Shows in New York! 244
Family Fun: 50 Places to Go with Kids in the City 246
Chelsea Piers 254
Sports for All Ages 254
Sports: For Spectators 257
New York after Dark 258

Index. 267

Acknowledgments

I guess it's only fair to start off by thanking New York City for being such an exciting place in which to grow up. It's not hard to take it for granted; there's so much of the world at your disposal. From an early age, my dad and I went to Mets games at Shea Stadium, within a mile of our home. And as a youngster, I remember attending the World's Fair nearly every weekend for two summers. My first visit to the United Nations was in the fifth grade on a class trip, and I took my first voyage to the Statue of Liberty in high school when I realized that I had never been there and simply took off from school to see it!

I attended Queens College in New York, and on the weekends my friends and I would set out for Greenwich Village, Sheepshead Bay, Jones or Rockaway Beach, or City Island. Today, my family and I are lucky enough to live less than half a mile from Central Park. The great park is our "neighborhood park," and I watch as my daughter climbs the rocks that I climbed as a kid.

Seeing my son's face when he looks up at the dinosaur in the Museum of Natural History or my daughter's face when we went to Madison Square Garden to see *The Wizard of Oz on Ice* can only remind me of how lucky we are to be part of such a great center of culture, art, and excitement. So, thank you, New York City.

I'd like to thank my wife Carol, more so than I usually do regarding my books. She's a great source of support, and I love her . . . and she's also a native New Yorker. Thank you, Eric and Rebecca, for putting up with Daddy's working so many evenings.

I'd also like to thank R. J. Marx for some jazzy help; Donna LaStella and Tom Wengelewski for lending a helping hand; the New York City Convention and Visitor's Bureau; Debra Markowitz for helping put Long Island into focus; Gina Guttman and Wayne Miller for being the voices of Staten Island; Alexander Wood at Big Apple Greeters for helping people with disabilities get around the city; London Towncars limousine service for some map clarification; the people at the Central Park Conservatory for their help; and Pam Liflander at Adams for reading all of this quickly and being a calm, collected editor who's never frazzled. And I dedicate this book to my parents, who just celebrated their fiftieth wedding anniversary, right here in New York City.

Introduction

The Big Apple, the City That Never Sleeps, One Hell of a Town—that's New York, New York. No matter how you refer to it, New York City is a one-of-a-kind metropolis offering something for everyone. It is a city rich with excitement and chock full of happenings and landmark sights. The World Trade Center, the Empire State Building, the Statue of Liberty, Central Park, Broadway shows, world-renowned museums, Lincoln Center, Greenwich Village, Coney Island, incredible shopping, historic settings, the Mets, the Yankees, and much more can be found in this city of attractions and activities of all kinds. Commencing with the breathtaking view of the skyline, New York City is like no other, with sights, sounds, and an atmosphere unmatched anywhere in the world.

The fast-paced city does take some getting used to. From Wall Streeters to street vendors, much of Manhattan resembles a film on fast-forward during a busy weekday, with everyone hurrying to reach his or her appointments, make the sale, or close the deal. Billions of dollars worth of business transactions take place in a single hour. Most of the largest companies in the world have at least an office or a base in New York City, and thousands of small businesses start up there every year.

The city is also the cultural mecca of America, with more museums to stroll through than in any other city and a performing arts base second to none. There is a nightlife like no other, with clubs of all kinds and an endless array of restaurants at which to enjoy any type of cuisine you can think of. You can play any sport or attend any kind of major league game. In fact, you can buy, see, or do just about anything if you look hard enough! As the New York State Governor's Office of Motion Picture and Television Development says in their motto, "If it's in the script, it's in New York." The same can be said for your vacation plans. Short of skiing, or seeing an active volcano, "If it's in your vacation plans, it's probably in New York."

Nearly eight million people call New York City home, and some nineteen million live in what is called the Metropolitan New York area, or the tri-state area, which includes neighboring New Jersey and Connecticut. In addition, New York City attracts over

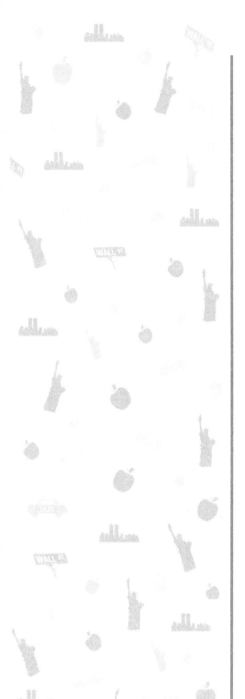

thirty million visitors annually, topping thirty-three million in both 1998 and 1999.

Visiting or vacationing in New York City takes planning. According to the New York City Convention and Visitor's Bureau, some sixty-three thousand hotel rooms await you. This makes for careful choosing when you have just a week or two to spend in such a vast metropolis. It's important to determine how long you will be vacationing in the Big Apple and to plan accordingly. Put your own personal slant on your vacation itinerary! While one visitor may want to spend more time in New York's fabulous museums and at Lincoln Center, another visitor may want to take in a ball game at historic Yankee Stadium, ride the Cyclone at Coney Island, or hit the wide array of dance and jazz clubs the city has to offer at night.

Whatever you plan to do, it is a good idea to make up a basic list of places you'd most like to see and things you'd most like to do. Have family members decide what they would most enjoy doing as well. While the Statue of Liberty, the World Trade Center, the Empire State Building, and Central Park are on most visitors' lists, you can branch out according to individual interests and certainly not feel obligated to hit every major tourist attraction.

Sometimes just walking around neighborhoods, enjoying local color and ambiance, can occupy a significant portion of your day. Central Park can provide entertainment, exercise, people watching, bird watching, and sightseeing, all in one marvelous place.

I don't need to mention that shopping alone could take up a week-long visit and cost you as much money as you're willing to spend. Browsing fashionable stores is a shoppers delight, while the shrewd shopper can find offbeat shops in the East Village, the boroughs, and local neighborhood flea markets.

When visiting New York City, you should keep your budget in mind. Most hotels are costly (in comparison to the rest of the country), while sights and museums are not particularly expensive. The variables regarding expenses will come from food, entertainment, and transportation. Four-star restaurants, Broadway shows, and taxis will obviously cost you more than off-Broadway shows or cabarets, moderate-priced restaurants, and public transportation. Many visitors plan to mix the best of both worlds, seeing a Broadway show one night and enjoying a day of inexpensive fun at the Bronx Zoo the next.

However you decide to spend your time in New York, remember one thing: New York is a state of mind. How much you enjoy the experience is really up to you, determined by your attitude and planning.

"We spent a marvelous day taking in Brooklyn while going to Coney Island and enjoying the beach, the old-style boardwalk, and a Nathan's hotdog" is one way of looking at your day. "We wasted so much time getting to Coney Island, and then all we did was go to the beach, walk the boardwalk, and I'm still hungry after having just a hotdog" is quite another way of looking at it. If you want to enjoy New York City, approach it with an attitude of embarking on an adventure. Unlike a theme park in which everything you do is predetermined and the same experience each time, New York City provides a unique experience every time you leave your hotel room.

Beyond that, good planning is key. Be prepared, well packed, and have everything in order regarding travel and accommodations. While you can be spontaneous about which restaurant to eat in, the basic structural plans of your trip should be set up well in advance and carefully thought out. Once in the city, giving yourself rough itineraries will also help you see all that you want to while avoiding wasted time in traffic or landing in the wrong parts of town.

Among the plans you'll be making will be when to go, how to get there, and what to pack, all of which are addressed in the second chapter, along with a look at where to stay (featuring a guide to over thirty of the many New York City hotels). Chapter 3 will help you get around within the city, with some suggested tours, for those who want an overview, and a number of restaurants listed for your consideration. Then it's on to the can't-miss sights and museums, Central Park, the neighborhoods of Manhattan, and the best of the boroughs. The final chapter highlights fun things to do for everyone in the family. We'll start out with a brief history of the city. It's *The Everything Guide to New York City*!

Chapter 1

New York City,
A Brief History

So, you're heading to New York City! Do you know how this vast metropolis came to be the hustling, bustling melting pot of ethnic cultures and major industries that it is today?

So much has transpired in the nearly five hundred years since the territory was first discovered. The city has a pulse of its own, the culmination of years of growth and change. From the thousands of early settlers to the millions of present-day New Yorkers, being in New York has meant being in an exciting, prospering location. Having the advantage of sitting along the Atlantic Ocean in the northeastern part of the continent, New York was (and still is) the first place that many travelers heading west from Europe encountered. And for that reason, New York was able to grow rapidly. It accounts for the city's great ethnic diversity and explains why so many crafts from different parts of the world emerged into industries in New York.

To visit New York is to take in all the ambiance the present-day city has to offer. However, to fully appreciate what is today one of the largest, most significant cities in the world (financially, architecturally, and culturally), it may serve you well to read up on the history of New York in this abridged version that spans centuries, noting a small few of the many major events and contributions that went along with the city's growth.

Many of the sights visitors will see in their travels around the city are part of the city's rich history; others are named for famous explorers, settlers, governors, and statesmen who helped define what the city became.

How It All Began

Nearly a hundred years after an Italian captain, Verrazano, sailed along New York harbor, an English navigator, Henry Hudson, was hired to find a route across the continent of North America. He set out with intentions of ending up on the western shores of the continent. However, he failed and found himself traveling north along a

Mayors of the Big Apple

Although there were many mayors prior to the city's consolidation, since the five boroughs of New York City became a single entity in 1898, there have been seventeen mayors presiding over the great city.

Robert Van Wyck was the first mayor of consolidated New York City. His term in office was highlighted, perhaps blighted, by so many scandals that Governor Theodore Roosevelt was petitioned to remove him from office. He was allowed to remain in office until the end of his term, then slipped away from the political scandals to become an attorney. He was best known for helping the city get the first subway system under construction. For that accomplishment the Van Wyck Expressway in Queens bears his name and is home to endless congestion to and from Kennedy Airport.

passageway that headed up to Canada. His journey wasn't a complete failure, however, as the Hudson River was later named in his honor.

Despite their efforts, neither Verrazano, for whom a bridge is named, nor Hudson led settlers into the region. In fact, neither stopped there at all. It was the Dutch who saw the area as fertile territory for fur trading and who first colonized what would soon become New Amsterdam (now Lower Manhattan) in 1625.

After a few less competent executives led the fur trading expeditions, the West India Company put Peter Minuit in charge of protecting the corporate interests, making him one of the first Manhattan corporate executives. It was Minuit who, in 1626, purchased the island now known as Manna-hatin from a local tribe, the Canarsie Indians (Canarsie is now a section in Brooklyn) for a mere $23.70. The island today is valued at somewhere around $75 billion. As it turned out, Minuit did not get a great bargain, since it was later learned that the Canarsie Indians didn't own the land.

By the 1640s, New Amsterdam would begin to resemble the city of today in one respect—its variety of cultures. Immigrants from all throughout Europe, Brazil, and other parts of the world began settling at the port that was becoming a very popular stomping ground for explorers and travelers looking to leave their native lands. Although the city, or settlement, didn't extend beyond what would now be Houston Street, the population soared to over one thousand by the late 1640s. The most popular establishment for the traders and farmers would become (what else?) the tavern. There were taverns all over, and many were in the English style, as English settlers were becoming more prevalent in the Dutch-owned territories.

Stuyvesant

Not unlike Mayor Koch many years later, Peter Stuyvesant would eventually govern New Amsterdam for an extended term; it lasted some 17 years. For his efforts, he has not only a housing development but also a prestigious high school and a Brooklyn neighborhood named after him. The first big problem Stuyvesant would face was disharmony between the settlers and the Indians who lived in the area. For those who thought skirmishes with Indians were only

Mayors of the Big Apple

Seth Low was next in line after Van Wyck. A competent mayor, he lowered taxes, improved the schools, and introduced the civil service to the city. He did such a good job that he was kept in office for only one term. He proceeded to champion the rights of unions and labor issues.

Mayors of the Big Apple

George McClellan followed Low and held two terms in office; he was elected under the age of forty. He was in office during the building of the Manhattan and the Queensboro Bridges (which seem to be perennially under construction). McClellan made one mistake and that was to defeat publishing tycoon William Randolph Hearst for his second term in office. He learned that Hearst held the power of the press, and good old "Citizen Cane" blasted McClellan in the papers for everything he did and didn't do. After leaving office, he became a professor of economic history and served in World War I.

part of Westerns, New York history shows numerous battles in the 1600s in and around Manhattan and the territories that would later become the boroughs. In fact, a wall was built in 1653 in Lower Manhattan to guard against a possible Indian attack (and possible attack by the British settlers, who were not in harmony with the Dutch). By 1700 the wall had been torn down and Wall Street remained in its place. Meanwhile, the Native Americans had claims to land in several areas and towns. Mineola, Massapequa, and other parts of the city and Long Island are named for the tribes that had first settled there.

Besides the battles with Indians, Stuyvesant, who was not very tolerant of the various religious groups that were settling in the area, created other problems. The 1650s saw Quakers, Lutherans, and the first Jewish settlers, among other groups. Stuyvesant decreed that only Dutch Reformed religious services would be allowed in public, so other groups were forced to worship privately in their homes.

Despite his uncompromising religious views, Stuyvesant's years in office saw the city grow with new shops, bakeries, factories (manufacturing a wide range of goods), and, of course, taverns. Although the city was growing in some respects, it was not progressing in others; in fact, slaves from Africa were brought in to build some of the many buildings.

While the Dutch Colony was thriving, the British were moving into Long Island and other surrounding areas. In time they would grow to outnumber the Dutch colonists. By the end of the 1660s, without a battle, the British would take New Amsterdam and the surrounding area of the New Netherlands, and they would rename it New York.

The 1700s and Growth!

Through the early 1700s, the city grew rapidly. By 1740 there were nearly eleven thousand people of a wide range of ethnic backgrounds living in the city, and by the start of the Revolutionary War, the population was over thirty thousand. Printing, fur trading, and the garment industry led the way as the economy grew. The 1700s also saw the establishment of a standing police force, volunteer fire companies, and the opening of New York Hospital.

The British rule became increasingly tighter on the colonies in the mid-1700s, and New York was no exception. Tea was one of the key concerns, as the British Parliament proclaimed that only East India Company tea could be purchased in the city (the company was owned by the British, of course). Even then, New Yorkers did not like being told they have no choice, and once news spread of the famous Tea Party up in Boston, New York's own brand of rebellion was imminent. When the British ship *Nancy* sailed into the harbor, New York rebels took action and fired a canon warning the British not to dare unload. This tea rebellion was a small step in New York's entry into the Revolutionary War. It may also explain why there are so many trendy cafés and few tea houses in the city today.

When the Revolutionary War began, New York was quite entrenched in the fighting. Battles on Long Island saw numerous American casualties, and the British advanced quickly through what is now Queens and up to the East River. More battles were fought by the river and onto Manhattan Island at what is now 34th Street. (Battles can still be found on 34th Street when Macy's has a sale on limited items.) The British outnumbered George Washington and his troops, and for a while George probably wished he had the bridge named for him built to head west into New Jersey. New York was ultimately taken over by the British, who set up their headquarters in the city for several years leading up to 1783, when the city was finally freed from British troops.

When the war began, New York City was perhaps the most prosperous city. Although it's not widely recounted (at least not in much of the city's history), New York took a fierce beating during the war and saw its population sliced in half, from nearly thirty thousand down to under fifteen thousand.

As has often been the case over the ensuing years, New York would rise from the battles of the Revolutionary War and take a giant step forward. Soon the city became the capital of the United States as the eighteenth century came to an end.

An Inauspicious Start to Better Times Ahead

The nineteenth century started off with a bang, literally, as Vice President Aaron Burr shot and killed Secretary of the Treasury Alexander Hamilton in a duel in 1804. And you thought politics today was rough!

In the early nineteenth century, manufacturing of all sorts of items, especially clothing, became prominent in Manhattan. Banking, commerce, and real estate were also thriving. John Astor bought up land around Manhattan for under $40,000 and would later (over 30 years later) turn that into over $20 million. Printing became a major industry in the city, and the book publishing world was underway, joined in the 1830s by newspapers including the *New York Evening Post* and the *New York Tribune*. The *New York Times* would first publish in 1851.

The arts also thrived in the 1800s; going to the theater became the thing to do. Numerous artists settled in the city, and the first grand opera, the *Barber of Seville*, was staged.

Through the 1800s, the city grew in every respect. The settlements of Manhattan, which were initially in only the lower portion of the city, expanded north until the entire island was populated. The four other boroughs also grew as New Yorkers opted for "the suburbs." Business, industry, and commerce grew rapidly, thanks to the harbor and little additions like the Erie Canal. Wall Street became the nation's financial center, Central Park became the city's place to play, and baseball became the game to watch. In 1886 the State of Liberty was unveiled to watch over the harbor and the city. And in 1891, Tchaikovsky conducted the opening night gala at Carnegie Hall.

All throughout the nineteenth century, immigrants flocked to the city, from Germany, Ireland, and all throughout Europe, many settling on the Lower East Side, by the new Brooklyn Bridge. In 1898, New York united the five boroughs and became one city with a population of over three million, making it the world's largest city.

As the twentieth century began, immigrants just kept coming to the city. In 1902 alone, some half a million immigrants landed at the new home of immigration, Ellis Island. Great concern grew that

Mayors of the Big Apple

John Mitchel was a mere 35 years old when he became mayor in 1914. The young mayor brought in a new accounting system and established zoning laws. He was effective in office and, therefore, like Seth Low, not re-elected. In 1918, he was killed in a plane crash at the age of 38.

• • •

John Hylan, a farm boy who came to New York as a teenager, was next in line. He would fight hard to maintain the $.05 subway fare. Hylan, nicknamed Honest John for his dedication and devotion, was mayor for 7 years, until 1925.

the "outsiders" were taking over the city, and a great deal of anti-immigrant articles and propositions were bandied about. It was estimated that nearly 70 percent of the city's population was living in tenement housing because there were just not enough houses to go around. The early tenements were row houses built on lots originally intended for single family homes. The conditions were barely livable, but the immigrants flocking to a new land of freedom managed to make do.

Meanwhile, in the first several years of the century, major league baseball was established with three New York teams, the Yankees, Giants, and Dodgers, and city workers were busy building the underground maze of railways that would become the New York City subway system. Macy's department store opened on 34th Street, and the Manhattan and Queensboro Bridges were constructed to open later in the first decade of the twentieth century.

By 1910 there were over 80 miles of subway below the New York City streets. The city continued to grow, with significant building projects such as Penn Station, which took 6 years to build and was completed in 1910, and the 42nd Street New York Public Library, which cost some $9 million to build. Today, it is still one of the foremost research centers in the world, and its striking architecture, protected by two giant lion statues in front, has become a national icon.

Despite a troubled Wall Street in 1907, the city continued to thrive as the financial center of the nation. Municipal services improved, horse-drawn carriages on Fifth Avenue were replaced by automobiles, and the immigrant population continued to grow. In 1907, Ellis Island set a new record for immigrants at over 1.25 million. And in 1908, the *New York Times* kicked off what would become a long-standing New York City tradition, dropping the giant ball at Times Square to ring in the new year. And what did New Yorkers do for entertainment, besides the popular taverns and saloons and those early (pre-strike) major league baseball games? They went to see the Ziegfeld Follies or to the early silent films, many of which were shot in New York. However, the mayor at the time, George McClellan Jr., decided that he would clean up

Mayors of the Big Apple

James "Jimmy" Walker would follow. One of the more colorful New York mayors, Walker spent much of his 6 years in office making sure all was running properly in the nightclubs around the city by frequenting them. He had a penchant for hanging out with celebrities, taking long vacations, partying, and even writing songs. Unfortunately for Walker, he was in office when the Great Depression hit. The problems of the city grew, and a fun loving mayor wasn't what the city needed. To make matters worse, the personable Walker was brought up on numerous charges of corruption. He eventually resigned the office.

the city, much like Mayor Giuliani has done in more recent times. The only difference is that McClellan decided to close all 550 movie theaters in New York City. The mayor claimed that the theaters were cramped, crowded, and dark and that "early film was also flammable." The truth was, he felt, that those who frequented movies had no moral scruples. Ordinances outlawed crime depictions in films, and the battle raged on. But by the start of the second decade, movie theaters were opened, and they were packed. By the end of the second decade, the city had become the leading pre-Hollywood home of movie making, despite the moral dilemma over those "morally reprehensible" motion pictures.

A Disastrous Decade and a Fun Decade

While the city grew financially and the population topped the two-million mark, the second decade of the 1900s saw its share of tragedy as well. A 1911 fire at the Triangle Waist clothing factory killed 146 people. In 1912, families awaited the arrival of the greatest ocean liner ever built, the *Titanic*, but it never made it across the ocean. In 1915, the *Lusitania* set sail from New York, but it too never reached its destination. Later, in 1916, a motorman would be responsible for the tragic subway crash killing 102 people.

The Triangle disaster sparked great debate over workers, safety, and over fifty reforms were instituted for factories. Unionization also became the talk of the town. In 1916, the city would endure its first garment industry strike and its first transit strike.

While the unions were bringing workers together, the war brought New Yorkers together behind the troops who fought the Germans. Unlike other parts of the country, the German population in New York City was not subjected to ridicule, harassment, and violence. And, at the end of World War I, the city welcomed its war heroes home.

The Roaring Twenties would bring in the post-war era of prohibition and speakeasies. It was a time of new hairstyles, nightclubs, flappers, jazz, and fun. Harlem became the hub of jazz in the city,

Mayors of the Big Apple

John P. O'Brien took over for Walker in 1933 and served for just 1 year to finish out the term and to put on his resume that he was mayor of New York.

with Duke Ellington and Louis Armstrong, among others, drawing crowds uptown, along with Paul Whiteman and a thirty-piece band, the kings of jazz. Along with the Cotton Club, other clubs around the city flourished, including Roseland on 52nd Street and the Savoy Ballroom. The Ziegfeld Follies were also going strong, having debuted in 1907, while New Yorkers and the country were doing the Charleston and the playboy mayor, Jimmy Walker, was hitting hot spots all over town. Broadway shows were also the rage, including a classic, *Showboat*, which opened in 1927.

In addition to the music and dancing, the New York Yankees were the talk of the world, with a new-found hero, Babe Ruth, picked up from the rival Boston Red Sox. In 1927 he would set the home run record with sixty homers, a record that stood until 1961. The Yankees would win twenty-five world championships throughout the century, far more than any other major league baseball team. And if the Yankees weren't enough to celebrate, the city threw a ticker-tape parade through the streets of lower Manhattan for Charles Lindbergh, who made the first ever solo flight over the Atlantic Ocean, also in 1927.

The fun, the dancing, and the revelry that marked the decade of the '20s came to a crashing halt when the stock market plummeted in 1929. Wall Street suffered Black Thursday and then Black Tuesday, and the bottom dropped out of the stock market. The city fell into the Great Depression, which swept across the nation.

Tough Times and Big Buildings

The 1930s saw a city headed in two directions. The people did whatever they could to get through the lean years, while the city hosted some major new building projects that kept it advancing forward.

While people were having a hard time finding jobs, the world's biggest office building, the Empire State Building, opened up. Within a few years, an ape would climb the building in the movies and the Museum of Modern Art, featuring the latest, if not the most controversial, art of the era would open. Work would also soon begin on a proposed fourteen-building project called Rockefeller

Mayors of the Big Apple

Fiorello LaGuardia took over in 1934, and unlike O'Brien, he stayed in office for 12 years, long enough to get one of the city's two major airports named after him. Of Italian and Jewish decent, LaGuardia was born in the Lower East Side. His family moved to the Midwest, but LaGuardia would return to the city he loved. A master of several languages, including Yiddish, German, and French, LaGuardia became the most productive mayor in New York history. A powerhouse at 5 feet 2 inches, LaGuardia united the city's three transit systems; built parks, hospitals, and low-income housing; improved the schools; cleaned up corruption; and basically did a tremendous job at pulling New York out of a depression in the wake of America's entry into World War II.

Good-Bye Trollies

Back in the early 1940's one way of getting across Manhattan to East 42nd Street and the lower tip of the United Nations would have been by taking the 42nd Street crosstown trolley. But the trolley service ended in 1946.

Center, and a massive hotel, the Waldorf Astoria, would open its doors. And, very quietly, without any great fanfare, a small experimental television station—W2XAB—would be set up by CBS. Nobody would realize the impact of that little station and others like it for years to come.

The problem faced by the city, however, was that while it was surging forward in some respects (such as development), in others it was losing money. Even the Empire State Building could barely find tenants who could afford to rent office space. By 1932 the city was nearly $2 billion in debt (which at that time was a lot of money). In fact, the rest of the country combined was not that much in debt. Nearly two million of the city's seven million inhabitants were receiving relief of some type. Some 164 bread lines were not enough to feed the hungry in a very troubled city. The charismatic mayor of the '20s, Jimmy Walker, was not so charming anymore as he faced charges of corruption and accepting bribes. Knowing that his fate was sealed, Walker resigned and packed his bags for France.

The city needed a take-charge mayor. In 1934 Fiorello LaGuardia stepped in. He was tough and ready to turn around the city he loved. He took over a $30 million deficit, with only $31 million left from a federal government loan that would run out just 8 months after he took the oath. LaGuardia instituted a sales tax and utility tax programs that were just the start of measures that over the next several years would pull the city out of its financial crisis. He also cracked down on crime, starting with the arrest of the city's most famous, most notorious, mobster, "Lucky" Luciano. LaGuardia cleaned up the city, put welfare recipients to work, and made a better New York. He even closed down the famous Minsky's Burlesque, much the way Mayor Giuliani cleaned up Times Square—a far more raunchy Times Square than the patrons of Minsky's could ever have imagined.

Despite the financial difficulties of the early 1930s, construction never stopped. Thousands of families moved into new housing projects, while the subway lines expanded and construction of New York City Municipal Airport began. The airport was later renamed LaGuardia.

Helping to build the city was the ever aggressive Robert Moses, parks commissioner with a mission. Despite coming under criticism for ousting tenants, Moses would build 5,000 acres worth of parks and set up over 250 playgrounds. One of the parks, created from a garbage dump, was Flushing Meadow in Corona, Queens; it cost nearly $600 million. But Moses was preparing the site for the fabulous World's Fair, a huge economic boom for the city. To help make Queens and the World's Fair more easily accessible, the Triborough Bridge and Midtown Tunnel were constructed, and New York City Municipal Airport opened.

As splendid as the World's Fair was, the news from Europe wasn't encouraging. Following the Pearl Harbor attack, security was increased on all bridges, tunnels, factories, and other significant points in New York City that were potentially prime targets for an attack. Goebbels reportedly wanted to destroy New York, which he called a "medley of races," none of which fit with the Nazi sentiment.

During the war, the lights of the spectacular New York City skyline went dark or were dimmed. The lights of Broadway were also dimmed, as was the enthusiasm of the city as soldiers went off to war leaving factories and production at a depleted level. While the mayor moved north into Gracie Mansion (originally built in 1804 and redesigned by Robert Moses), the people of the city watched and waited for news from overseas.

LaGuardia was unquestionably one of the most significant New Yorkers in history. During his final days in office, when the city's major newspapers went on strike, he read the Sunday comics aloud on his radio show.

After the city welcomed the war heroes home with a rousing parade, New York continued the building expansion of the prewar era, and the Yankees just kept on winning pennants. Along with the city's renewed expansion was the controversial proposal to build the headquarters for the United Nations in Manhattan. Eventually, after much debate, a block of land purchased by John D. Rockefeller in 1946 would soon become the home of the newly created United Nations. The focus of the world would be on New York City as host to this new international organization.

Mayors of the Big Apple

William O'Dwyer went from being a 20-year-old Irish immigrant to a police officer to district attorney and finally to the office of mayor of New York City in 1946. He was instrumental in the United Nations being located on First Avenue and was known for being tough on crime. Unfortunately, during his fight against crime, he made the wrong friends and became connected with organized crime. He was unable to shake that association. Worse than that, he allowed the subway fare increase from $.05 to $.10. New Yorkers could forgive the organized crime thing, but a subway fare hike, never!

Mayors of the Big Apple

Vincent Richard Impellitteri came to the United States from Italy in 1901; in 1950 he became the mayor of New York City. A former navy man and former district attorney, Impellitteri still holds the distinction of having the hardest name to spell of any New York City leader. A great deal of highways and various public facilities including housing were built during Impellitteri's 3 years in office. Unfortunately, much of the funding for these improvements came from increased taxes and the raising of the subway fares to $.15.

A Couple of Jackies and a Lot of Baby Boomers

As Jackie Robinson broke the baseball color barrier by joining the Brooklyn Dodgers in 1947 and a guy named Ed Sullivan took the stage (in what is now David Letterman's theater) to host his own really big variety "show," the city neared its fiftieth anniversary. The fiftieth anniversary would be the year that New York's second major airport, Idlewild (now Kennedy), opened (in Queens).

The city would enter the second half of the decade with nearly eight million people, not far from its current population. The postwar New York would see a return to tremendous manufacturing, led by the successful garment industry. A new industry called "television" would also join the fray, with early shows (including the *Honeymooners*, starring Jackie Gleason and shot in Brooklyn studios) being produced in the city. But while the city's economy was seemingly strong, with over a hundred thousand retail stores selling billions of dollars worth of goods, there were other problems. New York continued to lure anyone who felt he or she could achieve the American Dream. As the population grew with the postwar baby boom and immigrants, housing became scarce; the city was in need of new dwellings. The '50s would see numerous housing projects including the massive Stuyvesant Town on the East side of Manhattan. New laws to protect low-income housing were enacted, but the city was hard pressed to find enough homes for its population, which now exceeded that of nearly all the states in the nation.

Along with the housing situation came class and racial divisions that would eventually explode in the '60s. Harlem was in disrepair, and little effort was being made to rectify that situation. The rapidly growing Puerto Rican population faced a language barrier and discrimination and lacked job skills. To make matters worse, many city dwellers were heading for the suburbs. A house in Long Island and a commute to Manhattan became the way of life for hundreds of thousands of the middle class. And as if the growing uneasiness between races and classes wasn't enough, there was also the onset of the Communist scare. The Cold War had begun and midday alarms would blare loudly, signaling school children to duck under

their wooden desks, where it was believed they would miraculously survive the force of a Russian atomic bomb attack.

The seemingly tranquil postwar '50s had an undercurrent that made many New Yorkers feeling uneasy. Despite a trust in Mayor Wagner, the city was separating into factions. From the coffeehouse Beat poets of Greenwich Village to the ghetto inhabitants of Harlem, people stayed in their neighborhoods, where they felt safe, except, of course, from the prevailing threat of "the bomb," which was more evident in New York, since, after all, this was still the biggest manufacturing city and most populated city in the nation.

And while the city never experienced an attack, the blow of losing the beloved Giants and Brooklyn Dodgers, who packed up and moved 3,000 miles away to California, jolted their loyal legions of fans. Three teams remaining in one city, even good teams, was just not feasible with new horizons out west making attractive offers, including new ballparks to be built in coming years. While the Giants in the Polo grounds were missed by their Manhattan-based fans, they had always had to bask in the shadow of the Yankees across the East River. The Dodgers, however, were as much a staple of Brooklyn as Coney Island, idolized by the children of Brooklyn . . . and their dads. Although they only beat the Yankees in the 1955 World Series, they were so loved that their loss was mourned by the borough and their fans for years to come. Some, who are old enough, miss them dearly even today.

And Then Came the '60s!

The city entered the 1960s with new roadways, including the Throggs Neck Bridge, the Verrazano-Narrows Bridge, and the new second level of the George Washington Bridge. The New York Mets were born, taking the uniform colors of the departed Giants and Dodgers but not gaining the trust and enthusiasm of those teams' old fans, particularly since they played, in 1962, dreadfully.

Lincoln Center, the most advanced, spectacular showcase for the cultural arts in the world, opened on Manhattan's Upper West Side, despite protests over its displacing much needed housing.

Mayors of the Big Apple

Robert Wagner became mayor in 1954 and stayed in office until 1965. A lawyer and veteran of World War II, Wagner was instrumental in many city changes. In addition to improvements in the school system and the building of major new roads and bridges (including the Verrazano between Brooklyn and Staten Island), Shea Stadium, Lincoln Center, and other New York institutions opened while Wagner was in office. The NYU Graduate School of Public Service is named for Wagner.

Mayors of the Big Apple

John Lindsay was mayor of "Fun City" during the turbulent 1960s, with protests, marches, civil unrest, riots in the ghetto, a major blackout, a city-wide transit strike, and all sorts of events. His hair wasn't gray when he took the job. It was a wild ride for Lindsay. Even the fledgling New York Mets rose up and won the World Series during Lindsay's 8 years in office. Somehow Lindsay remained amenable, and he never lost the respect of the city. Although he did a good job in keeping the city in check through the '60s, he was not very successful in the presidential primaries in 1972. So, he did the next best thing and became a part-time television commentator.

As if a new ball club and arts center were not enough, the city also got the thumbs-up to host the second world's fair in 25 years in the same location, Flushing Meadow Park in Queens. Most exciting—to teenagers at least—was the American debut of the British phenomenon, the Beatles, who appeared on the *Ed Sullivan Show* and later at a relatively new venue in the city, Shea Stadium.

Despite all of that excitement, the city was facing a budget crisis from trying desperately to build housing and advance public programs, which now included City College, a college designed to give minorities an opportunity to receive a college education. The onetime melting pot, where immigrants from different nations lived together comfortably, had become a boiling pot, where minorities were not welcomed and racial tension mounted. Class separation was peaking in the early '60s, and the nation had a very mixed reaction to the war in Vietnam, evidenced by protests throughout the city (and the nation). While the new World's Fair showed the city at its best, drug use, crime, and poverty were rising and showing the city at its worst, but only to those who took the time to notice. In the summer of '64, riots rocked Harlem, with hundreds of fires, several deaths, and a public outcry for help.

John Lindsay was welcomed as the new mayor, but there was still great concern. The '60s were indeed turbulent in the nation's largest city, where protests, sit-ins, walkouts, and strikes, including a newspaper strike that lasted for months and a transit strike that cost the city nearly a million dollars in revenue, set the city on a spiraling path. The city was already in financial trouble from government programs and efforts to solve the postwar housing crisis. Headlines like the one in *Fortune* magazine, "A City Destroying Themselves," didn't set an optimistic tone either.

New York was divided in numerous respects in the late '60s. The concerns about poverty, the racial tensions, and events including the assassinations of RFK and Martin Luther King rocked the city and the country greatly. Much of the tension came to a head when violent demonstrations broke out at the prestigious Columbia University on the Upper West Side of Manhattan.

At the end of the decade, the New York Jets pulled off the improbable Super Bowl upset and the hapless Mets emerged from the depths to become World Champions. Heck, men even walked on the moon! But New York was still in trouble.

From Bad to Worse

While the tensions in the city eased somewhat in the early 1970s, the financial situation worsened. Much like the opening of the Empire State Building during the Great Depression, the new World Trade Center now towered over Manhattan while officials searched their pockets and the treasuries for enough money to keep the city from bankruptcy. By 1974 the Big Apple had hit rock bottom. The city was broke. The departure of the middle class to the suburbs, the mismanagement in government spending, the never-ending flood of immigrants, the attempts to solve the housing problems, and the expenditure of city funds on social services that could no longer be afforded ran the city into the ground. The city had simply operated in the red for too long.

Since New York City is, obviously, part of the larger New York State, the city turned to the greater body for funding. But when the Urban Development Corporation ran out of money and collapsed in early 1975, this did not bode well for the state's credit rating. The state, under Governor Carey, would, however, turn to the Emergency Financial Control Board and the Municipal Assistance Corporation (MAC), which would issue what became known as Big Mac Bonds. No, McDonald's was not taking over New York (not yet, anyway), but Mac bonds were sold with state backing, asserting their "moral obligation" to make good on all issues. A wage freeze on municipal workers, a transit fare hike, and cutbacks in all city agencies soon followed.

From the newspaper employees to garbage collectors to doctors at city hospitals, everyone was walking out on strike, angered that they were feeling the effects of the city's plummeting financial situation. The police, who at one point also went on strike, issued warnings to tourists to stay away from "Fear City." Crime was up, and the city was falling apart, as evidenced, literally, by a truck falling through the West Side Highway, which was sorely in need of road repair.

Mayors of the Big Apple

Abraham Beame was yet another immigrant to join the ranks of mayor. Beame was born in London in 1906, and 68 years later, he would become mayor of New York City. Despite the marvelous bicentennial celebration, the city was in major financial trouble and faced bankruptcy. Massive budget cuts and job cuts helped the city stay afloat, but it was a struggle over the 4 years in which Beame resided. His accounting and budgeting skills left a lot to be desired, and the city almost defaulted.

Finally, when even the state could not bail the city out, New York turned to Washington and asked President Ford for help. The president snubbed New York, yielding the *Daily News* headline "Ford to City, Drop Dead."

Ford's response, however, did not sit well with many constituents from other states who were already beginning to feel a ripple effect from New York's struggles. They reasoned that if the nation's largest city and most prominent manufacturing center, as well as financial center, collapsed, they would be in trouble as well. Thus, the federal government had no choice but to bail out New York City.

The 1976 bicentennial, featuring the tall ships sailing the Hudson River, celebrated not only the nation's two hundredth birthday but also the return of New York City. Broadway was revitalized, the struggling Yankees of the late '60s and early '70s returned to the top of the American League, and the city hosted a Democratic National Convention that would ultimately lead the party past Gerald Ford . . . how ironic.

The Late '70s, a Slow Comeback, Despite Disco

It took a few years, but the city began to put itself back on track. Not all was smooth sailing though; the city was terrorized in the summer of '77 by a crazed killer, David Berkowitz (The Son of Sam), and disco reared its ugly head. But slowly things were back on track, with tourists returning to a much-improved city.

With Mayor Koch at the helm, the city had hope for the '80s. But the first year ended on a somber, chilling note as John Lennon was gunned down outside of his Central Park West home, stunning the city and the world.

The city saw a resurgence in the early '80s, with new housing projects and new buildings providing more office space. Financially the city was finally back on track. The garment industry was going strong, as was manufacturing in general. The financial center was also enjoying the city's comeback. Tourists were once again heading to New York City.

By the latter part of the '80s, Yuppies could be found at numerous posh eateries and outdoor sidewalk cafes as the city basked in the consumerism that characterized that period. All of this showcased the city despite continuing racial tensions, the growing AIDS epidemic, and extreme corruption discovered in Mayor Koch's administration. Then, in late 1987, the stock market crashed, dropping over 500 points in a single day.

The results of the Wall Street plunge of '87 were nothing compared with the depression that resulted from the crash of '29. The city, and the market for that matter, recovered rather quickly. But as the '90s continued, there were echoes of the mid-'70s, and the fiscal budget came under scrutiny. Major department stores could no longer survive in a city that was becoming too expensive in which to run a business, so they shut down or moved out along with many smaller companies. Even worse, however, were a number of incidents of violence triggered by strained race relations. The economic, social, and overall turnaround of the late 1980s that saw New York prospering was now looking to make a U-turn. In fact, 1990 saw an all-time high for murders in New York City at over twenty-two hundred.

While Ellis Island reopened to celebrate immigrants coming to these shores, the people who were modern-day New Yorkers were at odds with each other. The streets no longer felt safe as crime and drug use increased. And as the homeless population increased, the number of welfare recipients hit an all-time high in 1993. Even terrorism, of an international flavor, rocked the city, with the bombing of the World Trade Center on February 26, 1993.

New York Comes Back, Again!

And then came Rudy. Not unlike Fiorello LaGuardia in many respects, Rudy Giuliani stepped into the office of mayor from an underdog party ticket, with a hard-edged, no-nonsense manner in a time of trouble for the city. Like LaGuardia, Giuliani took a tough-guy approach and a zero-tolerance approach to the violence and drug use that plagued the city and, in a few short years, made New York a city in which people, once again, felt safe.

Mayors of the Big Apple

David Dinkins, the city's first African-American mayor, held one term in office starting in 1990. The soft spoken, likable Dinkins championed social reforms and human rights. However, the city was once again heading into financial troubles, and the problems of the homeless, crime, drugs, and racial tension increased. Many New Yorkers began exiting for safer, cleaner neighborhoods.

Mayors of the Big Apple

Rudolph Giuliani, a native of Brooklyn, is the 107th mayor of New York City (if you return to the years before the five boroughs were unified to create the city we know today). When Giuliani took over the office of mayor in 1994, the city was nearing a low point. New Yorkers felt unsafe, the city was "dirty" (in many ways) and violence and drug dealing were causing city dwellers to consider moving elsewhere. You couldn't even stop at a traffic light without youngsters with squeegees rushing over to wash your car windows, whether you liked it or not—and then you had to pay them. Besides all of that, over a 3-year span taxes had gone up more than $1.5 billion.

Giuliani was a tough, hard-nosed district attorney, who some felt lacked charisma and charm. But, at that point, New York needed a tough guy more than it needed a nice guy. A Republican mayor in a city traditionally run by Democrats, Giuliani was an unwelcome change for some, but after a couple of years, New Yorkers began seeing a marked difference. Giuliani's zero-tolerance approach to crime put the emphasis on staying within the law for all New Yorkers, from jaywalkers to drug users. As a result, crime dropped by over 40 percent, and there were over 65 percent fewer murders during Giuliani's first 4 years in office. And there are no longer kids with squeegees. Indeed, New Yorkers now feel more comfortable in their own urban backyard.

The crackdown on crime had a ripple effect on the city. Areas like Union Square in Manhattan, instead of being a haven for drug trafficking, was able to re-establish itself as a viable place for businesses to grow. Times Square experienced a major turnaround, going from sleazy to Disney. Many other areas were able to attract new businesses, and their customers, thus stimulating the economy. Job programs replaced many welfare checks, saving the city millions of dollars and, thus, helping the economy of New York. And the film industry, among other industries, once again began to thrive in New York.

Giuliani won a second term easily. The second term, however, has not been the same Rudy lovefest. While the improvements of the first term have stuck, Rudy has faced criticism that his hard-nosed approach has gotten a little "too hard." He has met with much criticism of his handling of racial matters and of his policies regarding the schools, which are still (despite a number of new programs and safety measures) experiencing very low reading scores.

New York is a tough city. Ask any ballplayer who's gone through a week-long slump. Despite all that Rudy has done for New York, his popularity has dropped considerably in his second term. Despite this, he will perhaps be appreciated for all the good he did for the city. He turned New York City around, and it has not turned back. But, again, this is a tough town. A couple of errors in the field and you'll hear them booing you loud and clear.

Although the city's love affair with Rudy has faded over subsequent issues and events, there is no denying that the New York at the end of the 1990s was a far cry better than the New York of the early part of the decade. Almost on cue, the Yankees were world champions again. Broadway saw greater success than ever, Internet companies were booming in "Silicon Alley," welfare was down, tourism was up, and film and television were returning to the city in a big way. The year 1998, the hundredth anniversary of New York as a unified city, was one in which the city could take pride.

As New York City forges ahead into the new millennium, the city has over eight million inhabitants and is the leader in finance and manufacturing. The city sees more tourists than any other American city and is enjoying a period of growth both culturally and economically. Broadway is going strong, Times Square is looking cleaner, most of the professional sports teams are playing well (and certainly drawing crowds), Central Park is looking as beautiful as ever, Lincoln Center is enjoying sold-out performances, Radio City is refurbished, many neighborhoods are enjoying a resurgence, and, while the subways can be hot and crowded, they are still a fast, affordable way to get around town. It's a great time to visit New York City!

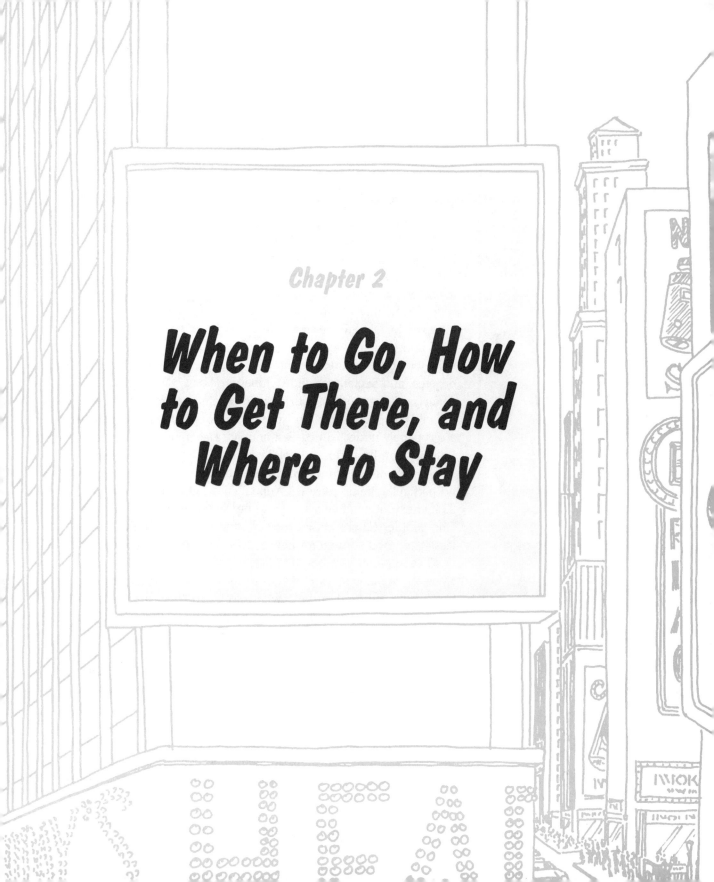

Chapter 2

When to Go, How to Get There, and Where to Stay

When to Go

There is no "wrong" time to visit New York City. The chilly temperatures of January and February will dissuade some travelers, but the hotel rates are lower during those two months, and there is always plenty to see and do.

From ample snowfall to sizzling summer heat, New York is a city with very distinct seasons and a wide range of temperatures. In June, July, and August temperatures are in the 80s, with high humidity coming into play in July and August. April and May are pleasant and mild, with temperatures around 65 degrees, and September and October are perfect walking months, with a range of temperatures from the mid-60s into the 80s. In November through March, temperatures are generally under 55 degrees, and late December, January, and February can be bitter and cold, with single-digit windchill factors.

New York sees an average of 40 inches of rain annually, with no particular "rainy season." Annual snowfall is often around 20 to 25 inches but has been known to be significantly more or less. Only Mother Nature knows for sure, but you can certainly expect at least one good snowstorm between December and March.

The summer can be quite hot, thanks to the humidity. However, Manhattan experiences a weekend exodus as city dwellers head to Long Island and elsewhere to try to "beat the heat" and hit the beach. Thus, traffic can be lighter and hotels less expensive. Just make sure your hotel room is air conditioned!

December is a joyous time in New York, with the glow of the famous Christmas tree at Rockefeller Center and a holiday spirit that's hard to match. The festivities end with the world-famous New Year's Eve party in Times Square. This is the peak tourism season, with high-priced hotel rooms that fill up fast.

Spring and fall may be the best times to visit the city, if your schedule permits. April/May or September/October offer you the opportunity to enjoy most activities, from parks and zoos to base-

ball games to the Philharmonic or the opera. Temperatures are not too hot or cold, and there are many festivals and special city events. Hotel rates are neither at their highest nor lowest points and tend to fluctuate from year to year and from economy to economy. Often you can get package deals or special offers. Ask.

How to Get There

After you decide when to go, you have to plan how to get there. There are several options: car, plane, bus, train, or even boat!

By Car

Driving will save you the cost of airfare and is certainly a popular choice when coming from nearby cities. However, having a car in New York City means paying for garages, since parking is at a premium. If you plan to use public transportation once you arrive—which is advisable in Manhattan—you can find a parking lot with a weekly rate, which will save you money. Most hotels have parking arrangements with lots (for a fee) where you can leave your car for the majority of your stay.

While Brooklyn and Queens are connected by land, the boroughs are otherwise connected to each other and to neighboring New Jersey by bridge or tunnel. Coming into New York via car through the George Washington Bridge, Lincoln Tunnel, or Holland Tunnel will cost $4. Have money ready for tolls and be prepared for a 15 to 20 minute wait at the tunnels and bridges (longer at rush hour and shorter late at night).

Use AAA or any map of major roads leading to New York to plot out a direct route. It's a big city, and signs will say New York City from hundreds of miles away. It's hard to miss!

Note: Fill up with gas, say in New Jersey or Connecticut, prior to driving into New York City. Gas prices are high once you hit the city, and finding a gas station in Manhattan is not an easy task.

Tuning In

When approaching New York City, you might turn to WINS (1010 on your AM radio dial) or CBS-AM (880 on your AM radio dial). These are New York's all-news radio stations, and they have regular traffic updates.

Getting In and Out of Manhattan by Car

You have a number of choices when it comes to driving on and off the busy island. Many of these routes have traffic delays during the busier times of the day—particularly between 7 A.M. and 10 A.M. or 4 P.M. and 7 P.M. on weekdays. Some of these routes, as noted, have tollbooths as you head into but not out of Manhattan.

To and from New Jersey:

The three primary routes across the Hudson River include two under water and one over it. The **George Washington Bridge**, opened in 1931, has two levels of two-way traffic connecting Manhattan to Fort Lee, New Jersey, from 181st Street. Primary routes to the bridge are the Henry Hudson Parkway on the West Side along the Hudson River, and Harlem River Drive, which becomes FDR Drive, along the East River. **The Alexander Hamilton Bridge** connects the Cross Bronx Expressway directly with the George Washington Bridge, crossing into Manhattan. The bridge itself stands 200 feet above the Hudson River and is one of the most traveled bridges in the world. It connects easily with the Palisades Parkway, Route 80, the New Jersey Turnpike, and other major New Jersey roadways. You can also walk or bicycle across the bridge on outer walkways. The $4 toll is paid only upon entering Manhattan.

The **Lincoln Tunnel** connects Manhattan from West Thirtieth to Thirty-second Streets with Weehawken, New Jersey, and like the George Washington Bridge, intersects with most major Jersey routes. The tunnel has three connecting tubes that were completed in the late 1950s. Nearly forty million cars, trucks, and busses use it every year. The toll is $4 upon entering Manhattan only.

The **Holland Tunnel** connects lower Manhattan from Canal Street or Spring Street to Jersey City and provides easy access to Routes 1 and 9. The granddaddy of underwater travel, this tunnel dates back to 1927. There is a $4 toll when entering Manhattan.

If you are traveling from Manhattan to or from Staten Island, catch the **Staten Island Ferry**. The ferry leaves every 15 minutes from Whitehall Street next to Battery Park in Lower Manhattan and goes to the neighborhood known as St. George on Staten Island. The ride is free. The view from the third deck is quite pleasant. The 6.2 mile ride takes about 25 minutes and, if you bring your car on board, costs $3.50.

From Queens into Manhattan and vice versa you can take the **Queensboro Bridge,** which connects Long Island City in Queens with First and Second Avenues in Manhattan at 59th and 69th Streets. Although the bridge has two levels, it is likely that one of those levels will be closed for repairs in at least one direction. Nonetheless, the bridge is free! It provides easy access to Queens Boulevard, Northern Boulevard, and, via Van Dam Street, the Long Island Expressway in Queens.

The **Queens Midtown Tunnel** is at the west end of the Long Island Expressway. The tunnel deposits you in the East 30s in Manhattan, between First and Second Avenues. The tunnel toll is $3.50 in both directions and is **very** busy during rush hour. **The Triborough Bridge** connects Queens from the Grand Central Parkway to Manhattan at 125th Street, where you can easily go onto the FDR Drive going south or Harlem River Drive going north. The elaborately designed bridge also connects Queens with the Bronx, and the Bronx (from the Bruckner Expressway) with Manhattan. To confuse matters, the bridge also connects with Randalls Island. There is a $3.50 toll in all directions.

The Bronx connects with Manhattan at the **Triborough Bridge** and at other bridges, including the **Willis Avenue Bridge,** which connects the Harlem River Drive with the Major Deegan in the Bronx. The **Willis Avenue Bridge** (off the Harlem River Drive), **Third Avenue Bridge** (at 129th Street), the **Madison Avenue Bridge** (at 138th Street), and the **Macombs Dam Bridge** (at 155th street) also connect the Bronx with Manhattan.

On the West Side of Manhattan, you can take the Henry Hudson Parkway North, past the Cloisters, and connect with Riverdale (part of the Bronx), which goes directly into the **Henry Hudson Bridge**. There is a $1.75 toll in both directions. The road will become the **Saw Mill River Parkway** and heads north to Westchester.

One-Day Drives!

Several major cities are a one-day drive from New York City. They include:

Atlantic City
2½ hours
Baltimore
4 hours
Boston
4 to 5 hours
Montreal
7½ hours
Philadelphia
2 hours
Washington, D.C.
5 hours

Times are approximate depending on traffic, road conditions, weather, and holidays.

There are four routes connecting Brooklyn with Lower Manhattan. The famed **Brooklyn Bridge** will take you from Cadman Plaza or the Brooklyn Queens Expressway (BQE) into Manhattan, with easy access to the FDR Drive, or Park Row by City Hall. The **Manhattan Bridge** connects Atlantic Avenue or Grand Army Plaza in Brooklyn with Canal Street in Chinatown. The **Williamsburg Bridge** connects Metropolitan Avenue or the BQE with Delancey Street in Manhattan. All of these bridges are free.

The **Brooklyn Battery Tunnel** connects West Street in Manhattan, with easy accessibility from the FDR Drive or Henry Hudson Parkway (through elaborately designed tunnels at the lower tip of Manhattan) to the Gowanus Expressway in Brooklyn. The tunnel costs $3.50 in both directions.

By Plane

Every major airline and most of the smaller ones have frequent flights to New York City. It's always best to check with several carriers to find the best deals.

Try to make your reservations ahead of time. Airlines give good deals generally for 21 days advance booking. Check prices on various airlines and look for advertised specials. Also, if your schedule permits it, you'll almost always get a better airfare if your stay includes a Saturday night. If you're planning your visit around a major holiday, you need to book far in advance. During the holidays, the tickets do go quickly, particularly around Thanksgiving and Christmas. Airfares vary widely depending on where you are flying from, what type of seats you are purchasing, and when you purchase them. On an airplane, everyone on board can be paying a different ticket price.

These are the major airlines:

Air Canada	800-776-3000
American Airlines	800-433-7300
America West Airlines	800-235-9292

British Airways	800-247-8736
Continental Airlines	800-523-0280
Delta Airlines	800-221-1212
Kiwi Airlines	800-538-5494
Northwest Airlines	800-225-2525
Southwest Airlines	800-435-9792
TWA	800-221-2000
United Airlines	800-241-6522
US Airways	800-428-4322
Vanguard Airlines	800-826-4827
Virgin Atlantic	800-862-8621

Ask whether they fly from your city to New York City, preferably nonstop. Flights with stopovers, although often cheaper, can make traveling long and tiresome, particularly with kids.

Since New York City is truly a city that never sleeps, you can fly into one of the three major airports, get a cab, and check into a hotel at any hour. Just make sure the hotel knows ahead of time when you should be getting there. If it's not inconvenient, you can often avoid crowds at the airports and traffic en route to Manhattan if you fly at night.

When going to the airport, any airport, it's advisable to give yourself plenty of time to get there and to check in. Passengers have been known to get bumped from overcrowded flights because they showed up too late. Youngsters may enjoy watching planes take off and land while you relax before your flight, perhaps reading up on New York City. It's also important to arrive early, as there are added security checkpoints at airports. Have ready two IDs including a photo ID, such as your driver's license.

JFK International Airport

JFK International Airport is one of the world's busiest airports. Opened as Idlewild International Airport in 1948, the name was changed to John F. Kennedy (or JFK) International Airport in the '60s. All major carriers land at JFK. Transportation information counters are located on the lower level near baggage claim carousels, and taxis, busses, shuttles, and limousines pull up just

Important Phone Number

If you are in need of information regarding ground transportation from any of New York's three major airports, you can call the Port Authority Ground Transportation Hotline at 800-247-7433. They also provide information on parking at the three major airports.

outside. Car rental facilities are also nearby and can be reached by rental company shuttle busses.

Although the airport sits some 15 miles outside of Manhattan, travel by taxi to Manhattan from JFK, which is located in Queens, takes about 40 to 60 minutes, more during very busy hours. Taxis charge a flat rate of $30 plus tolls and tips, so don't let them tell you otherwise! The tip should be 15 percent, more or less, depending on service, for example, whether they put your bags in the trunk or simply open it for you to load up.

Ground Transportation

- **Carey Coach Express** bus service runs every 30 minutes from 6 A.M. to midnight and will also take 40 minutes or more. The cost is $13 per person. Call 1-800-678-1596.
- **Grey Line Express** runs every 20 minutes from 7 A.M. to midnight to the Port Authority Bus Terminal on the West Side of Manhattan and to Grand Central Station on the East Side.
- **Gray Line Air Shuttle** goes from the airport directly to over forty Manhattan hotels for $14 per person. Call 1-800-451-0455.
- **New York Airport Express Bus Service** goes directly to the East Side of Manhattan at Grand Central Station between 41st and 42nd Streets on Park Avenue. Another bus goes to the West Side, to the Port Authority Bus Terminal at 42nd Street and Eighth Avenue. Busses are $13 per person. Call 1-718-706-9658.

There are also van services, limousines (see Chapter 3), and rental cars available at the airport. If you rent a car, to get to Manhattan from JFK, you can take the Van Wyck Expressway to the Long Island Expressway heading west to the Midtown Tunnel, which will deposit you in the East 30s in Manhattan. You can also take the Grand Central Expressway and proceed over the Triborough Bridge (watch the signs because the bridge also goes to the Bronx) and follow the signs for Manhattan/FDR Drive. You can also take the Belt Parkway around Brooklyn to the Brooklyn/Queens Expressway and go over the Brooklyn Bridge to Lower Manhattan—

or follow signs to the Gowanus Expressway and take the Battery Tunnel into Lower Manhattan, but you'll have to pay a toll.

LaGuardia Airport

Smaller than JFK but larger than many major city airports, the 680-acre LaGuardia Airport handles all of the primary carriers and is home to, primarily, domestic flights. Originally opened commercially in 1939 as New York City Municipal Airport, the name was later changed to commemorate the former Mayor Fiorello LaGuardia. Located less then ten miles from Manhattan, the trip from this Queens-based airport is around 30 minutes but can be as quick as 20 minutes during the off hours. However, during busier hours, traffic can turn it into an hour. Taxis, charging by the meter, cost around $20 plus tolls and tips. They are easy to find at any number of taxi stands.

Ground Transportation

- **Carey Coach Express Bus** service will run $10 per person to Manhattan. Call 1-800-678-1569.
- **Gray Line Bus Express** costs $10 for a one-way ticket and will take you to the Port Authority Bus Terminal on the West Side of Manhattan and to Grand Central on the East Side.
- **Gray Line Air Shuttle** also runs from 6 A.M. to 11:30 P.M., at a cost of $14 per person (212-315-3006) and will take you to nearly fifty Manhattan hotels.
- **Delta Water Shuttle** can take you to Manhattan docks in 30 to 45 minutes. The cost is $15 for one way or $25 for round-trip. Call 800-543-3779 for the schedule and information.

There are also van services, limousines (see Chapter 3), and rental cars available at the airport. If you rent a car, to get to Manhattan from LaGuardia, get onto the Grand Central Parkway going west, and it will take you to the Triborough Bridge. Watch the signs as the bridge also goes to the Bronx. Look for the sign for Manhattan/FDR Drive. If you're going to Lower Manhattan, you can also get the Brooklyn/Queens Expressway from the Grand Central Parkway and head to the Williamsburg or Brooklyn Bridges.

Which Airport?

All three city airports are within similar proximity to Manhattan. Finding the best fares may help you determine which airport to land at. If you are staying in Brooklyn, Queens, or the Bronx, Newark Airport would be a last choice, since the other two airports are located in Queens.

Lost
Luggage?

Most luggage mix-ups are quickly resolved. However, you should always report lost luggage immediately. File a complaint with the carrier, including your flight and time of arrival. You can also call the U.S. Department of Transportation at 202-366-2220 or write to them at C-75, Room 4107, Washington, D.C. 20590.

Newark International Airport

In nearby Newark, New Jersey, is Newark International Airport, some 30 to 40 minutes from Manhattan (more during rush hour) by car or bus. New Jersey's largest commercial airport, Newark has enjoyed major renovations over the years, including monorail service from terminal to terminal. If heading to the West Side of Manhattan, you might consider flying into Newark, as the other airports enter the city from the East Side. Also, Newark is generally less crowded than Kennedy or LaGuardia because some consider it farther away. Without traffic it can seem closer. Taxis cost $40 to $50 plus tolls.

Ground Transportation

- **Olympia Trails Express Busses** leave for Port Authority every 15 minutes from 6 A.M. to 1 A.M. and cost $10. Call 212-964-6233 or 908-354-3330.
- **Gray Line Air Shuttle Minibus** service goes to nearly fifty Manhattan hotels for $18.50 per person. Call 212-315-3006.
- **New Jersey Transit** has 24-hour bus service to Port Authority every 15 minutes (or every half hour between 1 and 6 A.M.) for $7 per person.

There are also van services, limousines (see Chapter 3), and rental cars available at the airport. If you rent a car, to get to Manhattan from Newark, follow airport exit signs to the New Jersey Turnpike (95) North. Take the Turnpike, following signs for the Holland Tunnel, the Lincoln Tunnel, or the George Washington Bridge. The Holland Tunnel comes into Lower Manhattan, the Lincoln Tunnel comes into Midtown Manhattan, just south of 42nd Street, and the George Washington Bridge enters the city near the upper tip of Manhattan, around 178th Street.

By Bus

If you are heading to or from New York City by bus, be it Greyhound, Trailways, or any other leading carrier, you will most likely end up in the Port Authority Bus Terminal on Eighth Avenue in Manhattan, between 40th and 42nd Streets. The largest bus

terminal in the country, Port Authority sees busses coming from and heading to all points in the continental United States, plus Canada and Mexico.

Below are some bus services you might want to contact:

Adirondack Trailways	800-858-8555
Arrow Bus Line	914-658-8312
Bonanza Bus Lines	800-556-3815
Command Bus Company	718-272-0900
Gray Line	212-397-2600
Greyhound Lines	800-231-2222
Olympia Trails	212-964-6233
Peter Pan Trailways	800-343-9999
Pine Hill Trailways	800-858-8555
Shortline	800-631-8405
Triboro Coach	718-335-1000

For more bus information, call Port Authority bus information at 212-564-8484.

By Train

Amtrak is the leading carrier of passengers to and from points across the country in and out of New York City. For Amtrak information, call 800-872-7245 (800-USA-RAIL). Trains pull into Penn Station on the West Side of Manhattan between Seventh and Eighth Avenues just below 34th Street. From there you'll easily be able to take a taxi or bus to your hotel. Penn Station is very busy and crowded, so be sure to keep an eye on your property at all times. Cabs are easily found on surrounding streets.

For travel north and south, to and from other points in New York State, and even Connecticut, you can travel Metro North Commuter Railroads, which arrive at and depart

Airport Tip: Rides to the City, No Wait!

Taxi drivers are not allowed to solicit fares. Always wait in the taxi stand line when catching a cab from an airport. If a cab driver or anyone else meets you in the terminal and offers you a ride— even at a "low rate"— refuse it. So-called "gypsy cab" drivers are not legal and are not authorized by the city. Don't take chances. Get taxis at designated taxi stands and busses at designated bus areas.

from Grand Central Terminal on East 42nd Street at Park Avenue. Call 212-340-3000 for schedules and information.

Travel Agents

You can also make your airline arrangements and hotel plans all at once through travel agents. Through their "connections," they will often be able to put a package together for less money. This can save you both time and money. Travel agents are terrific to work with, but you must still get all the details to your liking. So ask questions about the flight and the room arrangements, as you would if you were making plans yourself. Also find out ahead of time what to do if you are dissatisfied with the accommodations and need to change them. Flexibility is important!

It's a good idea to read up on accommodations at various hotels so that you have an idea of what you are looking for. Then ask the travel agent about rates or discounts at those specific hotels. Also, if you are not renting a car, ask about arranging or at least providing details about the shuttle service to and from the airport. Good travel agents can also arrange transportation.

Deal with reputable travel agents and be careful with "too good to be true" deals advertised on the Internet or anyplace else. You can call the American Society of Travel Agents at 800-965-2782 to check on any travel agent. As is the case when dealing with anyone who is essentially working in your best interest, try to establish a good rapport with your travel agent or get a referral from someone you know and trust.

Packing for Your Trip

While the finer restaurants may require sport jackets for men, most restaurants, particularly those with family fare, do not have strict dress codes. Nonetheless, it's a good idea to mix in some dressy clothes along with casual attire.

Since the primary means of getting around Manhattan is walking, you will need at least two pairs of comfortable shoes

and/or sneakers. We can't emphasize this enough. A good pair of walking shoes can make the difference between a fun-filled, action-packed day and an all-out exhausting day. The same goes for layers: Be prepared for varying temperatures. Wearing layers of light and warm clothing will help keep you comfortable and happy while touring the city. The true characteristics of the four seasons are as defined as you'll find anywhere, but the weather within those seasons can sometimes be unpredictable.

If you are traveling to New York City for 10 days or less, it's to your advantage to bring 2 weeks worth of clothes, since doing laundry in many Manhattan hotels can be expensive, and Midtown Manhattan does not have many Laundromats.

Watching the Weather Channel or checking the temperature in New York in *USA Today* will give you an idea of the climate as you are planning for your trip. It's a good idea to have at least one small folding umbrella, since there's always the chance of a shower—particularly late afternoon thundershowers in the summer months.

The multitude of shops and 24-hour stores in New York City do allow for you to buy whatever you might leave at home. However, the city is pricey, and you don't want to have to buy items you just as easily could have brought along with you. So make a list before packing.

Make sure all bags have zippers or clasps that can be closed for security. If you are planning to carry bags onto the airplane, limit them to two per person but try to allow for one person to have a "free hand." Remember to label all bags so that they are easily identifiable at the airport luggage carousel.

If you bring things to do on the plane, tuck them away before you land so that you're not carrying anything besides your suitcases. Keep cameras tucked safely away until you are settled in your hotel. Unfortunately, there are some people in every major city who will try to take advantage of tourists. So be alert and don't accept offers of rides, tours, currency exchanges, or anything else from anyone you just happen to meet at the baggage claim area or on the streets of the city. And don't let anyone hold or guard your stuff for you. Exercise common sense at all times.

Airport Safety Tips

- Do not leave baggage unattended.

- Do not leave your wallet (or important papers) in one of your carry-on bags. Have it on your person, in a deep front pocket or a closed handbag (the bag's clasp facing you).

- If you use a cash machine or make a phone call with a calling card, do not let others see what numbers you are pressing.

Parking Safety Tip

Some New Yorkers use "The Club" while others post a "no radio" sign to ward off potential car break-ins. The most important precaution, however, is this: DO NOT leave anything of value in the car—or anything that might hint of a valuable item.

Where to Stay
New York Hotels

The sky's the limit when you look at hotel rooms in New York City. They range from no-frills $90 rooms to the $15,000 a night suites at the famed Plaza. For $250 a night or $1,500 a week (6 nights), you can stay in a double room (with your family) in one of the many fine hotels. Some offer discount packages and specials; it's worth asking about special offers.

You need to determine the type of accommodations that are right for your needs. A couple celebrating their twenty-fifth or fiftieth wedding anniversary may want to relax in style in a suite with all the trimmings, while a family with young kids may need a kitchenette and more practical surroundings. Determine the type of vacation you are looking for (sightseeing, romantic getaway, active and athletic, or a combination) and start planning accordingly. There is no right or wrong "style" of vacation. It depends on what you enjoy. New York is a city that can offer you accommodations to meet any flavor getaway you choose.

Amenities

What type of amenities meet your needs? A hotel featuring a business conference center, bars, and a special executive lounge may not be what you are seeking if you're traveling as a family. For a similar price, you might find a hotel such as the Double Tree Guest Suites more to your liking—they offer what's called the Kid's Quarter Club, which features interactive video games and other things for youngsters, plus a refrigerator and microwave in every room to save you money on a few breakfasts and lunches. So be practical.

Location

The obvious location choice is Manhattan, since you want to be in the middle of the action. Within Manhattan, you need to determine which area is to your liking. Hotels in and around Times Square are busy and certainly in the middle of the hustle and bustle. Since Times Square and 42nd Street are now "cleaned up" and Disney-fied, the area is more appropriate for families than it once

was. Times Square is ideal for theatergoing and sightseeing. Several midtown hotels in both the East and West 50s put you in close proximity to the sights and excitement of the city with slightly less hustle and bustle. As you approach Central Park, you'll find more lavish accommodations, particularly on Central Park South, where the Plaza and plush neighboring hotels overlook the park. These elegant hotels are in a less touristy area than Times Square and cost quite a bit more. Here, instead of the glut of souvenir shops you'd find in Times Square, you'll find elegant stores such as Tiffany's and Saks.

Heading downtown, there are many fine hotels in the 30s, on both the East Side and West Side. Some of these are a little quieter and less expensive, since they're not in the "middle of the excitement." Often these hotels will be surrounded by office or residential buildings. Since taxis are abundant and mass transit covers the city, it is not hard to get wherever you are going from these hotels. Streets in the downtown 30s, however, can be quiet at night, and you may not feel as safe walking around. Also, if something looks too inexpensive, be careful.

Way downtown in Lower Manhattan, you'll find some of the newest, most fashionable hotels in the city, in and around the World Trade Center. While this area can be quiet at night and on weekends, it is bustling during the day. If you are planning to see the Statue of Liberty, Ellis Island, the South Street Seaport, and other Lower Manhattan sights and are not as attracted to the midtown nightlife and Fifth Avenue museums, you may enjoy staying at these hotels, which are often frequented by business travelers in town for meetings in the financial district. You might appreciate more elbow room on the weekends as the business execs hit the road. On the other hand, if you plan evenings at the theater, want to spend days in Central Park and at the United Nations, and enjoy being in the heart of the action, this might not be the area for you.

Decide what you plan to do during your stay, your price range, and the atmosphere you are looking for when you step both into and out of the lobby and then determine which part of town best suits your needs.

Once you look through the hotel listings and determine those that fit your price range, consider these factors:

Travel Agent Tips

1. Deal with reputable, well-known travel agents.

2. Call for airfares ahead of time. Then you'll have a frame of reference for comparing prices to make sure you're getting a good deal.

3. Don't be talked into something you do not feel comfortable about—after all, it's you who will be taking the flight and staying in the room, not the travel agent.

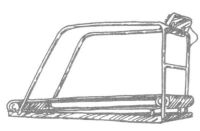

- Is there an extra charge per night for children staying in your room? Are there special children's rates or family packages?
- Is there a kitchenette in the room? A refrigerator? Microwave?
- What kind of restaurants are in the hotel? For family dining, a casual restaurant is more practical if you want to grab a quick, inexpensive breakfast or lunch. All major hotels have room service, but the prices can be eye-openers. (You're better off in a neighborhood with stores nearby to buy a few items rather than ordering room service.)
- Is there easy access to public transportation?
- Does the hotel have bus or van service to the airport?
- Does the hotel have a concierge? In New York City, a hotel concierge is far more common than a hotel swimming pool. It is also more practical, as the concierge can help you with directions, reservations, and all sorts of services.
- How much does the hotel charge for phone calls? Phone calls made from hotel rooms (anywhere) can be quite costly. It's to your advantage to make calling card calls or to use a cellular phone. You might also ask about a jack for using your laptop. Most New York hotels now offer two-line phones and jacks for computers. Being able to go on-line and look up your next destination can be a plus.
- Is there a safe in the room? Whenever you travel, it's important to know you can protect valuables. (Of course, it's not advisable to travel with too many "valuable" items.)
- What is the parking situation? If you drive to the city, ask your hotel about parking availability and cost. Even some of the biggest finest hotels in the city have tiny (fee) garages or arrangements with local lots for a certain number of spots. Also ask what the fee is for re-entry to the lot and whether the lot is near the hotel.

Hotel List

New York City is packed with hotels. Although the city has millions of visitors each year, there are still more rooms than there are

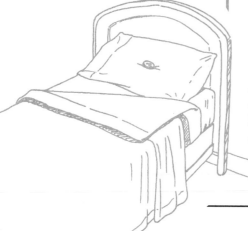

tourists and business guests. With that in mind, most hotels offer first-rate services to secure your business and have you return. They also know how valuable "word of mouth" is and want you to tell others about the accommodations. Room rates are not inexpensive; moderate rates are around $200 per night. And then there's a 13.25 percent hotel tax, plus a $2 per night room tax! **Always ask about special packages.**

Standard fare in New York City hotel rooms include televisions with cable access, movie choices (some for a fee and some free), stereos, and often CD players. Some hotels have video rental libraries; beyond that, it's not hard to find a video store in New York City. Two-line phones are common in most hotel rooms, along with modem and computer accessibility. Hair dryers are also commonly found in the rooms, along with toiletry items. The policy of nonsmoking floors has become standard, so if the reservation clerk doesn't ask you, ask him or her about a nonsmoking floor. Also, individual climate control is fairly common in all hotels.

New York hotels are famously expensive, and they're often luxurious. In the more lavish hotels, they really pile it on. However, if you plan to spend less time being pampered and more time out and about perusing the sights of the city, you may not need the marble bathtub or Louis XIV draperies. It's all up to you. You can choose to be treated like royalty, or you can look for more basic accommodations at a better price.

Figure out which amenities you are looking for and ask whether the particular hotel can provide them; then ask which are included and which have an extra cost attached.

For example, does the hotel have a health club? Find out whether it is open to all guests, whether you need to pay an additional fee, and what its features are. Is there a swimming pool? Swimming pools are uncommon in city hotels, although some of the huge modern facilities, such as Millennium in Lower Manhattan, have them.

If you're traveling with children, find out what the hotel offers for kids. If the person on the other end of the phone hesitates at the mention of children, this may not be the best place for you. Some hotels are more child friendly, with children's menus, videos for kids, and a game room. Depending on the deal, time of year,

Fitting In Tip

New Yorkers move at a rapid pace. Everyone is in a hurry—it's simply the pace of one of the world's most invigorating cities! Therefore, if you choose to stop to take a picture, to read the map, or just to look around, it's advisable to step away from the hustle and bustle of a busy Manhattan sidewalk. Step into a doorway or an alcove, or find somewhere to sit for a minute. This will keep you out of the path of people in a hurry and will make you less of a target for pickpockets.

and policy of the hotel, some offer "children stay free" plans to kids under 17.

When calling the hotel, you will often be linked up to "reservations." The person on the phone may be prepared to book you into the hotel but may not be able to answer your questions. Ask for brochures or for the hotel's Web site so that you can see for yourself what the accommodations look like.

Hotel chains are often a good bet: they are in the business of hospitality in a broader sense and have established a reputation for service. Hyatt, Hilton, Marriott, Loews, and international companies like the Fitzpatrick Group from Ireland have established reputations for hospitality and are all part of the vast New York hotel scene. This doesn't mean that a smaller hotel with personal service or a more intimate/elegant hotel can't be the perfect location for you.

Keep in mind that rates in New York City hotels vary almost as much as airfares. There are numerous rates offered for different seasons, weekdays, weekends, packages, and so on. Sometimes, like airlines, they are based on availability. It's good to check with several hotels and shop around. *When you read "Rates are subject to change," they definitely mean it in New York City.* The most popular, high-rate seasons are the fall and the December holiday season. The rates listed below are the lowest rates in the off-season. Therefore, you need to add at least $100 to $200 or more during peak seasons.

Although this listing is geared for leisure travelers, it should also be noted that almost every major New York City hotel has a business center. These range from a few computers and fax machines to expansive two-, three- and even five-floor mega business centers featuring state-of-the-art technology plus secretarial, messenger, and courier services. Since several million business travelers touch down in the city in a given year, the hotel industry is determined to stay at the forefront in regard to meeting their needs. If you have business needs, inquire about what is offered in the hotel business center and the hours of availability. In New York City, you should be able to find anything you need!

The listing of hotels that follows includes a few in each part of Manhattan, with an emphasis on accommodations for vacationers and families.

Midtown (East Side)—42nd Street to 59th Street

Beekman Tower
3 Mitchell Place
Between 49th Street and First Avenue
800-ME-SUITE; 212-355-7300

Overlooking the United Nations and the East River, this lavish art deco style hotel, built in 1928 offers 172 handsomely furnished studio, one-bedroom, and two-bedroom suites.

One of ten Manhattan East Suites properties in the city, the Beekman Tower suites feature complete kitchens with full stoves, refrigerators, microwaves, dishes, and utensils. Luxury baths, plush robes, and cable channels, plus in-room movies and in-room safes are included in your accommodations. The facility also offers a health club with saunas, a concierge, valet parking, a coin-operated laundry, a grocery shopping service, and more.

Essentially this is an opportunity to rent a luxury apartment in New York City for a week, complete with (in some cases) a terrace and a river view. In fact, you're one up on apartment dwellers–you can get room service! The kitchens can save you some money if you buy food and eat in, or you can use the valet grocery shopping service to have groceries delivered to your door.

The Zephyr Grille restaurant features continental American cuisine, while the Top of the Tower on the twenty-sixth floor overlooks the city and serves lunch, dinner, or cocktails.

Rates start at $229.

Other Manhattan Suites East Hotels in the city include the **Dumont Plaza, Eastgate Tower, Lyden Gardens, Lyden House, Plaza Fifty, Shelbourne Murray Hill**, and **Surrey Hotel**—all located between 34th and 76th Streets on the East Side. The Southgate Tower is on Manhattan's West Side, by Penn Station. Call 800-ME-SUITES for reservations at any of the properties.

Tipping Is Appreciated

Taxi drivers usually get 15 to 20 percent. Baggage handlers and bell-hops generally get $1 per bag. Waiters and waitresses get 15 percent—or more if the service was particularly good. For large groups, usually at least eight people or more, gratuities may be added to the bill, so look at your check carefully.

"Taxi Speak"

Cab drivers in New York are from all over the world. Be sure you are very clear about where you are going and make sure they understand. Check a map ahead of time so that you can be certain you are not going the wrong way.

Crowne Plaza at the United Nations
304 East 42nd Street
Between First and Second Avenues
800-879-8836; 212-986-8800

This forty-year-old, twenty-story high-rise is a fashionable hotel in the quaint surroundings of Tudor City, just a block away from the United Nations and a bus ride across town to Times Square. High on hospitality and comfort, the Crowne Plaza is a popular stop for tourists and for visiting dignitaries with business at the U.N.

The hotel has a classic old-world charm, with marble floors and velvet furnishings. The tiny Tudor City area, a quiet street tucked away behind the hotel, is just off 41st Street. Most New Yorkers have probably never seen this little two-block area overlooking the United Nations.

As for the three-hundred-room luxury hotel, which enters off the more popular East 42nd Street, guest rooms include in-room movies, mini-bars, digital safes, large beds, Italian marble bathrooms and a warm, comfortable, yet modern atmosphere. The hotel includes a fitness center, concierge, parking, and some marvelous views from the higher floors. For a few dollars extra you can enjoy complimentary breakfasts and cocktails in the Crowne Club Lounge. (Only in New York can you find complimentary amenities for a fee.) Nonetheless, this is a first-rate facility in a prime, safe, and easily accessible location run by a worldwide hotel chain.

Cecils' Bistro, featuring both American and French cuisine, is on the premises.

Rates start at $199.

Fitzpatrick Grand Central Hotel
141 East 44th Street
Between Lexington and Third Avenues
800-367-7701; 212-351-6800

The newer of the two Manhattan East Side hotels run by the Irish-based Fitzpatrick Hotel Group, this is the larger slice of Dublin, with 155 rooms including eight suites and two garden suites. Rooms feature canopied beds, Irish linens, and plush bathrobes, and you can probably even order Irish coffee from 24-hour room service.

A short walk from the United Nations and ten blocks north of the Empire State Building, this hotel's cozy lobby sports a couple of old-fashioned wood-burning fireplaces and a comfortable setting that sets you apart from the busy Midtown location.

Concierge service is also included. Perhaps the biggest drawing card of the Fitzpatrick hotels is the personalized, friendly service.

The Grand Central Fitzpatrick is home to the Wheeltapper, a quaint "old-world Irish railroad-themed pub" with a full menu and a children's menu called "The Wee Folk."

Rates start at $325 for a double and $395 for a double suite. Special packages are offered frequently.

The Fitzpatrick Manhattan Hotel
687 Lexington Avenue
Between 56th and 57th Streets
800-367-7701; 212-355-0100

The second of the two Fitzpatrick hotels is a small inn in the heart of Manhattan, just two blocks from Bloomingdales and close to Rockefeller Center. Consisting of fifty-two one-bedroom suites and forty guest rooms, all impeccably, tastefully furnished, the Fitzpatrick offers the personal touch. Cozy accommodations, such as carefully chosen fabrics and furnishings, terry cloth robes, and soft lighting, help make your stay relaxing.

The hotel also provides a comfortable, charming lobby with a warm atmosphere, plus amenities that include laundry service, a health club, and a concierge. An Irish pub along with Fitzers Restaurant, serving Irish delights as well as American cuisine, are all part of this property. There are weekend rates and specials for children, including a complimentary VCR and a video library.

Perhaps the most significant features of the Fitzpatrick Manhattan, like its sister hotel, are the personalized attention and ideal location of the property.

Rates start at $295 and $365 for suites.

Smart Money-Saving Tip

Saving money is a concern for most people, but not at the cost of a safe and enjoyable vacation. A deal that sounds "too good to be true" or is notably out of line with other prices may mean you are venturing into either a scheme, whereby you pay more money later, or a dangerous situation, or both.

On a more subtle note, if you are driving, you may be told of a route that saves you money by avoiding a $4 toll bridge. If, however, the route takes you through a high crime neighborhood after dark, it may not be worth saving the $4.

Be smart when trying to save money!

Grand Hyatt New York
Park Avenue at Grand Central
800-233-1234 or 800-243-2546 (for instant check-in);
212-883-1234

With over thirteen hundred rooms, the Grand Hyatt is indeed "grand"! Donald Trump built the hotel; it opened in 1980 and was refurbished with a $100 million face-lift in 1996. The Hyatt is a short walk from Broadway theaters, the United Nations, the finest shopping on Fifth Avenue, and other attractions. Sports fans may enjoy catching a glimpse of the ballplayers who stay at the hotel when the "visiting" teams are in town.

The Hyatt's rooms including sixty-three suites, are well lit, sleek, and comfortable, with in-room movies and other amenities. A health club, concierge, laundry service, and outdoor garden are all part of the Grand Hyatt, which features a sprawling plant-filled atrium lobby, complete with a cascading waterfall. It's quite impressive, but that's typical "Trump" stylings.

Three restaurants include the glass enclosed Sun Garden Lounge, which serves Mediterranean fare and overlooks 42nd Street; the Crystal Fountain, which serves American cuisine and champagne Sunday brunches; and the small Cigar Room, featuring fine dining and exquisite cigars.

Rates start at $219 on weekends and $265 on weekdays. Ask about holiday rates.

Loews New York
569 Lexington Avenue
At East 51st Street
800-23-LOEWS; 212-752-7000

Built in 1961 and designed by the same architect as the famed Fontainebleau (in Miami), this recently renovated 728 room hotel sports an art deco lobby plus two restaurants and several stores below. While the views aren't spectacular, the stylish East Side/Midtown area offers an array of shopping and restaurants. It's also convenient to all transportation.

Essentially a quality hotel, without the elegant trimmings, Loews offers a good value, comfort, safety, cleanliness and some amenities

in a good location. The Club 51 concierge level provides special amenities including complimentary breakfasts and evening cocktails.

Rooms are comfortable and feature an in-room safe, modern decor, a marble bathtub, an in-room modem line, and a refrigerator. Other amenities include a modern fitness center, a concierge for special requests, and reasonable parking (for Manhattan) at $30 a day. On the premises you'll find a gourmet coffee beanery, a nail salon, a barber shop, and a W. H. Smith newspaper and magazine shop.

The Lexington Avenue Lounge offers an intimate setting for cocktails, snacks, or supper, complete with a multitude of television screens with news, sports, and videos. The Lexington Avenue Grill is a popular location for standard American Cuisine in a warm, "casually elegant" environment.

Rates start at $189.

Marriott East Side
535 Lexington Avenue
Between 49th and 50th Streets
800-228-9290; 212-755-4000

Once upon a time this was the Shelton Towers (built in 1924). Over the years, it has been a stomping ground for many performers, including Harry Houdini, who performed escape tricks from the pool. Band leader Xavier Cugat, Peggy Lee, and Eddie Fisher also performed there—but not in the pool. Shelton Towers was also the first major New York City hotel to employ female bellhops.

Today, the property is a landmark Marriott Hotel. Its East Side location is ideal for visiting Rockefeller Center, the United Nations, and many other popular city locations. The grand lobby, complete with columns and a lavish interior, welcomes you to this fashionable, but not ostentatious, hotel.

Some 643 guest rooms and 12 suites offer a "Servi-Bar" (snacks) and in-room movies as part of their well-appointed, fashionable accommodations. There are six deluxe concierge floors available, plus amenities for all guests, including a theater, tour and travel desk, health club, video message center, safe deposit boxes, and gift shop.

After Dark

New York city is known as "the city that never sleeps." This is because there are clubs, bars, and restaurants operating at all hours. HOWEVER, this does not mean that many, if not most, city streets do not get quiet after 10 P.M. (and earlier in some places). Even the busy Times Square, as it gets later, can have a seamy element (despite the cleanup of 42nd Street). Therefore, while it's great to enjoy the city's nightlife, it's ill advised to walk around most of New York City late at night unless you are in a busy area such as Greenwich Village or perhaps around Lincoln Center or the Upper West Side on the main streets. City side streets can be very quiet. Be careful.

The Shelton Grille features continental dining throughout the day, and the lobby lounge provides an intimate setting for cocktails and conversation.

Rates start around $200 and suites around $400.

New York Palace
455 Madison Avenue
Between 50th and 51st Streets
800-697-2522; 212-888-7000

Set in a newly refurbished 1882 landmark estate, the eight-hundred-room hotel—the former Helmsley Palace—is now a luxurious facility with a lavish decor, spacious first-class accommodations, and easy access to everything Midtown has to offer. Features include three dual line phones, in-room safes, and fully stocked refreshment bars.

Hotel amenities include a concierge and 24-hour laundry service plus a 7,000 square-foot first class health club complete with TV monitors and headphones at each treadmill. A separate "Towers" section has 175 guest rooms and suites with a separate check-in, butler service, and a host of other niceties including room service from one of New York's premier restaurants, Le Cirque 2000. If all this isn't enough, high atop the Tower sit the Triplex suites—three-floor accommodations with their own private elevator, marble floors, fully equipped kitchen, master bedroom, a solarium, and private outdoor terrace for sunbathing.

The Palace is home to the world famous Le Cirque 2000, recently renovated and reopened, and Isetan, featuring Mediterranean cuisine. It also neighbors Sushusay, one of the city's best Japanese restaurants.

Rates start at $475 and $900 for suites. Ask about seasonal specials.

Regal U.N. Plaza
One United Nations Plaza
At 44th Street and First Avenue
800-222-8888; 212-758-1234

Part of the Regal International Hotel chain, The U.N. Plaza, directly across from the United Nations, offers quiet elegance rising

some twenty-eight stories high. Elegant tapestries with designs dating back as far as the ninth century adorn the property, reflecting the multinational ambiance of the neighborhood.

Several of the 427 brilliantly decorated guest rooms are suites. Some have kitchenettes, and all have great views of either Midtown or the East River and Queens. Rooms include mini-bars, HBO, and in-room movies, and the hotel offers valet parking, a concierge, a heated indoor pool, fitness center, massage and sauna, indoor tennis courts, and covered parking. You can also exchange currency at the front desk if you are traveling from abroad.

A special section of rooms, the Regal Class, is available for long-term leasing.

Restaurants include the Ambassador Grille, a casually elegant (highly acclaimed) eatery, and the Ambassador Lounge, which serves light lunches and cocktails.

Rates start at $300 for guest rooms and $500 for Junior Suites. Children under 17 can stay free if sharing a room with their parents.

St. Regis Hotel
2 East 55th Street
Between Fifth Avenue and Madison
800-759-7550; 212-753-4500

The height of elegance, the St. Regis offers guests an unparalleled level of comfort and luxury. Originally opened in 1904 (as New York's tallest building at the time) and recently restored with a $100 million, 3-year face-life, this is *the* lap of luxury, complete with high ceilings, crystal chandeliers, velvet-covered armchairs, silk wallpaper, mahogany paneling, valuable antique tapestries, and Tiffany dinnerware. There is even butler service in every room. Needless to say, the St. Regis is among the priciest hotels in the city . . . no, make that the world.

The 315 rooms, featuring 92 suites, provide the modern-day amenities, including mini-bars, in-room safes, and fax machines. A concierge, laundry service, beauty salon, library (featuring leather-bound volumes and a librarian), health club, baby-sitting service and parking are among the various amenities offered. Designer stores, including Bijan, Odica, and Christian Dior, are located in the building.

Complimentary Breakfast

A complimentary breakfast can save you $25 for a family of four per day. It is included at the following hotels:

The Avalon,
16 East 32nd Street
(212-299-7000)

The Bentley,
500 East 62nd Street
(212-644-6000)

Comfort Inn Manhattan,
42 West 35th Street
(212-947-0200)

East Side Inn,
201 East 24th Street
(212-696-3800)

The Midtown Inn,
243 West 55th Street
(212-489-0808)

Roger Smith Hotel,
501 Lexington Avenue
(212-755-1400)

Roger Williams Hotel,
131 Madison Avenue
(212-448-7000)

The St. Regis is certainly not for your typical vacationer. It is for an extremely upscale clientele or perhaps for a very special weekend anniversary or celebratory trip.

Restaurants include Lespinasse, one of the city's most prestigious four-star dining experiences, and the King Cole Bar and Lounge, featuring the Maxfield Parrish "King Cole" mural. The Astor Court, an elegant tea lounge, is also featured.

Rates start at $520, and suites can go for as high as $10,500 a night.

Declared a New York City landmark in 1988, the St. Regis has won numerous hotel awards.

The Waldorf Astoria
301 Park Avenue
Between 49th and 50th Streets
800-WALDORF; 212-355-3000

Originally opened in 1893 on 33rd Street, the Waldorf you see today has been at its current location since October of 1931. Over the years, the classic hotel has undergone some $200 million in renovations to maintain its art deco look and New York City landmark status.

There is a great history to the grand hotel. Over the years, the Waldorf has seen its share of dignitaries, including numerous American presidents, King Hussein, Charles de Gaulle, and Queen Elizabeth II, among others. It was, for many years, the site where Guy Lombardo and his orchestra ushered in the new year. The Empire Room was and still is home to great entertainment, including Frank Sinatra on the bill on a number of occasions. The hotel was even the residence for three five-star generals: Douglas MacArthur, Dwight Eisenhower, and Omar Bradley.

Today, the Waldorf has some 1,380 guest rooms and over 200 suites, each designed in a slightly different manner. The rooms have luxuries ranging from marble bathrooms to the modern in-room premium cable and video, plus in-room checkout features.

The hotel also features not one, but two lobbies, one of which (on the Park Avenue side) has a 148,000-piece mosaic called "Wheel Of Life." A concierge is available, plus an international concierge service desk providing assistance in over sixty languages.

There is a theater desk, a tour desk, and a Plus One fitness center with six personal trainers and full-time massage therapists. When you're finished with your 30-minute personal training session, you can treat yourself to a 30-minute, or longer, shopping spree at one of several posh, luxurious boutiques that are also part of the Waldorf. A gift shop and florist are also on the premises.

A highlight of the Waldorf is the dining. Four restaurants, with a shared kitchen that takes up a city block, are the pride of this classic hotel. Peacock Alley serves up French cuisine featuring many specialty items. The popular Bull and Bear is known for steaks and fine seafood. You can sit at the mahogany bar and enjoy a pre-dinner cocktail while watching the stock quotes pass by on an electric ticker. (If your stock goes up, you can buy everyone dessert!) Oscars is an American bistro serving classic American dishes in a relaxed setting. Inagiku is a Japanese restaurant serving a variety of classic and contemporary dishes. There is also a lounge, the Cocktail Terrace, overlooking the art deco Park Avenue lobby, featuring an informal Wednesday night fashion show to the strains of Cole Porter piano music from 4 to 7 P.M.

The Waldorf is not only an elegant place to stay but also a sight to visit on your trip. With that in mind, the Waldorf gives guided tours—how many hotels can say that? Their Landmark Tours can be scheduled for groups of twelve starting at 9 A.M. for a cost of $300. (It's the Waldorf—nothing comes cheap!) For a visiting group, the hotel tour is a unique venture that takes 90 minutes and goes behind the scenes to see how this small city within a city operates. Guides will recount some of the hotel's great history and take you through the immense kitchen and four-story grand ballroom, where the big bands once played. For tours call 212-872-7227.

Even if you consider a tour to be "a bit much," you should stop and see this hotel and perhaps plan to dine at one of the restaurants. Dinner at the Waldorf is a nice touch on any visit. If you plan to stay, book well in advance.

The Waldorf offers several packages, including the romance package with plenty of champagne, the Bounceback Weekend Package with continental breakfasts, and the Weekend at the Waldorf package . . . call for details.

Rates start at $300 and suites at $500.

Pets Allowed!

Pets are allowed at the following hotels:

The Michelangelo,
152 West 51st Street
(212-765-1900)

Hilton New York Hotel and Towers,
1335 Sixth Avenue
(212-586-7000)

New York Marriott Marquis,
1535 Broadway
(212-398-1900)

The Plaza,
768 Fifth Avenue
(212-759-3000)

SoHo Grand Hotel,
310 West Broadway
(212-965-3000)

Midtown (West Side)—42nd to 59th Streets

The Algonquin
59 West 44th Street
Between Fifth and Sixth Avenues
800-555-8000; 212-840-6800

This classic hotel is famous for its Algonquin Roundtable literary gatherings, which included such writers as Dorothy Parker and James Thurber. For many years, it was the "in" place to meet for writers, and it housed visiting actors, playwrights, and others in the arts, including Helen Hayes, Sinclair Lewis, Maya Angelou, George S. Kaufman, and so many other notables. Built in 1902, the Algonquin is now a historic New York landmark and, if you're not staying within, worth a visit.

The hotel is rich with history, and it is also fresh off a $5.5 million restoration designed to return the property to an earlier period, with furnishings from the turn of the century. The antiques that make up the Algonquin decor were carefully chosen to recreate the ambiance of a bygone era.

Today, the 165-room hotel combines the elegance and charm of the early twentieth century with the functionality of the early twenty-first century. Specialty suites are dedicated to and feature the works of Dorothy Parker, with warm, comfortable furnishings in all guest rooms, plus movies, safes, and fax machines as part of the in-room amenities.

A small 24-hour fitness center would seem out of place, but if you read while on the treadmill, you will at least be maintaining the literary theme of the hotel. Concierge and laundry service are available, and also on premises is (appropriately) a library.

The Oak Room, for dining by day, becomes a cabaret at night. The cabaret features dining and entertainment Tuesdays through Saturdays, with dinner beginning at 7 and the curtain going up on first-rate entertainment at 9. The Blue Bar serves cocktails and food, and the Spoken Word is a place for literary programs that range from discussions about books to readings of short plays.

Rates start at $325 January through March.

Ameritania Hotel
230 West 54th Street
Corner of Broadway
212-247-5000

A hip, trendy 207-room hotel includes 39 rooms with king-sized beds and 13 suites. The interiors and guest rooms were refurbished in 1998, and the marble and fashionable decor is quite pleasing.

A stone's throw from the Ed Sullivan Theater and home to *Late Night with David Letterman*, the Ameritania is just a short walk from Central Park, the Theater District, and Fifth Avenue shopping. Amenities include valet laundry service, a concierge, and discounted parking. A comfortable, well-situated hotel, the Ameritania is one of several Amsterdam Hospitality Group Hotels around the city, all designed to provide quality accommodations at reasonable (for Manhattan) prices. One such property, the Amsterdam Court Hotel, is very similar to the Ameritania and sits just four blocks away at Broadway and 50th Street. Call the Amsterdam Court at 212-459-1000.

The Ameritania features the popular Bar 54, a restaurant/bar with standard fare, serving all meals and cocktails in a sky-lit atrium.

Rates start at $185 and $265 for deluxe suites.

Best Western Manhattan
17 West 32nd Street
Between Fifth and Sixth Avenue
800-567-7720; 212-246-8800

Best Western provides your standard clean, comfortable hotel room at a good price. The "Manhattan" is in the fashion district, which is hectic by day and quiet by night. For sightseeing, you are in the shadows of the Empire State Building and close to Times Square and the Theater District. You can also stroll over to nearby Macy's for some shopping with the money you save on your room.

The 176 rooms are basic with on-demand movies, irons, coffeemakers, and typical fare. The hotel has a fitness room, beauty salon, and laundry service and provides complimentary continental breakfast.

Bring Your Bathing Suit!

Swimming pools can be found at these hotels:

Crowne Plaza Manhattan,
1605 Broadway
(212-977-4000)

Holiday Inn Midtown,
440 West 57th Street
(212-581-8100)

Le Parker Meridien New York,
118 West 57th Street
(212-245-5000)

Millenium Hilton,
55 Church Street
(212-693-2001)

Bring Your Bathing Suit!

Swimming pools can be found at these hotels:

New York Marriott Financial Center,
85 West Street
(212-266-6145)

Regal U.N. Plaza Hotel,
One United Nations Plaza
(212-758-1234)

Sheraton Manhattan Hotel,
790 Seventh Avenue
(212-581-3300)

Skyline Hotel,
725 Tenth Avenue
(212-586-3400)

Travel Inn Hotel,
515 West 42nd Street
(212-695-7171)

Best Westerns are good hotels. In Manhattan, where luxury and pricey amenities are abundant, this is comparatively a no-frills deal, but for the "get up and go" traveler who plans to get out each day and see the city, this fits the bill nicely.

Restaurants include Manhattan Café, which serves American cuisine; Dae Dong, serving Asian food (located next door with an entrance from the lobby); and the Skybar, an outdoor rooftop bar that is pleasant for snacks and drinks in the warm weather.

Rates start at $99 and $129 for suites.

Note: Another Best Western hotel, the Best Western Woodward, is located at 210 West 55th Street (800-336-4110).

Crowne Plaza
1605 Broadway
Between 48th & 49th Streets
800-243-6969; 212-977-4000

At a marvelous location—just north of the busy Times Square area, south of Central Park, and within a short walk of the Theater District, Rockefeller Center, St. Patrick's Cathedral, and Fifth Avenue shopping—sits the forty-six-story, upscale 770-room Crowne Plaza Manhattan.

The views are terrific from the higher floors. Rooms feature an in-room refreshment center, free movie channels, makeup mirrors, ironing boards, and in-room safes. Children under 19 stay for free if sharing a room with their parents—a nice touch for families. The hotel also offers a room service kiddie menu.

The on-site health club is huge—nearly 30,000 square feet—and is run by fitness managers with trainers on hand. And yes, the health club has one of the city's largest hotel indoor swimming pools. The pool and wide array of fitness equipment are first class amenities, as are classes offered in boxing, yoga, ballet, and water aerobics.

Crowne Plaza sports a friendly atmosphere and provides laundry service, a concierge, and on-site valet parking. Restaurants include the 136-seat Balcony Café, which is ideal for breakfast and lunch; the Sampling Bar, which is a lively bar/restaurant for pre-theater fare with a wide variety of wines; and the Broadway Grill, which is a casual 120 seater with memorabilia from the Broadway shows.

Rates start at $199 and suites at $450.

Days Hotel
790 Eight Avenue
Between 48th and 49th Streets
800-572-6232; 212-581-7000

Part of the Loews Hotel Group, Days Hotel is a standard facility offering quality rooms at a comparatively good price. Featuring 367 recently renovated guest rooms, the hotel is within walking distance to the Theater District for Broadway shows, Rockefeller Center, and Radio City.

Rooms are sizable, with on-demand movies and plenty of cable channels and in-room climate controls, plus refrigerators (in some rooms). The gift shop doubles as a concierge, making tour arrangements and helping arrange for theater tickets.

The Days Hotel is, essentially, not unlike hotels you'll find along the highways of America. This is your standard "place to stay," not elegant, not fancy, but comfortable and a good choice for the family with plenty of things to see and do. The neighborhood, once an outgrowth of "seedy" Forty-second Street, has improved with the Times Square cleanup and is crowded with theater goers in the evenings.

There is a garage with a rate of $15 or higher per day, depending on whether you use the car. You can pay more money if you want valet parking, but why would you?

The Metro Deli serves standard American fare and is open from 6 A.M. to 11 P.M.

Rates start at $150 ($350 in December).

Doubletree Guest Suites
1568 Broadway
Between 46th and 47th Streets
800-325-9033; 212-719-1600

"Suites" is the operative word here, with forty-three floors featuring some 460 suites. And, like everything else these days, you have a wide range of choices, including king suites, queen suites, double/double suites, executive conference suites, family suites, handicap suites, nonsmoking suites, and two presidential suites.

Suites include private bedrooms and separate living rooms, plus sofa beds, wet bars, microwaves, refrigerators, two televisions with

Kid-Friendly Hotels

Amenities for kids are featured at the following:

The Paramount Hotel, 235 West 46th Street, (212-764-5500), includes a well-stocked children's playroom

The Plaza, 768 Fifth Avenue (212-759-3000)— includes a Young Plaza Ambassador's Club, where kids from 6 to 19 receive various gifts, plus free Sunday brunch and "Plaza Dollars" for special discounts.

The Lap of Luxury

You can get champagne popsicles at the Premier, 133 West 44th Street (212-768-4400).

cable, and more space then many New York City apartments. They are all well decorated.

The hotel features a state-of-the-art fitness center, valet service, and a family floor with child safety features—plus a dedicated Kids Club that offers video games and fun activities for children ages 3 through 12. A gift shop and laundry are also on premises.

The Doubletree is in the heart of the Times Square action, towering high, with a glitzy, modern look and an off-the-street lobby (common in the Times Square hotels) that affords privacy and safety. It is a very child-friendly hotel, featuring freshly baked chocolate chip cookies and play activities. The suites, at essentially the same rates as comparable guest rooms in the area, provide that much-needed room for family traveling.

The Center Stage Café offers American cuisine with a Broadway theater ambiance. The Cabaret Lounge provides piano music in a lavish show biz setting while you sip cocktails.

Rates start at $200.

Hilton New York and Towers
1335 Avenue of the Americas
Between 53rd and 54th Streets
800-HILTONS; 212-261-5870

Located in the heart of Manhattan is this forty-six-story Hilton with a special "Towers" section overlooking the city below.

It's hard to go wrong with a Hilton property. This massive hotel is a city in a city, providing all sorts of conveniences. Guest rooms are clean and roomy and sport modern decor plus refreshment centers, pay movies, and various basic amenities.

The hotel itself has a lot to offer, including a state-of-the-art fitness center, concierge service, foreign currency exchange, computerized checkout, and an AT&T language line offering 140 languages, plus elevators with CNN newscasts to keep you abreast of what's going on in the world during your ride. There are numerous shops located in this mass structure, including boutiques, a gift shop, drugstore, ticket booth, and beauty salon/barber shop. The Hilton also has fifty-two rooms specially designed for people with disabilities; the rooms are equipped to accommodate guests in wheelchairs.

The Towers is a special private sector from the thirty-eighth through forty-fourth floors, featuring a private lounge for complimentary breakfast, afternoon tea, hors d'oeuvres, and more. There are various other amenities for the Tower clientele.

The Hilton has long been a favorite of visitors to the city because of the first-rate service, easy accessibility, and wide range of amenities. They draw families in with their "children under 18 stay free" policy (providing they share a room with their parents or grandparents). They also have a "Vacation Station"—a toy lending station and a folder of activities for kids to do around the city (it's open during the summer months).

An eight-level underground parking garage has 24-hour valet parking.

Restaurants include Etrusca, the new Italian eatery, plus the New York Marketplace, a sidewalk café that is ideal for breakfasts or lunches. There are also the Bridges Bar and the Lobby Lounge for a nightcap.

Double rooms start at $250 and suites start at $525.

Marriott Marquis
1535 Broadway
Between 45th and 46th Streets
800-843-4898; 212-398-1900

In the heart of the Theater District, and housing a Broadway theater within, the fifty-story Marriott Marquis is one of the premiere hotels in the Times Square area. The modern skyscraper is accentuated by a thirty-seven story open atrium with glass enclosed elevators that provide a spectacular ride.

The nineteen hundred rooms are modern and spacious, with in-room safes and service bars, plus on-command video and the latest in climate-control conveniences. The hotel is a small city unto itself, with shops, restaurants, lounges, three bars, a beauty salon, and a health club. Amenities include laundry service, concierge, parking (limited and for a fee), baby-sitting, airport service, and a tour and transportation desk.

Marriotts are usually well run, and this big, bold, bright Broadway hotel is no exception. The energy and excitement of the Theater District is prevalent throughout, but with the main lobby several floors above the street, there's also a feeling of being secure and away from the hustle and bustle of the busy area.

Restaurants include the View (a rooftop restaurant that revolves), the JW Steakhouse, Encore, and the Atrium Café. While you browse the premises, which in itself can take a day, you'll also find the Top of the View Lounge, Clock Lounge, and Broadway Lounge. Get a map or you'll get lost.

If the city doesn't have enough to offer, the hotel has more than its share of places to visit and to stop by for a bite to eat.

Rates start at $220 and $450 for suites.

Novotel
226 West 52nd Street
Between Broadway and Seventh Avenue
800-NOVOTEL; 212-315-0100

Smack in the busy Times Square/Theater District, the Novotel offers European hospitality and easy access to the sights of Midtown Manhattan.

The spacious lobby is safely tucked away on the seventh floor of the high-rise hotel with its 480 modern guest rooms. Rooms include an in-room safe, multiple pay movie choices, a mini-bar, and a large bathroom.

Part of the worldwide Novotel hotel chain, the property is well run and offers standard city amenities including a new fitness room, a theater ticket booth, and gift shop. The hotel also offers several packages including a three-day theater lovers plan and a kids under 16 stay free policy (if they share a room with their parents). Children also receive a complimentary breakfast.

The location, plus their kid-friendly status, safe and clean environment, and comparatively good rates (for New York City), puts the Novotel in strong competition with the Marriotts and more familiar name hotels.

Restaurants include the Café Nicole, featuring French and American specialties, along with a piano bar with nightly entertainment.

Rates start at $605, for a 3-night double-room package, and are higher in the fall.

Ramada Milford Plaza
270 West 45th Street
At Broadway
800-221-2690; 212-869-3000

A Ramada property, the Milford Plaza put a lot of money behind its advertising campaign, which featured the tune "Lullaby of Broadway" to appeal to the theatergoers—as the hotel is smack in the middle of the Theater District. The campaign apparently worked; Milford has established a presence amid several more luxurious hotels rich with amenities and designed for the business traveler.

Some thirteen hundred rooms were refurbished in 1995; they are comfortable and safe and feature cable TV and in-room movies. While they are not lavish, they are sufficient if you are planning to spend the bulk of your time seeing the sights and/or taking in the Broadway shows.

A spacious lobby complete with fountains, chandeliers, and flowers awaits you as you enter. Once inside, the Milford features a theater ticket and sightseeing desk, a game room for the kids, a fitness center, valet services, and parking at $14 per day (if you don't use the car that day). There is also a gift shop.

Restaurants include the Celebrity Deli and the Honolulu Steamship Company. Both are more than adequate.

The Milford Plaza provides no-frills rooms at a good price in a great location.

Rates start at $129 for two persons, suites at $200.

Sheraton New York Hotel and Towers
811 Seventh Avenue
Between 52nd and 53rd Streets
800-223-6550; 212-581-1000

Sheraton is another highly trusted top name in the hotel business, and this 1,750-room skyscraper is no exception. A host of suites can also be found, including special Tower Rooms, Hospitality Rooms, and VIP Suites with parlors.

In-room amenities include "refreshment centers," coffeemakers with complimentary Starbucks coffee (in some rooms), in-room movies, and video checkout. Through an affiliation with the

Booking Your Room: Some Tips

1. Book your hotel room several weeks in advance using a major credit card.
2. Make note of the name of the person who takes your reservations, and always get a confirmation number.
3. Call a few days before you arrive to confirm your reservation. If, for some reason, the hotel cannot find your reservation when you get there, tell the desk clerk the name of the person who took the reservation, the date of the transaction, and the confirmation number. Armed with such backup material, you might even get an upgrade! The adage "The customer is always right" still holds true, especially in New York City, where—believe it or not—people most often aim to please.

Voyager's Collection, a hotel shopping catalog is also available, featuring hundreds of products via in-room interactive TV.

The hotel itself is a few blocks north of the Theater District, Times Square, Radio City Music Hall, and Rockefeller Center and just south of Carnegie Hall and Central Park. In short, it is a prime location. The Sheraton offers a theater desk and a 4,000-square-foot fitness center and health club, complete with everything from personal trainers and steam rooms to fresh fruit (but don't eat it in the steam room).

The Sheraton Towers is a hotel within a hotel, with a special "elite" group of rooms that include personal butler service, private check-in, and a lounge on the forty-ninth floor.

Restaurants include the Streeter's New York Café, a large glass-enclosed cafe that seats 180 people on various levels for breakfast, lunch, and dinner; Hudson's Sports Bar and Grill, which is home to numerous sporting events on large-screen TVs; and the Lobby Court Lounge and Cigar Bar, with a unique mix of martinis and appetizers, located off 53rd Street. A singer/pianist performs Tuesdays through Saturdays from 8:30 to after midnight.

The location, amenities, security, and history of success at Sheraton properties makes this one a good choice.

Nearby is the renovated Sheraton Manhattan at Seventh Avenue and 51st Street. Guests of the Sheraton New York Hotel and Towers can run across the street and use the Sheraton Manhattan's 50-foot-long swimming pool. The Sheraton Manhattan features Russo's Steak and Pasta Restaurant and typical Sheraton amenities.

Rates run from $179 to over $300, and suites from $450 to $700.

The Time Hotel
224 West 49th Street
Between Eighth Avenue and Broadway
800-877-TIMENYC; 212-246-5252

One of the city's newest hotels, the Time Hotel is a "luxury boutique hotel" in the middle of Times Square, featuring just 164 rooms and 28 suites.

Rooms are sleek and modern, with bold colors. Curtains in place of closet doors, TV sets in canvas covers and essays on the choice

Traveler Tip

If you are heading to New York City to primarily enjoy the sights and sounds of Manhattan, it's not necessary to rent a car for your entire stay. If you take a day trip to Long Island or one of the other four boroughs, simply arrange ahead of time to rent a car for just that day. Better yet, take the bus, the subway, or a commuter train! There's no reason to have a car to get around Manhattan, when cabs and mass transit will do the job for you, and you'll save on parking, rental fees, gas, and headaches!

of color for the room will be part of this unique (*somewhat eclectic*) experience in Manhattan. And if that isn't enough, the primary color (red, blue, or yellow) will continue throughout the entire room, plus a special red-, blue-, or yellow-inspired scent in the bathroom.

Basic amenities include a mini-bar, an in-room safe, Web TV along with cable and movie channels, complimentary bathrobes, and in-room fax machines. The Time also offers a concierge, fitness center, personal shopper service, laundry and dry cleaning service, valet service, express checkout, and a second-floor lounge. Essentially the hotel provides large hotel amenities in a smaller setting. While the "designer rooms and fragrances" aren't going to be for everyone, the hotel is modern and still has that "new hotel smell." The hotel's smaller size, compared to its Times Square counterparts, can be comforting, especially when waiting for an elevator.

The Palladin restaurant is, like the hotel, eclectic, with a contemporary flair from an internationally known chef. While you can order food up to your room from the Palladin, don't be discouraged if it doesn't match the room's primary color. The Time Lounge on the second floor has a "tapas" menu, plus cocktails and specialty drinks.

Rates start at $200.

Travel Inn Hotel
515 West 42nd Street
Between Tenth and Eleventh Avenues
800-869-4630; 212-695-7171

West 42nd Street underwent the first wave of revitalization on the city's major cross street. The Travel Inn sits right in the middle of that area's "new look," just a few blocks from the Javits Center and not far from Times Square.

Nothing too fancy, but a good value, with clean rooms and two very unique amenities: an outdoor pool with a deck and FREE parking, yes, that's free parking. The hotel's 160 guest rooms are reasonably large with the standard hotel fare. A fitness center, gift shop, and tour desk are also included within.

The River West Café/Deli, located within the hotel, is a pleasantly designed little coffee shop with standard American cuisine.

An "outside Manhattan" hotel placed in Manhattan, the Travel Inn is in a convenient location, particularly for visiting the Intrepid Museum or taking a ride around Manhattan on the Circle Line or another of the many water cruises. Crosstown busses on 42nd Street are frequent, and Broadway and the major theaters are not far away. If you're not seeking luxury and, particularly, if you're driving into the city (with kids), this might be worth checking out.

Rates start at $150 for a single or double.

The Westin
112 Central Park South
Between Sixth and Seventh Avenues
800-WESTIN-1; 212-757-1900

It was the Ritz Carlton; now it's the Westin. The name doesn't conjure up the same lavish image, but don't let that fool you. The 208-room hotel is as elegant as ever, sitting on the south end of Central Park.

The rooms, which were remodeled in 1994, include 14 one- and two-bedroom suites, plus a presidential suite. The views are marvelous, especially those overlooking the park. Guest rooms are spacious, comfortable, and more than stylish, including Italian marble bathrooms, individual climate control, lighted makeup mirrors, phones in the bathroom, pay per view entertainment, and VCRs upon request.

First-class service and accommodations include a concierge with theater ticket service, valet service, valet parking, valet packing (on request), complimentary periodicals, safety-deposit boxes, and a recently upgraded fitness center with a Stairmaster, lifecycles, locker rooms, and the whole 9 yards . . . but no pool.

The bottom line is that the Westin has maintained the level set forth by the Ritz Carlton, offering first-rate, upscale accommodations, excellent service, and a prime location, particularly if you want to enjoy the park, Lincoln Center, Carnegie Hall, and shopping on Fifth Avenue.

The highly rated Fantino restaurant is on the premises, featuring international cuisine. The Bar and Lobby Lounge offer cocktails and light dining.

Rates start at $359 for a standard room and $910 for a suite.

Downtown—below 42nd Street

Best Western Seaport Inn
3 Peck Slip
800-HOTELNY; 212-766-6600

One block north of the South Street Seaport and one block south of the Brooklyn Bridge you'll find the Seaport Inn tucked away in lower Manhattan.

A comfortable hotel with modern amenities and old-world charm, the Best Western is within easy access to all Lower Manhattan sites, obviously including the seaport. Rooms are large with quaint furnishings and modern amenities, including video players, voice mail, refrigerators, and safes. Some rooms include whirlpools or steam baths.

The hotel has an exercise facility and offers a continental breakfast. If you're looking for a Lower Manhattan location and are planning to see the sights and take in the neighborhoods—such as Chinatown, Little Italy, and, of course, the Financial Center—this is a cost effective, clean hotel with all the basics. In the winter months, the area around the seaport can get awfully quiet, and the brisk winds from the river make walking around the shops, ships, and eateries less fun. In the warm weather, however, it's a wonderful area. Also, the hotel is not widely known, so you should get more personalized attention.

There is no on-site restaurant, but there are plenty of places to eat near the hotel.

Rates start at $169.

The Carlton
22 East 29th Street
Between Fifth and Madison Avenues
800-542-1502; 212-532-4100

Situated on a quiet street between the Midtown sights and Greenwich Village, the 350-room hotel is billed as "distinctive." What is especially distinctive is that the hotel does a good job at being fashionable and luxurious and not at extraordinary prices.

Rooms are simple and comfortable and have king- or queen-sized beds, in-room movies, and Nintendo. The off-the-beaten-path location

The Basics

The city is comprised of five boroughs: Brooklyn, the Bronx, Queens, Staten Island, and Manhattan. They measure some 301 square miles combined. These boroughs are five independent counties that together make up New York City. The island of Manhattan measures only 23 square miles, which explains why buildings were built upward toward the sky.

(not on an avenue and not around Times Square), coupled with the size of the hotel, allows for a private, more tranquil atmosphere.

A concierge and valet parking are offered, and children under 16 can stay free if they share a room with their parents.

The Café Carlton is a warm, cozy restaurant, serving breakfast, lunch, and dinner.

Rates start at $205 and suites at $600.

The Millenium Hilton
55 Church Street (in Lower Manhattan)
800-835-2220; 212-693-2001

Opened in 1992 and renovated in 1998, this sleek modern marvel rises fifty-eight stories high, which would seem even more impressive if it weren't across the street from the World Trade Center. Nonetheless, the 561-room Millenium has a lot to offer, including king-sized beds in most of the guest rooms, in-room safes, mini-bars, and fax machines, plus makeup mirrors and video checkout. Guest rooms are large and modern and offer a warm residential ambiance.

The spacious lobby is filled with the sounds of the piano. Several floors above are a fitness center and a glass-enclosed pool. A concierge, laundry service, and baby-sitting service are also among the various amenities offered at the Millenium, a popular hotel with both business and leisure travelers.

Restaurants include the Taliesin, featuring American cuisine with Mediterranean and Asian influence, and the Connoisseur Bar and Grille, a comfortable bistro. There are three bars on the premises. Parking is available but quite limited (and for a fee).

Rates start at $135, and junior suites run from $185 to $509. There are various specials throughout the year.

New York Marriott Financial Center
85 West Street (in Lower Manhattan)
800-228-9290; 212-385-4900

One of two Marriotts in lower Manhattan, this Financial Center property houses 504 modern guest rooms complete with pay movies, mini-bars, and standard in-room fare. The hotel is located in the shadows of the World Trade Center and the World Financial Center; it's a short walk from Wall Street and the ferries to Staten Island, Ellis Island, and the Statue of Liberty. Amenities include an indoor pool, exercise room, saunas, concierge, theater ticketing center, and gift shop.

Since this is primarily a business hotel, you may find good deals on weekends and during the summer months, when there are fewer business travelers. You will be well taken care of, and the service will always be first rate. The Lower Manhattan location puts you out of the fast pace of Midtown, which is a plus or minus depending on what you are looking for and what sights you are looking to see. Though the hotel is in close proximity to the numerous downtown sights, there is less nightlife, and the museums of Fifth Avenue are a bit of a walk. It's a matter of choice.

Restaurants include P.W.'s, featuring American cuisine; Battery Park Tavern, which is casual; and Pugsley's Pub.

Rates start at $299 and vary depending on the season, availability, and numerous specials.

New York Marriott World Trade Center
Three World Trade Center
800-228-9290; 212-938-9100

Not unlike its sister hotel at the World Financial Center, this is a first-class Marriott at the Trade Center, tucked in between the twin towers. Slightly larger, with 818 rooms, this 4-year-old gem has a sky-lit lobby and boasts the largest hotel health club in Manhattan. An indoor pool, jogging track, sauna, and whirlpool are among the first-class features.

In-room safes, mini-bars, and other Marriott amenities are found in spacious rooms, and a concierge, lounge, valet service, and gift shop are part of the hotel. While the pros and cons of staying in Lower Manhattan remain the same as those mentioned for the sister hotel, one of the highlights of this Marriott is the easy accessibility to the World Trade Center complex, including the shopping mall with numerous restaurants as well as the famous Windows on the World restaurant and the observation deck within the Trade Center itself.

Free bus shuttle service will take you from Lower Manhattan to the busy Midtown area. A business oriented hotel during the week, the Marriott World Trade Center is an excellent place to stay for a long weekend; the area quiets down considerably, and you can enjoy all that is offered by the hotel as well as the mixture of historic settings and modern skyscrapers that make up Lower Manhattan.

Restaurants include the Greenhouse Café, for elegant fare, and the Tall Ships Bar and Grill, for more casual dining in a pub atmosphere.

Rates start at $289 for doubles. Ask about specials including "Can't Beat Friday" rates.

New Yorker Hotel
481 Eighth Avenue
Between 34th and 35th Streets
800-764-4680; 212-971-0101

Just a tad downtown, and close enough to Macy's to hear about a good sale just by opening your window, the New Yorker is a grand old hotel with a large old-style lobby. Opened originally in 1930 and later closed in the mid-1970s and transformed into the headquarters for the Unification Church, the building was sold, retransformed, modernized, and reopened in part in 1994. The remaining one thousand rooms opened in 1999.

A short stroll from the Empire State Building, Madison Square Garden, and the Jacob Javits Center, the 70-year-old hotel sports an art deco look with the ambiance of the '30s and the modern computerized technology of the '90s.

Comfortable rooms are fairly basic with free HBO plus on-demand movies. The hotel features a well-trained concierge desk staff; a sightseeing, tickets, and transportation desk; foreign currency exchange; state-of- the-art exercise center; convenience stores; a gift shop; and complimentary continental breakfast in the Sky Lounge on the thirty-ninth floor.

Restaurants include the Tick Tock Diner, for the basics; La Vigna Ristorante, for Italian food; and the Lobby Café, for cappuccino, espresso, and pastries.

Rates start at $195, mini-suites at $275, and deluxe suites at $495.

Soho Grand Hotel
310 West Broadway
Between Canal and Grand Streets
800-965-3000; 212-228-1500

Originally built in the late 1800s, the posh hotel sits in the heart of the trendy neighborhood of Soho, busy with galleries and cafes and surrounded by Greenwich Village, Chinatown, TriBeca, and Wall Street.

The fifteen stories, housing 369 guest rooms, sit atop a large lavish lobby with oversized sofas, tropical palm trees, pillars, lanterns, and draperies surrounding 16-foot-high windows. Different? Indeed. In fact, the hotel is going to the dogs. The Soho grand pet policy is unique. Pet amenities include in-room dining, toys, grooming brushes, and complete pet care—including walking exercise, pet transportation, and (no, we couldn't make this up) a pet toothbrush and toothpaste. Naturally, all of this will cost you extra. AND, if you do not have a pet, the hotel will ask you if you'd like to have goldfish in your room during your stay.

As for people, they too get some amenities. Rooms have large beds, mini-bars with (of all things) healthy foods along with the fun stuff, photographs adorning the walls, on-demand movies, in-room safes, and marvelous views of the city—the building is in an area not oversaturated with skyscrapers.

The hotel also has valet parking, a health club, and a special "Guest Satisfaction Hotline," which essentially means good concierge service.

The Canal House Restaurant, serving American fare, is in the lobby, along with the Grand Bar—and no, pets cannot sit at the bar . . . sorry.

This is an offbeat but quite luxurious hotel in a fashionable part of town that isn't too far from either the Lower Manhattan or Midtown activities.

Rates start at $335 and $1,099 for suites.

Safety Tip

Busses and subways can be crowded—so can the sidewalks for that matter. If you are in a tight squeeze with people all around you, keep a hand in your pocket on your wallet. Crowds are where pickpockets work best. Even if a bus or train is not very crowded, sometimes one party will get off the bus or train slowly, allowing his or her accomplice enough time to bump into (and pickpocket) you from behind. Be aware!

Not a "Car" Town

If you drive your car to the city, or rent one there, keep it in a garage by day and drive in the evenings. Daytime traffic will prove to be quite frustrating, and it is very hard to park in Manhattan unless you pay for a garage. By night, you can drive with less traffic, but parking can still be difficult in many areas, which means you will look for, and pay for, parking. However, using taxis and mass transit in the end will be cheaper and will save you a lot of time otherwise spent searching for a garage or a parking space.

Uptown—above 59th Street

The Bentley Hotel
500 East 62nd Street
Between First and York Avenues
212-644-6000

The 197-room hotel, with 36 deluxe suites, was, until 1998, a 21-story modern office building. Spectacular views of the East River can be had both from guest rooms and from the rooftop restaurant and bar. A modern facility, the Bentley offers spacious well-designed comfortable rooms. Amenities include complimentary continental breakfast, 24-hour cappuccino bar, concierge, valet laundry service, and on-site parking. The location is easily accessible to LaGuardia Airport, just off the FDR Drive, and a short ride to the United Nations and Central Park.

Away from other hotels, the Bentley provides an opportunity to be part of the residential Upper East Side of Manhattan, with numerous restaurants and plenty of shopping. If you don't want to stay "in the middle of it all" or you've been to the heart of the city before, this is a nice change of locale.

Rates start at $255 and deluxe suites at $455.

The Excelsior
45 West 81st Street
Between Central Park West and Columbus Avenue
800-368-4575; 212-362-9200

The Upper West Side is a trendy neighborhood with many prewar apartment buildings, fashionable cafés, plenty of shopping, and "old New York charm." The area is also home to the Excelsior, a landmark hotel rich with atmosphere yet complete with the modern amenities.

A stone's throw from the Museum of Natural History, the Excelsior has one- and two-bedroom suites, with some of the (recently refurbished) 116 rooms and 80 suites sporting balconies. The hotel features a fitness room, entertainment lounge, library, and continental breakfast buffet.

This is a hotel for those who want a small, quaint hideaway in Manhattan, just north of the action, to enjoy quiet nights, an afternoon stroll, or a picnic in Central Park, which is just a short walk. Lincoln Center is some fifteen blocks south.

The hotel is also just completing a new restaurant and lounge. Rates start at $149 and suites at $189.

The Lucerne
201 West 79th Street
Between Broadway and Amsterdam
800-492-8122; 212-875-1000

A treasured landmark, the Lucerne is nestled among the shops and cafés on the Upper West Side and is a short walk from Central Park, the American Museum of Natural History, and Lincoln Center. Featuring 250 large rooms and suites, the Lucerne is one of several Empire Hotel Group properties around the city.

Rooms feature marble and granite bathrooms, in-room movies, and other standard amenities; the hotel includes valet service, a concierge and tour desk, fitness center, and discount parking.

The location puts you in a busy neighborhood with easy access to numerous sights, while not being in the heart of the Midtown area. Service is also more personalized, since the hotel is relatively small.

Wilson's restaurant is a bar and grill with breakfast and dinner. Rates start at $160.

The Mark
77th Street
Between Madison and Fifth Avenues
800-THE MARK; 212-744-4300

Situated on the posh Upper East Side of Manhattan, the Mark is an elegant hotel within a short walk of Central Park, the Metropolitan Museum of Art, the Guggenheim, plus other museums, prestigious galleries, and fine shops.

Neoclassic decor, fine Italian marble, and floral motifs create the luxurious feel that defines this upscale property. A concierge, limousine service, and other "luxury services" (as they are billed) are offered. Some 160 guest rooms and 60 suites include junior suites, terrace suites, and a host of other suites that make up the hotel—which enjoyed a refurbishing in 1996.

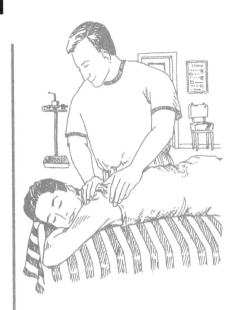

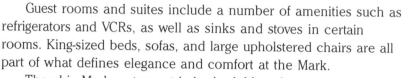

Guest rooms and suites include a number of amenities such as refrigerators and VCRs, as well as sinks and stoves in certain rooms. King-sized beds, sofas, and large upholstered chairs are all part of what defines elegance and comfort at the Mark.

The chic Mark restaurant is in the lobby where you can have dinner or an afternoon "tea" for $20 and up. The Mark's bar is located on 77th Street.

Rates start at $470 for singles and $540 doubles. Junior suites start at $650 and up.

The Regency
540 Park Avenue
Park and 61st Street
800-233-2356; 212-759-4100

One of the city's most exclusive hotels, the Regency is located on Park Avenue, also in Manhattan's "posh" Upper East Side. Having just received a $35 million renovation, the luxurious hotel, which opened in 1963, is the flagship property of the Loews Hotel chain. Celebrities are often spotted in and around the hotel, which houses some 351 guest rooms, including 87 suites with custom-designed furnishings.

The combination of traditional decor with contemporary stylings creates an atmosphere that is warm and comfortable as well as practical and functional.

Guest accommodations include an in-room safe, kitchenette with microwave and refrigerator, mini-bar, phone with caller ID, terry cloth robes, pay-per-view movies, goose down duvet comforters, and (of course) televisions in every bathroom. Suites have two bathrooms—which means yet another television.

The hotel itself has a full-service concierge, overnight valet service, complimentary Evian water and towels for morning joggers, on-site limo service (at a cost), and the Nico Salon featuring manicures, pedicures, facials, and more—for women and men. There is also a fitness center, with everything from free weights to Trotter Treadmills, Climbmax, and other state-of-the-art machines.

Michael Feinstein recently opened a nightclub at the Regency, which shares space with the 540 Park restaurant. The 540 features light lunches and dinners by a renowned chef. The Library is also on the premises, offering a residential-style lounge for breakfast and light snacks.

To give you an idea of how exquisite the Regency is, 50,000 square feet of marble was imported from Alicante, Spain, to be used in the guest bathrooms.

With suites ranging up to $3,500 per night, this is not the hotel for the family on the run or the average traveler, which isn't to say a slightly more affordable room at the Regency might not be a special place to spend a second honeymoon. There are also weekend rates, so inquire.

Rates start at $425 and $650 for suites. Ask about special rates.

Kid-Friendly Hotels

The Loews Loves Kids Program offers children a welcome kit with games and crayons, plus the use of a family video library. Participating hotels include the following:

Howard Johnson,
215 West 34th Street
(212-581-4100)

Howard Johnson Plaza Hotel,
851 Eight Avenue
(212-581-4100)

Loews New York Hotel,
569 Lexington Avenue
(212-947-5050)

The Regency,
540 Park Avenue
(212-759-4100)

CALL TO SEE IF THIS PLAN IS STILL IN EFFECT AT THE HOTEL YOU CHOOSE.

Chapter 3

Getting Around, Tours, and Dining

Getting Around

Now that you've arrived, how do you plan to get from your hotel to the Empire State Building? The Metropolitan Museum of Art? Yankee Stadium? Jones Beach?

The simple rule of thumb is this: If you are staying in Manhattan, use mass transit, take taxis, or walk. If you are venturing outside of Manhattan, drive (unless you're going to one location in the heart of Brooklyn or Long Island City in Queens).

Navigating Manhattan is easy; it's laid out logically as a grid. Numbered cross streets run east and west and ascend from 1st to 220th Street going north. Avenues run north and south.

Here are the primary avenues on the East Side, starting at the East River and going west:

- York Avenue runs both ways between 53rd Street and 96th Street.
- First Avenue runs north.
- Second Avenue runs south.
- Third Avenue runs north, with two-way traffic below 24th Street.
- Lexington Avenue runs south to 22nd Street.
- Park Avenue runs both ways.
- Fifth Avenue, which runs south, is the dividing line for the East and West Sides of Manhattan. All cross-street addresses are designated East or West, and proceed in ascending order from Fifth Avenue. Therefore, 12 East 59th Street will be just east of Fifth Avenue and 12 West 59th Street will be just west of Fifth Avenue. Always specify East or West when taking down an address on numbered streets.

Here are the primary avenues on the West Side:

- Sixth Avenue, also known as Avenue of the Americas, runs north to Central Park.
- Seventh Avenue, also known as Fashion Avenue, runs south from Central Park.
- Eighth Avenue runs north and becomes Central Park West at 58th Street.

- Ninth Avenue runs south and becomes Columbus Avenue above 59th Street (Columbus Circle)
- Tenth Avenue runs north and becomes Amsterdam Avenue above 59th Street.
- Eleventh Avenue runs two ways above 42nd Street and south below it; it becomes West End Avenue above 59th Street.
- Twelfth Avenue runs north, and ends at 59th Street.
- Riverside Drive runs both ways from 72nd Street to the George Washington Bridge (Between 178th and 179th Streets).
- Broadway cuts diagonally on the Upper West Side and slants east as it travels through Manhattan and the financial district all the way to the lower tip of the city at Battery Park. Thus, you can "give your regards to Broadway" while traveling the entire length of Manhattan from top to bottom.

The East Side has a highway running along the East River called the FDR Drive; it becomes the Harlem River Drive above the Triborough Bridge. The West Side has the West Side Highway; it becomes the Henry Hudson Parkway as you head north from Lower Manhattan and runs the length of the city, with great views of the Hudson River and New Jersey.

Both East Side and West Side Parkways are two-way roads with narrow entrance and exit ramps that require you to proceed with caution. When not crowded, they are the quickest ways of getting uptown or downtown. Watch out for potholes!

When navigating Manhattan, the grid of numbered cross streets and primary avenues occupies the areas from Greenwich Village to Harlem and is relatively easy to follow (as you'll see on a city map). The Washington Heights area at the far northern end of the city is the narrowest part of the city and easy to navigate because you're never too far from either the Harlem River Drive on the east or the Henry Hudson Parkway on the west.

All bets are off, however, once you get into Greenwich Village (the widest part of Manhattan), particularly the West Village, where narrow streets cross and turn in all directions. The East Village, also known as "Alphabet City," brings you to avenues A, B, C, and D, in a new grid leading to the Lower East Side.

Getting to the Boroughs

Maps of the "outer boroughs," which are the four boroughs other than Manhattan, will provide directions. If going by car, use the main parkways and expressways to get to your chosen section of the borough, and once you've exited carefully follow local street directions Main expressways in the boroughs include:

The Bronx:
   Bruckner Expressway
   Cross Bronx Expressway
   The Major Deegan

Brooklyn:
   Prospect Expressway
   Brooklyn Queens Expressway
   Belt Parkway

Queens:
   Long Island Expressway
   Grand Central Parkway
   Van Wyck Expressway

Staten Island:
   The Staten Island Expressway

The Lower East Side, Soho, Tribeca, Little Italy, Chinatown, and the Financial District, which are all essentially part of Lower Manhattan, require careful navigation and good map reading or directions. Church Street, Center Street, Broadway, and Bowery are your primary north/south avenues; major cross streets include Houston (pronounced hows-ton), Canal, Delancey, and Church Streets (in the financial district). Wall Street is famous but certainly not a major thoroughfare!

Car Rentals and Car Services

Renting a car in New York City is not inexpensive. From $50 a day to over $400 a week, a car in the city can be costly, with tolls, gas, and parking costs added to your rental expense. There is also insurance, which can run an additional $15 to $20 per day if you are not covered under your own policy (check your policy). And finally there is a 13 percent tax on car rentals!

If all of that does not discourage you, or if you want to rent a car for part of your stay to visit destinations outside of the city, look for discounts in advance of your trip. You might get a percentage off of your rental if you are a member of AAA or belong to a group or organization that has discounts on rental cars. You should also book in advance and be careful to reserve for a time you are fairly sure you can pick up the car—New York City, with so many car rentals (many Manhattanites don't have cars, so they rent on weekends), the companies are not known for holding cars past the scheduled pick-up time. Be sure to choose a major rental company with a good reputation and a good service record.

Rental car companies:

Avis	800-331-1212
Budget	800-527-0700
Dollar	800-800-4000
Hertz	800-654-3131
National	800-227-7368

Safety Tips

Don't carry your wallet in a back pocket. In a crowded city, it is easy for a pickpocket to brush past you and grab it. Also, women, keep your hands on your handbags (as well as your shoulder bags) when you walk through crowded areas.

You need to be over 18 to rent a car (or to drive) in New York City, and you also need a major credit card. Children under the age of five, or under 40 pounds, are required to ride in car seats, which you can get from the rental car company (usually for around $3 a day extra). Have your reservation number ready when you get to the rental car window at the airport or at the rental car office. Don't let them talk you into a host of unnecessary extras. If you have the option, you may want to pay for a tank of gas in advance (if the deal offered is a good one) rather than agreeing to the traditional "return the car with a full tank" routine, since finding gas stations in Manhattan is difficult. If you plan to pick up the car at one location and deposit it at another, make sure this policy bodes well with the rental car company ahead of time, particularly if you are traveling to another city.

Limos and Car Services

For those who want to travel in style, there are a number of popular limousine services in New York offering standard cars as well as stretch limos. Sometimes the rates, $50 for standard cars, isn't all that much higher than taking a taxi cab. Major city limousine companies and car services include the following:

AAA Bay Car & Limo Service	800-479-3889
Allstate Car & Limousine	212-333-3333
Carey	718-632-0500
Chelsea Executive Car & Limo	212-777-7676
City Ride	212-861-1000
Fugazy	212-661-0100
Lincoln Car & Limo Service	212-666-5050
London Towncars	212-988-9700
Olympic Limousine	800-872-0044
Sabra	212-777-7171
Safeway	212-826-9100
Tel Aviv	212-505-0555

You can usually put these costs on a credit card—in fact, many companies prefer it. Either way, always TIP YOUR DRIVER. Also, ask the company you call whether they have limousines, if that is

Visitor Information

The New York City Convention and Visitor Bureau has been around for 65 years, helping visitors to the Big Apple. They have a visitor's information center at 810 Seventh Avenue, between Fifty-second and Fifty-third Streets and can be reached by phone at 212-484-1200 or 212-484-1222. You can find them on-line at www.nycvisit.com or www.newyork.citysearch.com.

what you are looking for. Some companies are limo services and others are not. It is not always implied in the title.

Mass Transit

In Manhattan the quickest way to travel is by subway. Busses, while slower, will get you where you want to go while giving you some views of the city. Busses and subways are $1.50 per person. Subways require tokens or MetroCards (see below), and busses require exact change (coins) or MetroCards. Busses offer free transfers for one trip on an adjoining bus; simply ask the driver for a transfer. They are good for 2 hours from the time issued.

New York City has numerous busses (over thirty-five hundred), all equipped for passengers with disabilities. There are also express busses to the outer boroughs that are not run by the MTA (Metropolitan Transportation Authority). When waiting at a bus stop, read the sign on the front of the bus that tells you where it is going. It's easy to get on the wrong bus, so ask if you are not sure. New Yorkers, in general, will be helpful. Drivers, although sometimes curt, will usually answer if you ask "Does this bus go to . . . ?"

The concierge at your hotel, or someone at the front desk, can help you plan your route for the day and tell you which bus or subway goes to where you are headed. Also, watch for "limited" busses in Manhattan. These are busses that stop only at major intersections. If you find yourself at an express bus stop, you're in luck. When there is no traffic, limited busses can get you where you want to go in a hurry, provided they stop near your destination. "Limited" busses are marked as such in the front window.

If you expect that you will be traveling by mass transit (busses and subways) a lot during your stay, you can save money by buying a MetroCard, which is good for several rides on either the bus or the subway. An unlimited MetroCard for $17 will last you for a week and may be perfect for your visit!

The Subway System

The New York City subway system is an intricate maze of underground trains covering over 700 miles and zigzagging under four of the five boroughs. Initially erected in the early 1900s, the subways see nearly four million passengers daily, riding in some six thousand subway cars and stopping at 469 stations. It is still the quickest and easiest way to get around, and probably the noisiest. The most popular station is Grand Central Station, at Forty-second Street in Manhattan; it sees nearly every train that heads into the borough.

A ride costs $1.50—use either tokens or a MetroCard. There are discounts for a purchase of $15 or more. To save time, it's to your advantage to stock up on tokens or to buy a MetroCard for the number of rides you anticipate during your stay. The card just swipes through as you enter the train. MetroCard allow you to transfer free from bus to subway or vice versa within 2 hours of the previous ride. Tokens, or bus transfers when you pay in coins, do not allow such a bus/train transfer.

Going from subway to subway is free, provided the two trains you need to take connect somewhere. Subway maps tell you at which stations several trains stop.

A free copy of the subway map is readily available at any subway station book and in many hotels. During morning and evening rush hours (6 A.M. to 10 A.M. and 5 P.M. to 7 P.M.), the trains are very crowded, so if you can travel at other times, do so. You can plan numerous connections to take you where you want to go. Be aware and follow the signs carefully; finding connecting trains can be confusing at busy stations such as Forty-second Street or Union Square (14th Street) in Manhattan. Subway entrances often indicate "uptown only" or "downtown only," meaning you need to cross the street and look for the train going in the other direction. If you pay attention, you won't join the many visitors, and New Yorkers for that matter, who have taken the wrong train—it happens.

Note: It's generally not advised to ride the subways past 11 P.M., particularly if you're alone. AND, if you are at a rather quiet, unoc-

Bus and Subway MTA Phone List

Subway and
Bus information
718-330-1234

Service Status hotline
718-243-7777

Customer Service
718-330-3322

MTA Staten Island Railway
718-966-7478

cupied subway station, once you enter through the turnstiles, stand near the token booths. The city does have transit cops; however, there are more stations than cops, and more often than not, the transit cops are busy watching the turnstiles (so that no one gets through without paying) rather than the platform.

Walking

In Manhattan, one of the best ways to get around is to walk. Whether it's window shopping along Fifth Avenue or strolling the narrow streets of the Wall Street area or Little Italy, walking is a marvelous way to enjoy the sights and sounds of New York City. It also beats sitting in traffic. One thing you must remember when walking is to look very carefully when stepping off a curb. Just because the light has changed does not mean a cab driver is going to stop . . . many consider red lights to be a mere suggestion. Bicycle messengers do not adhere to traffic lights, and pedestrians have been known to be hit by them. Always wait a moment before crossing, or go with the crowds of people at a busy intersection.

Walking through New York City can be exhilarating. Times Square, Greenwich Village, Broadway, Fifth Avenue, Wall Street, the Upper East or West Sides—they all offer a host of stores, restaurants, street vendors, and excitement found nowhere else in the world. People watching is often half the fun. From a film crew to a clown or mime, anything can be spotted on the streets of New York. For those interested in architecture, the city is a paradise, mixing cultures and periods from corner to corner. An ornate nineteenth-century church standing next to a sleek black glass skyscraper is not at all uncommon. When you walk around the city, you can truly appreciate that New York City indeed has it all!

Taxis

When traveling by taxi, here a few things to remember:

1. Clearly explain where you are going to the driver. Giving street coordinates, such as Thirty-fourth Street and Fifth Avenue are usually the best way to get where you want to go, rather than giving addresses . . .

Phone Calls

There are still many pay phones in New York City, despite the fact that everyone is carrying their cellular phones. Pay phone calls are $.25 within New York City, which includes the five boroughs. The city area codes are 212 for Manhattan and 718 for the other boroughs (Roosevelt Island is 212). Long Island and Westchester will cost you more money. The area code for Long Island is 516 and for Westchester it is 914.

If you're staying in a hotel, keep in mind that hotels add on a significant surcharge for phone calls, so consider making calling card calls when in your hotel room, or when calling from pay phones—it's cheaper.

The Subways of the City

New York City subways are named with either a letter or a number. They cover four of the five boroughs; Staten Island has its own Staten Island Railway system.

Here are some popular destinations and the subway routes you can take to get there. Keep in mind that you can switch for free at stations with connecting trains. A complete and updated map is provided on the inside cover of this book.

Brooklyn Bridge, South Street Seaport, or City Hall—take the 4, 5, 6, J, or M.

Central Park West and the Museum of Natural History—take the B or C.

Grand Central Terminal or East 42nd Street (closest to the U.N.)—take the 4, 5, 6, 7, or S.

JFK Airport—take the A, then an airport shuttle bus to the terminal.

La Guardia Airport—forget it—take a cab or Greyline bus.

Lincoln Center—take the 1 or 9.

Macy's, 34th Street area—take the B, D, F, Q, N, or R.

Metropolitan Museum of Art—take the 4, 5, or 6 and walk two blocks west.

Rockefeller Center—take the B, D, Q, or F.

Shea Stadium—take the 7 from Grand Central or pick it up at Queensboro Plaza.

Times Square—take the 1, 2, 3, 7, 9, N, R, or S (cross-town shuttle)

Upper East Side of Manhattan or East Harlem—take the 4, 5, or 6.

Upper West Side of Manhattan or Washington Heights—take the 1, 2, 3, or 9.

World Trade Center—take the A, C, E, N, R, 1, 2, 3, or 9.

Yankee Stadium—take the B, D, or 4.

Subway Tips

1. Hold children by the hand and keep all bags closed or zipped.
2. Be very aware of what you are carrying and what is in your pockets. Pickpockets lurk on crowded trains (and busses for that matter). Leave nothing unattended.
3. If a platform is too crowded, step back and wait for the next train.
4. Stand behind the yellow lines. Leaning over to see if the train is coming does not make it come any faster.
5. Tuck chains in and don't tempt fate with lots of jewelry when riding the subways.

2. As you would in any other car, make sure you and your children are secured in seat belts.
3. Have your money ready as you approach your destination. The driver gets the amount on the meter plus a tip (usually 15 percent). He or she may not ask for more, except for tolls incurred. JFK Airport has a flat rate ($30). Rules and rates are posted clearly in the back of the cab.
4. Watch carefully when getting out of a cab; the driver may leave you off in a busy area, and bike messengers think nothing of zipping past a taxi on the passenger side. Look before getting out.
5. Check to make sure you take your belongings. When you pay, you should ask for a receipt not only for your travel expense records, but also so you'll have the taxi ID number in case you leave something behind in the cab. Call 302-TAXI or 212-676-1000 (the New York City Taxi and Limousine Commission) if you need to track down a lost article left in a taxi or if you need to complain.
6. Always check to see that the driver's name and license number are clearly posted inside the vehicle as mandated by the New York City Taxi and Limousine Commission.

The best thing about taxis is that they are plentiful, at least in Manhattan, where over ten thousand cabs drive zealously in pursuit of their next fare. They are available at all hours and get you places quickly. Taxi fares currently begin at $2 and increase $.30 for every 1/5 mile. There is a $.50 surcharge at night between 8 P.M. and 6 A.M.

Outside of Manhattan, you need to call a taxi or car service. In Manhattan, however, you can get a taxi through the concierge at your hotel, at a taxi stand, or, most commonly, by standing on the corner and signaling with your arm up and extended. Be aggressive when hailing a cab, particularly in busy areas—watch how New Yorkers do it; it's an art. The toughest times to get taxi cabs are during rush hours or whenever it rains.

Driving

If you are driving in New York City it is important to be patient; there is a great deal of traffic. Here are a few things to remember:

1. Don't block intersections.

2. Be extremely careful of cab drivers; many drive like maniacs.

3. You cannot make right turns on a red light in New York City unless there is a sign that says you can, which is rare.

4. People frequently cross against the light in Manhattan, so watch out for pedestrians.

5. Do not leave your car unattended unless it is parked and locked.

6. Read all traffic and parking signs very carefully. Metered parking is regulated closely, so make sure to feed the meter (usually it's $.25 for 20 minutes and meters only go up to 1 or 2 hours). Read at what times the meters are operating. During rush hour, the metered streets often become no parking at all (7 to 10 A.M. or 4 to 7 P.M.). After 7 P.M. many metered streets become free. Read the signs; there are numerous variations and exceptions. AND, Tow Away Zone means you may find your car in the police lot on the West Side of Manhattan and pay a high fine to get it back—do not park in Tow Away Zones!

7. Watch very carefully for bicycle messengers who weave through traffic in Manhattan.

8. It's a good idea to have a cell phone when driving around the city, though it's not a good idea to use it while driving. BUT, if you have car troubles, it will come in handy, and you won't have to abandon your car.

Traffic, the impossibility of street parking, expensive parking lots, bus only lanes, bike messengers, pedestrians, those pesky cabbies, horse-drawn carriages around Central Park, pot holes, and street construction make it really less than desirable to drive around Manhattan . . . particularly if you want to enjoy your visit.

Getting Around the City, for People with Disabilities

New York, like the rest of the country, has become more and more accessible for people in wheelchairs. All newer buildings, and many of the older ones, are wheelchair accessible, and city busses pick up wheelchair passengers at the curb by lowering the steps in the backdoor stairwell.

Most hotels, major sights, and theaters provide access for wheelchairs or anyone who cannot climb stairs. It is advisable to call ahead and ask where the entrance is and how to navigate once inside. Facilities like Madison Square Garden and other arenas, theaters, and stores have elevators. When booking your hotel, you should inquire about accessibility as well as in-room facilities such as hand railings in the shower/bathtub, and so forth. Newer hotels are more likely to meet the needs of people with disabilities than are older ones.

One significant program that is designed to assist travelers with disabilities is called the Access Project. It is associated with Big Apple Greeters, a volunteer program that connects visitors to the city with residents of the city for 3- or 4-hour personalized visits/tours. The Access Project works in conjunction with the New York Convention and Visitors Bureau and the Mayor's Office on People with Disabilities and other organizations, plus the MTA, to provide information and easy access to the sights, hotels, theaters, and transportation of New York City to people with a wide range of disabilities and mobility problems. Big Apple Greeter's Access Project can be reached at 212-669-3602. They help make New York accessible to all visitors.

Many Broadway theaters offer discounts for theatergoers with disabilities. The Shubert Organization, which runs some fifteen theaters, allow a wheelchair user and one companion orchestra seats for as little as $7.50 each (such tickets generally run over $50). Other theaters offer substantial discounts.

Phone numbers for people traveling with disabilities include the following:

The MetroCard Pays Off

The latest trend in New York City mass transit is the MetroCard. You can purchase a 7-day unlimited card for $17. If there are two of you traveling around the city and you anticipate at least one trip each way per day, you will be making twenty-eight trips, fourteen each for $34. If you were to pay for each fare individually you'd spend $42. Chances are you will actually use the card more than twice a day, so it is a savings. You can purchase MetroCards at 3,500 neighborhood stores, not to mention all subway stations.

- MTA (subway and bus) 24-hour Access Hotline, 718-330-1234, TDD 718-596-8273
- MTA NYC Transit, Access-a-Ride, Paratransit, V 212-632-7272, TDD 212-333-3147
- RJV Transport ambulette, 516-867-1900
- Wheelchair Getaways, accessible vans with lifts, 800-379-3750
- The Lighthouse (national service organization for the blind), 212-821-9200
- New York Society for the Deaf V and TDD 212-777-3900
- *Able Newspaper*, 516-939-2253
- New Mobility, 800-543-4116
- Travelin' Talk Network (for travelers with disabilities), 615-552-6670
- *We Magazine*, 800-WEMAG26
- Mayor's Office for People with Disabilities, 212-788-2830
- The Andrew Heiskill Library for the Blind and Physically Handicapped, 212-206-5400
- Disability Rights, 800-514-0301, TDD 800-514-0383

For a more detailed list including sightseeing in New York, contact the Access Project at 212-669-3602.

Tours

New York has tours for every interest and level of adventure. While bus tours are popular, considering traffic, you might make better time on a walking tour. The city offers both. There are also customized tours, ethnic tours, food tours, multilingual tours, water tours, and even helicopter tours available.

When calling a tour company, ask questions such as the following:

How many stops do you make?
Do stops mean that you can get out and take photos or that you stay on the bus or van?
What is the "rain" policy on walking tours or boat tours?
How much walking does the walking tour entail?
How long do the tours run?

Bicycling

In Central Park, or in one of New York's other parks, where bike riding is allowed, by all means, pedal away. Bicycling on the city streets is not advised for newcomers (it's not the safest thing to do for anyone). Drivers (particularly cab drivers) are very aggressive, pedestrians jaywalk from all sides, and cars and trucks double park where they shouldn't. What all of this means is that in New York City, bike riding is not something you should do for transportation—only for recreation.

Does the tour return to the same place from which it departs?
What is included in the price?
If you are with a group of ten, twelve, or more, can you get a group rate? (Most companies do offer group rates for tours.)
How many people are usually on a tour?

The last question may tip you off to whether you are dealing with a large or small tour outfit. Large, established tour companies such as Gray Line or Circle Line may provide more flexibility in departure times, with many tours running daily, and they can also offer a variety of tours and rates. On the other hand, larger does not always mean better. If you ask "When does the tour leave?" and you are met with the response "When can you get here?" you are dealing with a small outfit. Some visitors enjoy the more casual, more personalized approach, with fewer people and an opportunity to ask more questions. Smaller tours are sometimes more specialized, so if you have a particular cultural or historical interest, taking a small, specialized tour can be a wonderful way to get to know the city.

Generally, from talking on the phone for a few minutes with someone from the company, you'll get an idea of how well they know the touring business. Again, this is not a matter of size. Some two-person operations can provide greater expertise then some high-profile companies. Since there are many to choose from, ask questions before making a decision. The tour may be your first real impression of the city, so try to pick a winner!

Below are several popular city tours, large and small, on land, sea, and in the air, followed by a few "specialty tours."

Bus Tours

Gray Line New York Sightseeing Tours: In business since 1910, Gray Line is the bus tour sightseeing leader. One of its many tour offerings combines a double-deck bus ride around Manhattan and a trip to the World Trade Center Observatory. From their 21/2 hour Holiday Lights tours to their 81/2 hour Manhattan Comprehensive, Gray Line has a host of tours to offer with professional tour guides to lead the way on motorcoach and

double-deck busses. Jazz and gospel tours are also among the packages. The Grand Tour/World Trade Center Observatory package takes over 6 hours and departs at 9 A.M., 11 A.M., and noon daily. The tour runs $43 for adults and $27 for children ages 5 through 11. Call 212-397-2600 for schedules and rates.

New York Apple Tours: You'll see their old double-deck busses around the city, with their prominent advertising on them. Offering a Full City Tour covering nearly forty sights, a Manhattan tour, a Brooklyn Tour, a Night City Tour, a Harlem Gospel Tour, and other tours in various languages, New York Apple Tours appears to have the city well covered. Full city tours, as of 1999, started at $39 for adults and $22 for children under 12. Call 800-876-9868 for information.

Boat Tours

Circle Line Tours: For 50 years the Circle Line has been sailing the waters around Manhattan, pointing out the sights along the way. You will see and learn from an educated tour guide about key attractions including the Statue of Liberty, Ellis Island, the World Trade Center, Yankee Stadium, and many other sights of the city as you sail under the Brooklyn Bridge, George Washington Bridge, and past the piers and South Street Seaport. Take a sweater or jacket, as it can get breezy. Three-hour sightseeing tours are $22 for adults, $19 for seniors, and $12 for children under 12. Various other tours are offered, including Music and DJ Tours, Seaport Liberty Cruise, Semi-Circle Cruises (shorter versions of the Circle Line Full Tour), and more. Call 212-563-3200 for a schedule and ask about other tours offered. Food and drink, including snacks, sandwiches, and hot dogs, are available on board. Ships sail from 42nd Street at Pier 83.

Note: For those who want to see the sights with a bit more "excitement" and in only 30 minutes, Circle Line offers "The Beast," a speedboat that takes up to 145 passengers on a fun-filled ride around the harbor (at 40 knots or about 45 miles per hour). Adults pay $15, and children under twelve pay $10.

Hospitals

New York City has some of the most, prestigious hospitals in the world. While these are not the places you would want to visit on your trip, here are some numbers of hospitals in Manhattan—just in case:

Beth Israel Memorial Hospital,
First Avenue and 16th Street (212-420-2840)

New York Hospital,
Cornell Medical Center, York Avenue—entrances on 68th Street and on 70th Street (212-746-5454)

Lennox Hill Hospital,
100 East 77th Street (212-434-3030)

Mount Sinai Hospital,
Fifth Avenue and 101st Street (212-241-7171)

St. Luke's-Roosevelt Hospital,
Tenth Avenue at 59th Street (212-523-6800)

Chelsea Screamer: Another speedboat, "The Screamer" takes off at 40 miles per hour from Pier 62 at Chelsea Piers on West 23rd Street and takes you on an exhilarating wind-in-your-hair trip around Lower Manhattan, passing the Statue of Liberty, and then heading up the Hudson for a look at the Intrepid (the floating seaside museum). Chelsea Screamer speedboats run from May through October and cost $15 for adults and $10 for children under 12. Call 212-924-6262 for more information.

Spirit Cruises: From Pier 61 at Twenty-third Street you can set out on one of several lunch or dinner cruises around Lower Manhattan, in a climate-controlled environment with large glass windows, an outdoor deck, and a sumptuous menu. Dancing and entertainment cruises are also offered. From $30 to $70, you can set out for a 2- or 3-hour cruise. Call 212-727-2789.

New York Waterways: Several cruises are offered by this company that hit the waters in 1986. A 90-Minute Complete New York Harbor Cruise heads an impressive and varied list that includes Twilight Cruises, Broadway Music and Disco Cruises, Day Trips to Long Island and Westchester, and even Yankee Clipper and Met Express Baseball cruises. The baseball cruises include a hot dog, a beverage, and a souvenir to get you in the mood for the game; after the game, they bring you back to Manhattan. Most cruises run from $10 to $20, less for children. The longer day trips cost more. Fifty million people have sailed New York Waterways over the years. You can call them at 800-533-3779 for more information.

World Yacht Dining Cruises: Since 1984, the World Yacht has set sail, offering luxurious, romantic dining experiences at sea. The ship sails down the Hudson River and past the Statue of Liberty and Ellis Island as musicians play and dinner is served. It's a highly recommended, very special dining, sailing, and sightseeing experience for visitors and New Yorkers alike. Three-hour cruises depart from pier 81 on West 42nd Street and set sail at 7 P.M. (Board at 6 P.M.). Cruises cost $67 per person Sundays through Thursdays and $75 on Fridays and Saturdays. Brunch cruises also

run during part of the year. Jackets are required for men on the dinner cruises. For information, schedule, and reservations call 212-630-8100.

Helicopter Tours

Helicopter Flight Services, Inc.: Since these sky high tours only accommodate two guests at a time, advance reservations are required. Tours run from $99 to $139 per person, depending on the length of the flight. Tours leave from Twelfth Avenue and 30th Street or downtown heliport at Pier 6 and the East River. Call 212-355-0801 for reservations and information.

Liberty Helicopters: An award winning company for helicopter safety, Liberty has some ten choppers offering flights (Mondays through Fridays) from Twelfth Avenue and 30th Street or downtown heliport at Pier 6 and the East River. A variety of tours (routes) are available, ranging from 5 to 15 minutes. They cover numerous sights and cost from $46 to $159 per person. Call 800-542-9933 or 212-967-6464 for schedules and more information.

Walking Tours

Citywalks: Citywalks offers a private tour guide and features tours of downtown, the Lower East Side, Greenwich Village, and more. John H. Wilson conducts private tours for two people starting at $100 or for groups of around ten for $250. In a corporate world, Citywalks offers old-fashioned, personalized service. Call 212-989-2456 for more information.

Heritage Trails New York: Since it's next to impossible to drive around the Lower Manhattan area, with its traffic and narrow streets, the best way to tour it is on foot. Heritage offers a World of Finance Tour starting at the Museum of Financial History and covering Wall Street, the Stock Exchange, and more. The tour takes 2 hours and is offered every Friday at 10 A.M. It costs $15 for adults and $10 for students, seniors, and children under 12. Heritage offers other tour options, including self-guided tour maps outlining various

Directions

I'll say it again: New Yorkers can be both friendly and helpful. Asking someone (who isn't hurrying to get somewhere) directions will generally be met with a helpful response. Often those in uniform, including doormen, police officers, and postal workers, give the best directions.

Street Vendors

Around the city streets, a vast number of street vendors sell books, clothing, umbrellas, drawings or prints, toys, and more. A few vendors even sell scripts from popular movies and TV shows. Most vendors are licensed (the police try to monitor them carefully). While there is nothing wrong with buying something from a vendor, keep in mind that you cannot return the merchandise if it does not work or does not fit. Therefore, buy only simple items such as books, toys, gloves (try them on), and so on. Anyone selling something that is "too good a deal," such as a "genuine" Rolex watch, is not likely to be a licensed vendor. So use common sense when buying from vendors.

routes of interest through historic Lower Manhattan. Call 212-269-1500 for information.

92nd Street Y: The 92nd Street Y has a wide selection of walking tours of different areas of the city and outer boroughs. The tours offer journeys to areas of historic, social, artistic, and cultural importance. Some walking tours available are Castles in New York, Governor's Island and Battery Park, Jewish Harlem, and Gracie Mansion. The tours run from 2 to 4 hours and cost $15 to $25. If you register for five or more tours, you will receive a 10 percent discount. All tours meet in the neighborhoods visited. For information and registration call 212-966-1100.

Other walking tours are run by the **Municipal Arts Society** (212-935-3960) and **Harlem Your Way! Tours Unlimited,** which offers customized tours of Harlem, including gospel and jazz tours. Call them at 800-382-9363.

Other Tours

New York Southerland Hit Show Tours including two, three, or four nights at a hotel, a Broadway show, tours, and dinner. They offer lots of packages with lots of hotels included. Call 800-221-2442 for information.

Big Apple Greeters provide personal tours by New Yorkers themselves who, as volunteers, show you around a neighborhood on a one-to-one basis. It's a marvelous way to get a feel for a neighborhood while enjoying a personalized experience, as opposed to a boilerplate tour. You might also enjoy meeting a Big Apple Greeter as the perfect compliment to a "grand" tour of the city. Contact them at 212-669-8159 at least 2 weeks in advance.

Doorway to Design offers tours of the fashion and art world plus architectural tours with an architectural historian. Call 718-339-1542.

Urban Park Rangers (New York City Department of Parks) provide free tours of the many parks in New York City, with an emphasis on plant life, bird watching, wildlife, and geology. Call 800-201-PARK.

Central Park Bike Tours are a marvelous way to see the great park and get exercise at the same time. Call 212-541-8759.

Ragtime Theater Tours take you inside one of Broadway's newest and most exciting theaters. Call 212-556-4750.

Other tours (listed in Chapter 4) include Radio City Music Hall, the Apollo Theater, and Carnegie Hall, among others—not to mention the museum tours!

Dining

There are thousands of choices when it comes to dining in New York City. From exquisite world class eateries with world renowned chefs to charming and eclectic cafés to fast food franchises—you can get anything you desire. The ethnic diversity alone is unmatched anywhere in the world.

The Manhattan restaurant market is highly competitive, with three or four restaurants on a single block. With all this choice and competition, you should not have to put up with bad service, although it's often hard to determine what you'll find once inside. The nicer restaurants should afford you the finest service, but that is not always the case. Nonetheless, as in other parts of the country, you should tip around 15 percent for decent service, or 20 percent or more for excellent service. Coat check is usually $1 per coat, and there is no reason to tip anyone else.

For family fare, the finer restaurants—anything starting with "Le" or billed as "elegant"—are generally not the best places to take the kids. Exotic, sophisticated menus rarely offer foods kids will like, and sitting for a lengthy meal is not easy for most youngsters. There are plenty of family-oriented restaurants all over the city, including a seemingly endless array of pizza places. You can always ask about a children's menu or look at the menu posted outside and see what your children might like. New Yorkers are known for their menu browsing, so take a look before you enter. Also peek inside, and check out the following:

21 and Over

Since the Dutch settled in New York, the city has been known for numerous drinking establishments. The law states that no one under 21 can be served alcohol in New York State. It also sets the closing time as 4 A.M. Sunday morning for those staying in the clubs through Saturday nights. Bars and restaurants cannot serve alcohol on Sundays until noon. Furthermore there is no dancing allowed in bars unless a dance floor is specifically defined as such. The last ruling is new and, in protest, hundreds of New Yorkers held a mass hokey pokey protest outside of City Hall.

- Check the menu choices for something you like or something for the kids.
- Check the prices.
- Check the style of cuisine.
- See if there's anyone inside (an empty restaurant at 7 P.M. is not a good sign).
- See if the ambiance is what you are looking for (loud and busy versus cozy and intimate).
- See how you are greeted. The host, hostess, or maitre d' should make you feel welcome. If he or she is abrupt, rude, or simply too busy with the "regulars," you should go elsewhere. There is always another restaurant in New York City, and the stiff competition often eventually catches up with the pretentious places.

Note: Smoking is prohibited in most New York City restaurants, except in outdoor seating, in bar areas, or in designated smoking areas.

Finding Restaurants!

Here are the best ways to find restaurants in New York City:

1. Word of mouth. What places have people you know enjoyed when they were in New York City? Ask in your hotel. The concierge or even the folks at the front desk will have recommendations.
2. Check *New York Magazine, Where Magazine,* weekend newspaper dining sections, or local New York publications, often available for free when entering stores such as Barnes and Noble.
3. Visit key dining areas such as the Upper East Side or Upper West Side of Manhattan, Union Square, Restaurant Row on West Forty-sixth Street, Little Italy, or Chinatown. Browse the neighborhoods and read the menus.

The 57th Street area has its share of restaurants as well, but watch for high "touristy" prices at mediocre places. It's hard not to

Pesky Taxes

New York City has an 8.25 percent sales tax. Only supermarket food is not taxed. There have been a few well-promoted weeks in recent years in which the city has dropped the sales tax on clothing and shoes. If you're lucky, you'll land in New York City during one of those weeks. Some New Yorkers, when buying large items such as furniture or looking to make a day of shopping, travel over to New Jersey, where the sales tax is only 6 percent and there is no tax on clothing. New York hotel rooms are taxed at 5 percent, plus $2 per day. Parking taxes are an obscene 18.25 percent, and rental car tax is a whopping 13.25 percent.

On the Radio

Among the major radio stations you will find on the New York dial catering to a variety of tastes are the following:

AM

660 WFAN—Sports and more sports, including Mets, Knicks, Jets, and other games
710 WOR—Long-time talk and news station
770 WABC—Talk station with name personalities; also home of Yankees baseball
880 WCBS—All news station
930 WPAT—Adult contemporary music and talk
1010 WINS—"All news all the time"
1600 WWRL—Gospel music and talk

FM

92.3 WXRK—K-Rock, Howard Stern, and classic rock
93.9 WNYC—New York's National Public Radio station, mostly classical music
95.5 WPLJ—Top 40 hits
98.7 WRKS—Popular urban contemporary station
100.3 WHTZ—Top 40 hits
101.1 WCBS-FM—New York's oldies station
101.9 WQCD—Smooth, cool, contemporary jazz
103.5 WYNY—New York's only country music station
104.3 WAXQ—New popular rock station
105.1 WMXV—Adult contemporary (one of nine stations labeled as such)
106.1 WBLI—"Lite" music
107.5 WBLS—Long-time popular urban contemporary station

find a restaurant in New York; the trick is to find one you'll enjoy. All major hotels have restaurants. Some are excellent; others are simply overpriced.

When planning to eat out, it's advisable to do the following:

1. Call ahead to determine that the restaurant is open.
2. See if you need reservations.
3. Find out if there is a dress code. Many "nice but trendy" restaurants don't require jackets and ties but expect you will dress well. Use good judgment.

101 Places to Eat!

Below are 101 places to choose from in Manhattan, plus a few in the outer boroughs. Also look in the hotel section of the book for restaurants that are not included in the list below—some of which (like Le Cirque 2000) are top rated.

The list that follows is not simply the four-star favorites of the upper-crust crowd or Yuppie trend-setting places. It's a combination of some of the finest and fanciest and some basic fun fare for families. It also serves up a mix of ethnic and culinary styles along with some classic, famous eateries for good measure. Families might enjoy some of the big "family style" Italian restaurants, with their massive portions to share; couples may opt for the more romantic, smaller French settings.

This list of "101" is a drop in the doggie bag when it comes to the wide array of restaurants that you'll find in New York City. Included in each entry is the type of cuisine, the address and phone number, a few key details, and a price classification: Expensive (generally over $40 per person, including a drink); Moderate ($20 to $40 per person); and reasonable ($10 to $20) per person. This is, of course, a rough estimate, depending on what is ordered. Many restaurants around Manhattan offer Sunday brunch specials or price-fixed lunches (or even dinners) on certain nights. Ask.

Lower Manhattan

Accapella. 1 Hudson Street at Chambers (212-240-0163)
Northern Italian, fine food, fine service, ambiance.
Expensive

Allison on Dominick. 38 Dominick Street between Varick
and Hudson (212-727-1188)
Fresh French country cuisine, charming, romantic, lots of
wines. *Expensive*

Aquagrill. 210 Spring Street and Sixth Avenue (212-274-0505)
Seafood, fine cuisine at one of the trendy "in spots."
Expensive

Balthazar. 80 Spring Street between Crosby Street and
Broadway (212-965-1414)
Picture perfect French bistro, great food and celebs.
Expensive

Cendrillon. 45 Mercer Street between Broome and Grand
Streets (212-343-9012)
Filipino, pleasant setting with interesting creative choices.
Moderate

Chanterelle. 2 Harrison Street at Hudson (212-966-6960)
French, impeccable ambiance, classy food and service, $75
price-fixed dinner. *Expensive*

Hudson River Club. 4 World Trade Center at Vesey Street
(212-786-1500)
New American, marvelous waterside view and cuisine, three
hundred wines! *Expensive*

Katz's Deli. 205 East Houston Street at Ludlow Street
(212-254-2246)
Landmark sprawling Jewish Deli, bring your appetite.
Reasonable

Montrachet. 239 West Broadway between White and Walker
Streets (212-219-2777)
French bistro, one of city's top-rated eateries, elegant low-
key setting. *Expensive*

Nobu. 105 Hudson Street at Franklin Street (212-219-0500)
Top-rated Japanese restaurant in the city, phenomenal forest
setting. *Expensive*

Magazine Listings

New York magazine is widely known for stories about the city as well as entertainment listings. *Time Out New York*, along with magazine sections and pullouts in the *Sunday New York Times* and *New York Daily News*, tell you plenty about what is going on in the city.

One if by Land, Two if by Sea. 17 Barrow Street (212-228-0823)
Continental, elegant seventeenth-century townhouse setting, pianist, romantic. *Expensive*

Peking Duck House. 22 Mott Street between Park Row and Pell Streets (212-227-1810)
Chinese, Szechaun, Chinatown favorite. *Reasonable*

Thailand Restaurant. 106 Bayard Street between Baxter and Mulberry Streets (212-349-3132)
Among best Thai food in city, excellent bargain in Chinatown. *Reasonable*

Windows on the World. 1 World Trade Center (212-524-7011)
International, elegant, fine food, extensive wine list, incredible view! *Expensive*

Downtown (Below Thirty-fourth Street)

Basta Pasta. 37 West 17th Street between Fifth and Sixth Avenues (212-366-0888)
Italian, prepared by Japanese chefs, bright, popular, good with kids. *Reasonable*

Chosi. 77 Irving Place at 19th Street (212-420-1419)
Japanese, indoor and outdoor dining, sushi, sashimi, price-fixed dinners. *Moderate*

Cowgirl Hall of Fame. 519 Hudson Street at West Tenth (212-633-1133)
Southwestern, BBQ, onion rings, fun place for kids. *Reasonable*

E.J.'s Luncheonette. 432 Sixth Avenue by Tenth Avenue (212-473-5555)
American, old-fashioned coffee shop, great shakes and fries, fun for kids. *Reasonable*
(Also at 1271 Third Avenue at 73rd Street and 474 Amsterdam Avenue, between Eighty-first and Eighty-second)

El Cid. 322 West 15th Street between Eighth and Ninth Avenues (212-929-9332)
Spanish, known for tapas, cozy, unpretentious, lots of wine. *Moderate*

Gene's. 73 West 11th Street between Fifth and Sixth Avenues (212-675-2048)
Old-fashioned Italian, large portions, atmosphere, family friendly. *Reasonable*

Gotham Bar & Grill. 12 East 12th Street, between Fifth Avenue and University Place (212-620-4020)
American, one of the city's most popular, highly rated eateries. *Expensive*

Gramercy Tavern. 42 East 20th Street between Broadway and Park Avenue South (212-477-0777)
American, one of city's most popular, great food, fashionable. *Expensive!*

Grey Dog's Coffee. 33 Carmine Street between Bedford and Bleeker (212-462-0041)
American, Greenwich Village coffeehouse, good light food and drink. *Reasonable*

Internet Café. 82 East Third Street between First and Second Avenues (212-614-0747)
Surf the net, read a book, enjoy music/poetry/games, eat good food. *Reasonable*

Kiev. 117 Second Avenue at 7th Street (212-674-4040)
Eastern European, East Village dive with great blintzes and more (no credit cards). *Reasonable*

Marchi's. 251 East 31st Street between Second and Third Avenues (212-679-2494)
Italian family style, one price, and they keep bringing great food all night. *Moderate*

Mesa Grill. 102 Fifth Avenue between 15th & 16th Streets (212-807-7400)
Southwestern, Tex Mex style, big place, big food, big crowds. *Moderate*

Old Homestead. 56 Ninth Avenue between 15th and 16th Streets (212-242-9040)
Steakhouse, from 1868, big portions, gourmet shop next door. *Expensive*

Patria. 250 Park Avenue South at 20th Street (212-777-6211)
New Spanish, vibrant food and atmosphere, specialty drinks, fun. *Expensive*

Seafood Lovers

While New York City isn't as legendary as New England for great seafood, New York does have many excellent seafood restaurants for any fish lover's fancy. Even if you do not venture out to City Island, you can enjoy the Captain's Table in the East 40s (212-697-9538), the Oyster Bar in Grand Central Station (212-490-6650), Pisces, Avenue A in the East Village (212-260-6660), City Crab & Seafood Company, Park Avenue by 19th Street (212-529-3800), or the Seagrill in Rockefeller Plaza (212-332-7610).

Midtown

American Festival Café. 20 West 50th Street at Rockefeller Center (212-332-7620)
American, watch skaters in winter, dine outdoors in summer, enjoyable. *Moderate*

Aquavit. 13 West 54th Street between Fifth and Sixth Avenues (212-307-7311)
Scandinavian, extraordinary cuisine and ambiance, even a waterfall. *Expensive!*

Bombay Palace. 30 West 52nd Street between Fifth and Sixth Avenues (212-541-7777)
Indian, excellent food, great lunch buffet in a charming atmosphere. *Moderate*

Café Botanica. 160 Central Park South between 6th and 7th Streets (212-484-5120)
International, creative/gourmet dining by Central Park, garden decor. *Expensive*

Carnegie Deli. 854 Seventh Avenue at 55th Street (212-757-2245)
Jewish deli, well known, hectic, crowded, big portions, good food. *Moderate*

Dawat. 210 East 58th Street between Second and Third Avenues (212-355-7555)
Indian, one of city's best, creative cuisine, sophisticated setting. *Moderate*

Docks Oyster Bar. 633 Third Avenue at 40th Street (212-986-8080)
Fresh seafood, raw bar, clambakes, upbeat and fashionable. *Moderate*
(Also at 2427 Broadway at 89th Street)

Ellen's Stardust Diner. 1650 Broadway near 51st Street (212-956-5151)
American, rockin' 1950s diner, burgers, fries and shakes, family fun, busy. *Reasonable*

Four Seasons. 99 East 52nd Street between Lexington and Park Avenues (212-754-9494)
Continental, celebrated, New York institution, still first rate, need reservations. *Expensive*

You Want to Eat Ethnic?

In New York City you can find everything! French, Chinese, Italian, Japanese, Indian, and Mexican restaurants are rather easy to find in Manhattan. And here are the not-so-easy to find:

French/Indian Try Pondicherry on West 58th (212-750-7474).

Greek Try Milos on West 55th (212-245-7400) or Periyali on West 20th (212-463-7890)

Scandinavian Check out Christers on West 55th (212-974-7224).

Vegetarian Buddist Try Zen Palate on Ninth Avenue by 46th (212-582-1669).

Russian How about Firebird on West 46th (212-586-0244) or Russian Samovar on West 52nd (212-757-0168)

Brazilian Visit Churrascaria Plataforma in the Belvedere Hotel on West 49th (212-245-0505) or S.O.B.'s on Varick (212-243-4940).

Chinese-Latin Try Twenty Twenty on Warren Street (212-513-0441).

Korean Drop by Hangawi on East 32nd (212-213-0077) or Woo Chon on West 36th (212-695-0676).

Cuban-Asian Visit the appropriately titled Asia de Cuba on Madison Avenue by 37th Street (212-726-7755).

Ligurian Try Cinque Terre on East 38th (212-213-0910).

Belgian How about Waterloo Brasserie on Charles Street in Lower Manhattan (212-352-1119) or Café de Bruxelles on Greenwich (212-206-1830)

Florentine Visit Est! Est!! Est!!! on Carmine Street Street Street!! (212-255-6294)!!!

Vietnamese Stop by Indochine on Lafayette (212-505-5111).

Chinese-Cuban Go to Bayamo on Broadway, near Washington Place (212-475-5151).

Cajun-Creole How about Acme Bar & Grill on Great Jones Street in the Village (212-420-1934)

Peruvian Try El Pollo on First Avenue near 90th (212-996-7810).

Turkish Check out Uskudar on Second Avenue by 73rd (212-988-2641).

Thai Try the Elephant on 1st Street by First Avenue, Vong on East 54th (212-486-9592) or the Thai Café on Manhattan Avenue in Brooklyn (718-383-3562).

And if you really don't know what type of ethnic cuisine you want, you can always try the **Galaxy Global Eatery** in Gramercy Park by 15th Street (212-777-3631), which serves a little bit of everything!

Lutece. 249 East 50th Street between Second and Third Avenues (212-752-2225)
French, famous, long-time top rated for excellent cuisine, price-fixed menu. *Expensive*

Manhattan Ocean Club. 57 West 58th Street between Fifth and Sixth Avenues (212-371-7777)
Seafood at its finest, Picasso art, enticing appetizers, long wine list. *Expensive*

Mickey Mantle's. 42 Central Park South between Fifth and Sixth Avenues (212-688-7777)
American, burgers and basics, a fun place for baseball fans. *Moderate*

Mars 2112. 1633 Broadway at 51st Street (212-582-2112)
American, right out of Star Trek, with spaceship rides and aliens, kids love it! *Moderate*
(Note: May scare young children)

Metropolitan Café. 959 First Avenue between 52nd and 53rd Streets (212-759-5600)
American, large, plenty of choices, outdoor garden, good with kids. *Moderate*

Petrossian. 182 West 58th Street at Seventh Avenue (212-245-2214)
Continental, ornate, marble/mink-trimmed room, caviar bar, outstanding cuisine. *Expensive*

Planet Hollywood. 140 West 57th Street between Sixth and Seventh Avenues (212-333-7827)
American, very touristy, loud and crowded, lots of movie memorabilia. *Moderate*

Redeye Grill. 890 Seventh Avenue at 56th Street (212-541-9000)
American, seafood galore, raw bar, spacious, fashionable. *Moderate to Expensive*

Shun Lee Palace. 155 East 55th Street between Lexington and Third Avenues (212-371-8844)
Chinese, delicious food, extravagant presentation, great $19.99 price-fixed lunch! *Expensive*

Siam Inn. 854 Eighth Avenue between 51st and 52nd Streets (212-757-4006)
Thai, interesting choices, comfortable setting, good for theatergoers. *Reasonable*

Smith & Wollensky. 201 East 49th Street at Third Avenue
(212-753-0444)
Steakhouse, well known, "old boys club" atmosphere, young
exec hangout. *Expensive*

Topaz. 127 West 56th Street between Sixth and Seventh
Avenues (212-957-8020)
Excellent Thai food, gets very crowded at lunch time, arrive
early. *Reasonable*

Uncle Nick's. 747 Ninth Avenue between 50th and 51st Streets
(212-245-7992)
Greek, enticing appetizers, tasty selections, simple setting,
outdoor garden. *Reasonable*

Upper East Side (above Sixtieth Street)

Atlantic Grill. 1342 Third Avenue between 76th and 77th
Streets. (212-988-9200)
Seafood, spacious, fairly new, popular and enjoyable.
Moderate

Aureole. 34 East 61st Street between Park and Madison
(212-319-1660)
New American, very highly rated, one of city's absolute
finest. *Expensive!*

California Pizza Kitchen. 201 East 60th Street (212-755-7773)
Pizza and more, toppings galore, trendy, good for the family,
lunch. *Inexpensive*

Coconut Grill. 1481 Second Avenue at 77th Street
(212-772-6262)
American, very popular, fine food, and sidewalk café in
summer. *Moderate*

Daniel. 60 East 65th Street between Madison and Park
Avenues (212-288-0033)
French Bistro, intimate, posh, marvelous dining darling,
reservations. *Expensive*

Focaccia Fiorentina. 1166 First Avenue at 64th Street
(212-593-2223)
Pasta in a wide variety of styles, plus focaccia, noisy but
good food. *Reasonable*

"Soup Nazi"

The famous Seinfeld episode is based on one of New York's several fine soup restaurants, Soup Kitchen International, on West 55th Street, where the soup is great and the service can be downright frightening. Other city souperies include Soup Nutsy on East 46th and the Soup Pot in Lower Manhattan at Broadway between Murray and Warren.

Il Vagabondo. 351 East 62nd Street between First and Second Avenues (212-832-9221)
Italian, old-world charm, very good food, generous servings and bocci. *Moderate*

Le Regence. 37 East 64th Street between Madison and Park Avenues (212-606-4647)
French, chandeliers, murals, fine cuisine, very elegant, refined. *Expensive*

Malaga. 406 East 73rd Street between First and York Avenues (212-737-7659)
Spanish, friendly, warm, excellent food and plenty of it. *Moderate*

Manhattan Grille. 1161 First Avenue between 63rd and 64th Streets (212-888-6556)
American, elegant yet refined, fine food, comfortable setting, music. *Expensive*

Matthew's. 1030 Third Avenue at 61st Street (212-838-4343)
Mediterranean, very beautiful, romantic setting, interesting choices. *Expensive*

Mimi's Macaroni. 718 Amsterdam Avenue at 95th Street (212-866-6311)
Pasta, kid friendly (with toys), good pasta, and cheery ambiance. *Reasonable*

Park Avenue Café. 100 East 63rd Street at Park Avenue (212-644-1900)
American, creative cuisine, excellent service, classy "Park Avenue" setting. *Expensive*

Serendipity 3. 225 East 65th Street between Second and Third Avenues (212-838-3531)
American, dessert heaven in quirky setting, fun for kids, gets crowded! *Moderate*

Silver Star. 1265 Second Avenue at 65th Street (212-249-4250)
American, 24-hour diner, good basic food, fast service. *Reasonable*

Tony's Di Napoli. 1606 Second Avenue between 83rd and 84th Streets (212 861-8686)
Italian family style, good food, big portions, very big crowds. *Reasonable*

West Side

Aja. 937 Broadway at 22nd Street (212-473-8388)
Asian/European, modern fusion of unique styles, trendy. *Expensive*

Barbetta. 321 West 46th Street between Eighth and Ninth Avenues (212-246-9171)
Italian, landmark, outdoor garden dining, classic old-style cuisine. *Expensive*

Barney Greengrass. 541 Amsterdam Avenue between 86th and 87th Streets (212-724-4707)
Popular Jewish deli, the Sturgeon King, since 1908, lox, herring, blintzes. *Moderate*

Café Des Artistes. 1 West 67th Street between Columbus Avenue and Central Park West (212-877-3500)
French, fine food, romantic setting with murals adorning the walls (reservations). Expensive

Carmine's. 2450 Broadway between 90th and 91st Streets (212-362-2200)
Family-style Italian, spacious, crowded, good food, bring your appetite. *Moderate*
(Also one at 200 West 44th Street between Broadway and Eighth Avenue)

Earnie's. 2150 Broadway between 75th and 76th Streets (212- 486-1588)
Italian, large popular place, good for families and groups, noisy. *Moderate*

La Boite en Bois. 75 West 68th Street between Central Park West and Columbus (212-874-2705)
French, very cozy little bistro, warm and inviting with delightful choices. *Expensive*

Le Bernadarin. 155 West 51st Street between Sixth and Seventh Avenues (212-489-1515)
French/seafood, exquisite dining experience! (reservations). *Expensive*

The Saloon. 1920 Broadway between 64th and 65th Streets (212-874-1500)
Continental, spacious, by Lincoln Center, speedy service, great for lunch. *Moderate*

Love Those Sandwiches

There are nine Cosi Sandwich Bars around the city, and they are becoming very popular for a quick and tasty lunch. Most are in Midtown, West 40s or East 50s, with two downtown in Lower Manhattan. If you see one, grab a bite—if you can get in.

The Shark Bar. 307 Amsterdam Avenue between 74th and 75th Streets (212-874-8500)
Southern, chicken wings, soul rolls, no sharks, popular, hip place. *Moderate*

Tavern on the Green. Central Park West between 66th and 67th Streets (212-873-3200)
American, renowned, grandiose decor, glorious views of the park, great desserts. *Expensive*

Vince & Eddie's. 70 West 68th Street between Columbus and Central Park West (212-721-0068)
American, intimate setting, very popular with Lincoln Center crowd. *Expensive*

Uptown

The Cotton Club. 656 West 125th Street at St. Clair Place (212-663-7980)
Southern, renowned Harlem nightclub with weekend gospel lunch. *Reasonable*

Sylvia's. 328 Lennox Avenue between 126th and 127th Streets (212-996-0660)
Best soul food in New York, comfortable, homey setting, patio dining. *Reasonable*

Well's. 2247-49 Seventh Avenue between 132nd and 133rd Streets (212-234-0700
Longtime popular soul food institution, music certain nights. *Reasonable*

Brooklyn

Cucina. 256 Fifth Avenue between Carrol Street and Garfield Place (718-230-0711)
Italian, rated among the best in the borough. *Moderate to Expensive*

Junior's. 386 Flatbush Avenue at DeKalb Avenue (718-852-5257)
Deli, old-fashioned, popular Brooklyn diner with great cheesecake. *Reasonable*

Lundy Brothers. 1901 Emmons Avenue at Ocean Avenue (718-743-0022)
Seafood, massive, landmark, inconsistent service but good fresh seafood. *Moderate*

Peter Luger's Steak House. 178 Broadway at Driggs Avenue (718-387-4700)
The Taj Mahal of steakhouses—the best! (reservations, no credit cards). *Expensive*

River Café. 1 Water Street (718-522-5200)
New American, great view of Manhattan, $68 price-fixed dinner. *Expensive*

Bronx

Crab Shanty. 361 City Island Avenue (718-885-1810)
Seafood, one of several fine City Island eateries, big portions. *Moderate*

Dominick's. 2335 Arthur Avenue between East 184th and 187th Streets (718-733-2807)
Southern Italian, noisy, hectic, home-style seating, food is worth the trip (no credit cards). *Moderate*

Jimmy's Bronx Café. 281 West Fordham Road, off the Major Deegan (718-329-2000)
Spanish, large, popular eatery with big portions and music. *Reasonable*

Lobster Box. 34 City Island Avenue (718-885-1952)
Seafood, in business 50 years, serves many variations of lobster, great views. *Moderate*

The Venice. 2107 Williamsbridge Road by Pelham Parkway (718-597-2360)
Italian, long established, popular, large family-style portions, if you choose. *Moderate*

Queens

Akroyiali. 33-04 Broadway at 33rd Street (718-932-7772)
Greek, seafood specialties in this out of the way eatery. *Moderate*

Dante's. 168-12 Union Turnpike (718-380-3340)
Traditional Italian, tasty, relaxing/comfortable setting. *Reasonable*

Joe's Shangai. 82-74 Broadway between 45th Street and Whitney Avenue (718-639-6888)
Chinese, very popular. *Reasonable*

Burgers

Burger Heaven is more of a coffee shop than your basic fast-food eatery. The burgers are good, the service is quick, and you don't have to stand in line or order into a clown's mouth. Nearly a dozen are scattered around Manhattan, and they are all quite similar and generally well run.

Pizza

It's hard to travel far without finding a pizza place in New York City, especially in Manhattan. Manhattan is full of numerous pizzerias, many making up numerous new concoctions with elaborate toppings in an attempt to top one another. While many chains have tried, they cannot top the authentic pizzerias you'll find around town. **Lombardi's** on Spring Street, **Mariellas** on 16th Street and Third Avenue and on West 57th Street, **Joe's** on Carmine and also on Bleeker, **Sofia Fabulous Pizza** on Madison Avenue by 79th Street, a few **Original Ray's**, five **Pizzeria Uno Chicago** restaurants, and, of course, four **Little Italy** pizzerias in—where else—Little Italy are just some of the many excellent pizza places you'll find scattered around the city. From thin crust to deep dish, lots of cheese, three cheese, pepperoni, or Sicilian, New York City is a home to a lot of great pizza.

(also on Thirty-seventh Avenue in Queens and on Pell Street in Lower Manhattan)

Lundon Lennies. 62-88 Woodhaven Boulevard at 63rd Drive (718-894-8084)
Fresh seafood, cavernous, long-time popular family favorite. *Moderate*

Portofino. 109-32 Ascan Avenue at Queens Boulevard (718-261-1239)
Italian, casual atmosphere, attentive staff, popular. *Moderate*

Staten Island

Aesop's Tables. 1233 Bay Street at Maryland Avenue (718-720-2005)
New American, intimate, eclectic dishes, and a great name. *Moderate*

The Cargo Café. 120 Bay Street, two blocks from Victory Boulevard (718-876-0539)
American food, casual, colorful, indoor/outdoor dining, good for families. *Reasonable*

Goodfella's Brickoven Pizza & Pasta. 1718 Hylan Boulevard (718-987-2422)
Award winning pizza and more, popular setting, good for families. *Reasonable*
(Also at 96-06 Third Avenue between 96th and 97th Streets in Brooklyn)

South Shore Country Club. 200 Huguenot Avenue (718-356-7017)
Continental, fine food, fine service, dinner shows, comfortable setting. *Expensive*

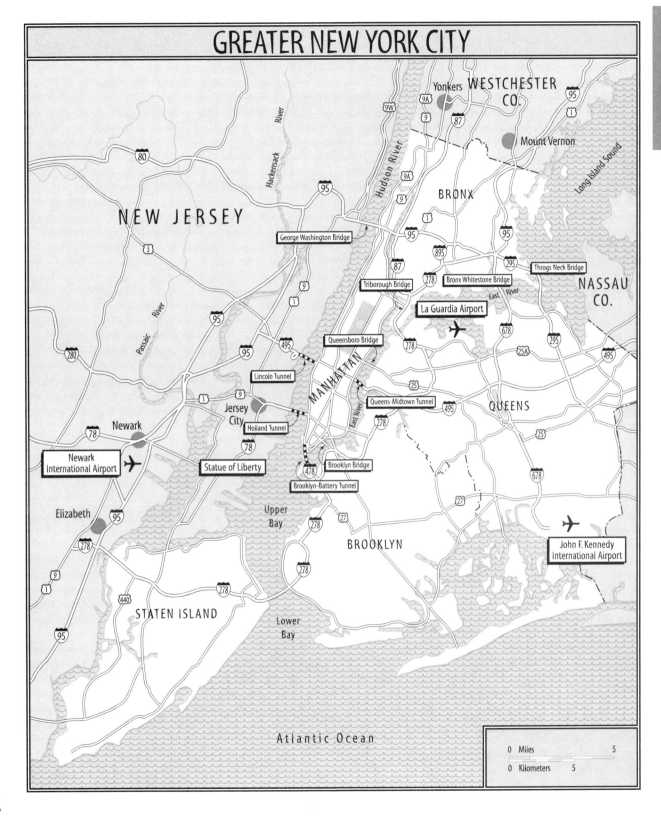

GREATER NEW YORK CITY

WESTCHESTER CO.

Yonkers

Mount Vernon

Long Island Sound

NEW JERSEY

Hackensack River

Hudson River

BRONX

NASSAU CO.

George Washington Bridge

Throgs Neck Bridge

Bronx Whitestone Bridge

Triborough Bridge

East River

La Guardia Airport

Passaic River

Queensboro Bridge

MANHATTAN

Lincoln Tunnel

Jersey City

Queens-Midtown Tunnel

East River

QUEENS

Holland Tunnel

Newark

Newark International Airport

Statue of Liberty

Brooklyn Bridge

Brooklyn-Battery Tunnel

Elizabeth

Upper Bay

BROOKLYN

John F. Kennedy International Airport

STATEN ISLAND

Lower Bay

Atlantic Ocean

| 0 | Miles | 5 |
| 0 | Kilometers | 5 |

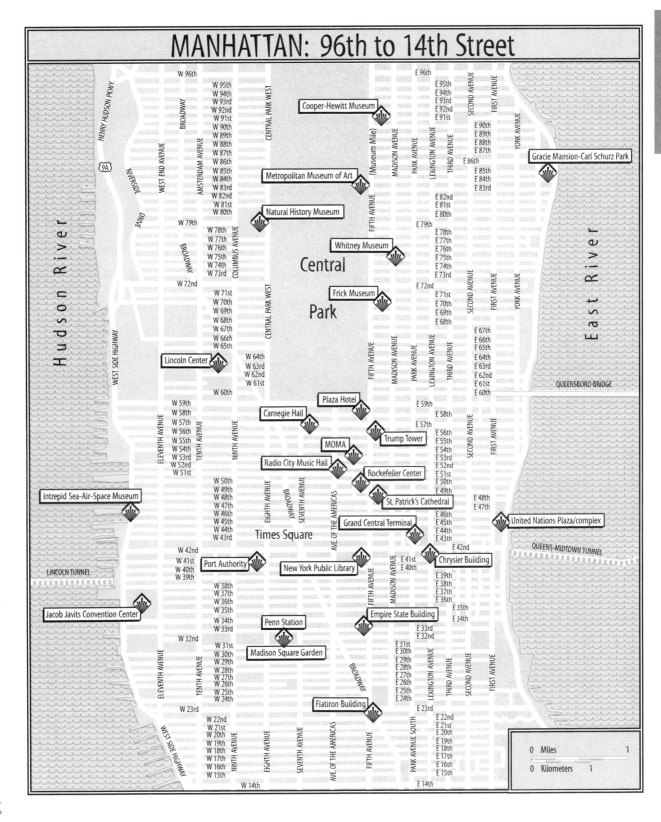

MANHATTAN: 96th to 14th Street

GREENWICH VILLAGE AND LOWER MANHATTAN

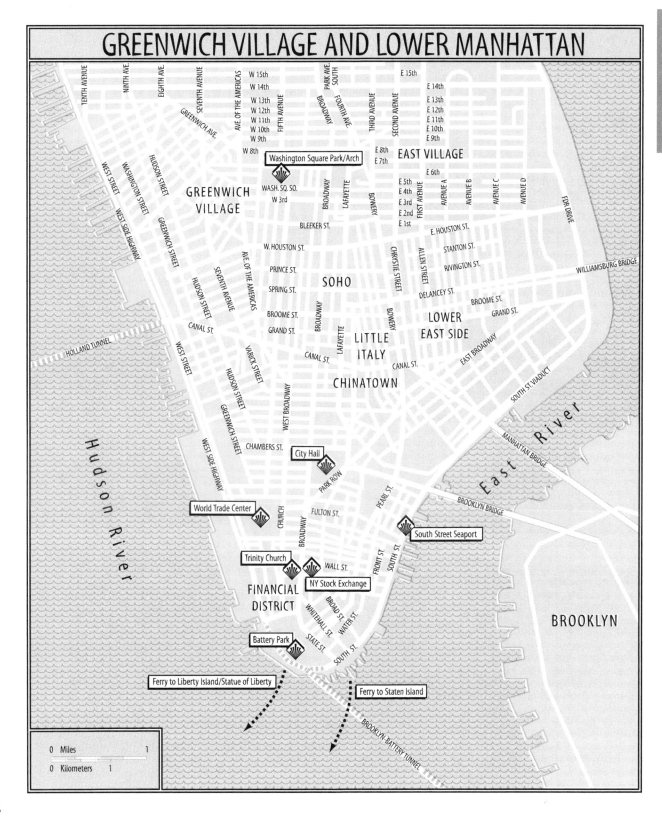

Chapter 4

"Can't Miss" Sights

The Brooklyn Bridge

From Frankfort Street and Park Row in Manhattan to Cadman Plaza in Brooklyn, the Brooklyn Bridge, completed in 1883 (it took 16 years to build) has taken millions of New Yorkers across the East River. The 6,000-foot-long bridge stands some 272 feet high and was built prior to the invention of the automobile, which explains the wide pedestrian walkways. The bridge was originally proposed by John Roebling and spearheaded on to completion by his wife and his son Washington after his death. Hundreds of suspension cables were used to support the vast structure.

Today, besides the ongoing traffic, numerous bikers, joggers, and walkers make their way across the bridge. The views from the bridge are spectacular. You can see the East River and the Southstreet Seaport, the skyline, and Brooklyn out in the distance.

Below are a few of the most popular, most visited sights New York City has to offer. Most of the sights on this list will take several hours to visit, with travel time, waiting, and so on. Some, such as Rockefeller Center, Radio City Music Hall, and St. Patrick's Cathedral, can be seen consecutively. Plan your itinerary based on approximately a ten-block radius of sights. Leave yourself time for tours—they can often take an hour—and don't forget to grab lunch along the way. Some of the most significant sights are the city's museums (see Chapter 5). If you plan to mix one of the major museums into your itinerary, rethink your plans; you'll need to allot 3 or 4 hours just to make a dent in the Museum of Natural History.

Since most sights will involve a fair amount of walking (or climbing steps—in the case of the Statue of Liberty), you should wear comfortable clothes, especially comfortable shoes or sneakers. Also, don't carry too many items with you; they will become cumbersome to carry all day, and there are not many safe places to leave bags and packages. If you plan to go shopping, schedule it for later in the day. Also, major sights have gift shops, and the paraphernalia you purchase can add up; therefore, consider opting for inexpensive mementos or postcards. If you plan to take photos (which is allowed at most sights), check your camera batteries in advance and bring an extra roll of film. Some stores don't carry batteries and film, and those that do may charge high prices.

Keep children within sight and, if they are young, within reach. Sights can get very crowded.

A week in New York City will hardly be enough time to cover all of the major sights, so pick and choose based on your interests, logistics, and the time of year. You may, for example, bypass the Seaport in the cold of January. Some sights may have rules and regulations regarding strollers, cameras, and bringing food inside. Some may have restriction; for example, pregnant women and young children are not allowed on the Skyride at the Empire State Building.

Hours and admission details are always subject to change, so you should call to confirm your options before setting out for the day. Most major sights are open between 9 A.M. and 5 P.M. every day, but tour hours do change, as do gift shop and restaurant hours. If applicable, it's to your advantage to carry a student ID

card or a card showing that you qualify for senior rates (generally, for those over age 62). Almost all sights have lower prices for seniors, and many do for students. Most major sights are handicap accessible, but it is advisable to call first to find out which entrance to use for wheelchairs and the location of elevators. (See Chapter 8 for descriptions of many other sights.)

The Apollo Theater

253 West 125th Street

This legendary Harlem theater was built in 1913 and opened to white audiences only. But by the mid-1930s it had emerged as the premier showcase for black talent and black audiences. For three decades, the Apollo was a first-rate show palace, with performers running the gamut from Ella Fitzgerald, Duke Ellington, Nat "King" Cole, and Billie Holiday to James Brown, the Jackson Five, Stevie Wonder, Aretha Franklin, Stephanie Mills, and numerous others. Comics such as Bill Cosby and Richard Pryor took to the famous stage as well. The popular amateur comedy hour began in 1935 and became an instant hit.

In the mid-1960s, Harlem fell into disarray, and the theater met with tough times. It remained shut down throughout most of the '70s, opening for a short time as a movie theater. Mired in bankruptcy, the Apollo seemed doomed as it entered the 1980s, until Percy Sutton's Inner City Broadcasting Company purchased it. By the end of the decade, it was given landmark status and, by 1992, not-for-profit status as well. By the mid-1990s, a refurbished Apollo reopened, and today is once again a hotbed of entertainment in Harlem.

While comedian Chris Rock and rap and rhythm & blues musical artists play to sold-out audiences, the Amateur Hour, on Wednesday nights at 7:30, is taped for television as part of the Evening at the Apollo television show, hosted by comic Steve Harvey. Tickets are hard to get. Call 212-749-5838 for show information.

The Apollo also offers an hour-long backstage tour that gives you the lowdown on numerous performers who've played the great hall, as well as a look at the theater, including the Walk of Fame and Tree of Hope. Also, you can participate in another version of Amateur Hour; no one will boo you if you're not very good. For a

The Slanted Roof

Clearly evident when looking at the New York City skyline from the east is "the building with the slanted top." It is the Citicorp building, built in 1977. A busy office building, Citicorp houses a comfortable atrium, the Citicorp Center (on the main level with delightful restaurants), an open sitting area, and some stores, including one of the city's popular Barnes and Noble superstores. It is a great place for lunch, and there are often musical performances throughout the day. Citicorp is located on Lexington Avenue, between 53rd and 54th Streets.

Six-Sight Special

If you're planning to stay in New York City for at least a week, City Pass is a new way to save money on New York attractions. Sights include the Empire State building, the Top of the World at the World Trade Center (the Observatory), and four of the world's foremost museums—the Metropolitan Museum of Art, the American Museum of Natural History, the Museum of Modern Art, and the Intrepid Sea-Air-Space Museum. The combined admission is $28 for adults, $21 for students 13 to 18, and $18.75 for seniors. This is half the price you would pay for all six sights individually. In fact, even if you go to five of the six, you're ahead of the game. Ask for City Pass at the first of these sights you visit. It's good for nine days. Call 707-256-0490 for more information or go on-line at www.citypass.net.

tour schedule, call 212-222-0992. Tours cost $8 per person. The gift shop sells books and other items relating to the Apollo.

Carnegie Hall

881 Seventh Avenue
Corner of 57th Street

At just over a century old, Carnegie Hall has been the standard for performance excellence in New York City and the world. Legendary musicians, vocalists, dancers, and even speakers, including authors and politicians, have graced the hallowed stage of this international institution. The tradition of the hall and the esteemed artists who have played there have built a rich history that is larger than the building itself.

Construction began on Carnegie Hall in 1890 at a cost of over $2 million. The six-story structure was designed to encompass a main hall seating 2,800, a recital hall (now the Carnegie Hall cinema) seating 1,200, and a chamber hall (now the Weil Recital Hall) seating 250. The building opened in 1891 with 5 days of performances that attracted New York's leading society folk. The Rockefellers, the Whitneys, the Fricks, and others, who now have museums or buildings named for them, sat and listened to the music of Peter Ilich Tchaikovsky, conducted by none other than Tchaikovsky himself. From that opening week forth, the hall—founded by Andrew Carnegie—was a huge success.

While many people acquaint Carnegie Hall with symphonies and all of the finest orchestras and conductors who have performed within, a wide range of other musical styles have been part of the ten plus decades. Jazz at Carnegie Hall dates back as far as 1912 and has featured performers such as Fats Waller, Louis Armstrong, Count Basie, Ella Fitzgerald, Miles Davis, John Coltrane, and Benny Goodman. In fact, since 1992, Carnegie Hall has had its own jazz band. Folk stars such as Woody Guthrie, Pete Seeger, and Arlo Guthrie also played the hall. Legendary performers such as Frank Sinatra, Judy Garland, Ethel Merman, Liza Minelli, Tony Bennett, the Beatles (in their third U.S. performance), the Rolling Stones, Bob Dylan, and Elton John have all graced the stage at Carnegie Hall.

Young people's concerts, radio and television programs, and speeches by Winston Churchill, Mark Twain, Booker T. Washington and Woodrow Wilson also are part of the legacy.

Almost demolished in the 1960s, when the New York Philharmonic Orchestra moved uptown to Lincoln Center, Carnegie Hall has had facelifts and has been refurbished in the '80s and '90s. Today, you can enjoy one of numerous performances at Carnegie Hall (call 212-247-7800 for a schedule) if seating is available or if you plan ahead. More likely you'll find time to fit in a tour. Hour-long tours are given on Mondays, Tuesdays, Thursdays, and Fridays at 11:30 A.M. or 2 or 3 P.M. Prices are $6 for adults, $5 for students or seniors, and $3 for children under 12. Tours take you behind the scenes and fill you in on the great history of the hall. Tour and dining packages are also offered for groups. For more information on tours, contact the Carnegie Hall tour office at 212-903-9790.

Carnegie Hall also houses a gift shop, and the Rose Museum, a small exhibit area featuring noteworthy items from performers who have graced the great stage.

Ellis Island

Ellis Island National Monument

Starting in the early 1890s and for some 60 years following, Ellis Island was the first stop on American shores for nearly sixteen million immigrants. They entered the United States from Ireland, Italy, Germany, Poland, and many other nations. They sought to build new lives on American soil. Their first stop was the federal immigration facility, which today is a significant tourist attraction, redesigned and reopened in 1990 as a testimonial to the people who made America their new home.

Today over one hundred million Americans, nearly 40 percent of the nation's population, can trace their roots back to these immigrants. The Ellis Island Immigrant Museum is a monument to these immigrants and to the roots and history of Americans. Located just north of the Statue of Liberty, the museum combines

Historic Trinity Church

This famous church dates back to the mid-1800s and is actually the third church built at its Lower Manhattan location. The first church was established in 1697. A stark contrast to the modern buildings of the neighborhood, the old church offers guided tours and a small museum. Nearby is the graveyard (of which you won't find many in Manhattan) where Alexander Hamilton is buried; there is also a monument for Robert Fulton, the steamboat designer. The church, located at Broadway and Wall Street, is open from 8 A.M. to 4 P.M. Call 212-602-0800.

photos and items from the past with modern technology—computers that help visitors trace their heritage.

Ellis Island attractions include the following:

- An Immigrant's Living Theater Presentation called *Ellis Island* Stories features reenactments of the immigrants' stories performed by actors.
- Two small theaters feature *Island of Hope, Island of Tears*, which recounts the history of the famed island.
- A spacious gallery houses photos and items from the immigrants.
- A learning center helps children learn about their roots.
- The American Immigrant Wall of Honor contains the names of over half a million immigrants, from the great-grandparents of George Washington to those of Jay Leno.
- The American Family Immigration History Center is a brand-new resource for immigration history, featuring state-of-the-art computer technology. It allows visitors to trace their roots, and you can even receive a print out of your family's background information.
- An outdoor restaurant on the premises offers a breathtaking view of the New York City skyline.

Ellis Island should be part of your visit to the Statue of Liberty, since they sit adjacent to each other, just off the foot of Manhattan, in the harbor, between New York and New Jersey.

Tickets go on sale at 8:30 A.M., and the museum is open from 9:30 A.M. to 3:30 P.M. daily. Call 212-363-3200 for a recorded message about the Ellis Island attractions. Prices are $7 for adults, $6 for seniors, and $3 for children and teenagers from 3 to 17. You can get to Ellis Island by ferry. The ferry runs every 30 minutes and costs $7. Ferries depart from Battery Park's Castle Clinton. Call 212-269-5755 for ferry information.

Visitor Information

Need 411?—information, that is. The Visitor Information Center at the Embassy Theater (1560 Broadway between 46th & 47th Streets) has ticket centers for Broadway shows and other New York City events, Metro Cards, computer terminals for Internet research, and even actual human beings who can answer your questions. You'll also find an international newsstand, CityStore (a NYC gift shop), and foreign currency machines. The center is open from 8 A.M. to 8 P.M. every day.

The Empire State Building

350 Fifth Avenue
Between 33rd and 34th Streets

The famed "Eighth Wonder of the World" was first opened in 1931 and for many years it was the tallest building in the world. Today it is surpassed by four other buildings, including the World Trade Center in Lower Manhattan and the Sears Tower in Chicago. Although it may no longer be the tallest building, the Empire State Building is rich with history and character, making it a very special part of New York history. King Kong climbed it in the movie bearing his name, and Tom Hanks finally met Meg Ryan atop its observation deck in *Sleepless in Seattle*. Many other films have featured this internationally recognized symbol of New York. Its upper floors are adorned with lights that change colors to match special occasions, casting a glow over the vast skyline that surrounds it. The view from the top is one that you'll never forget.

Nearly four million people visit this signature landmark annually, and over a hundred million have visited it in almost 70 years. The observatories, one on the 86th floor (1,050 feet high and outdoors) and the other on the 102nd floor (1,250 feet high and glass enclosed), offer a breathtaking view that on a clear day extends well beyond the city, into New Jersey and even into Pennsylvania. Tickets are sold on the concourse level, just above the ornate marble lobby.

An additional attraction for children in particular is the New York Skyride, an interactive flight-simulated tour of New York City. The 7-minute "wild" ride is located on the second floor of the building and costs $11.50 for adults, $9.50 for children over 12 and for seniors, and $3 for children 5 through 12. Four-year-olds are free. Pregnant women and children under four are not allowed on the ride. The Skyride is open from 10 A.M. to 10 P.M. daily. Call 212-736-3100 for information.

Observatory prices are $6 for adults and $3 for children under 12. There are discount rates for groups of ten or more. Call 212-736-3100 for more information. The

Staten Island Ferry

The fun boat ride heads from the southern tip of Manhattan into New York harbor and provides a terrific view of the Statue of Liberty (so take a camera) before it reaches Staten Island. You can then make the return trip. The ride is free; you can bring a vehicle for only $3.50. The Staten Island Ferry leaves from South Street and Peter Minuit Plaza and operates 24 hours a day, so you can travel by moonlight too!

observatory is open from 9:30 A.M. to 11:30 P.M. Combination tickets are available for the Skyride and Observatory.

A snack bar, ground-floor restaurants, and a well-stocked gift shop are also part of the New York City landmark. The best time to visit the Empire State Building is on any clear day.

F.A.O. Schwarz

767 Fifth Avenue
Between 58th and 59th Streets

Far more than another giant toy store, F.A.O. Schwarz is a tribute to toymakers, childhood, and imagination—and it's a unique foray into a paradise for youngsters. A tall clock tower, giant wooden soldiers, life-sized dolls, a glass-enclosed elevator looking down at a colorful sea of stuffed animals, enough Legos to build skyscrapers and rocket ships—this is what F.A.O. Schwarz is all about. And if you love Barbie dolls . . .

The store was started in Baltimore in 1862 by Frederick August Otto Schwarz. Broadway was the first of several New York City locations for the famed toy mecca. There are now stores in thirty-eight cities across the United States, but the New York City store is the flagship store.

A busy tourist shop, F.A.O. invites children of all ages to come in and simply have fun. Prices are on the high side, but the selection includes everything from the more traditional fare to more unique items, including the oversized piano keyboard Tom Hanks danced on in the film *Big*. From the latest in video and computer games to old-fashioned wooden trains and blocks, they have toys for all age levels. And over 30 percent of the toys are unique to F.A.O. Schwarz. There's also a candy shop within!

F.A.O. Schwarz is always busy, and on the weekends and during the weeks approaching Christmas, lines are known to stretch outside. Lesser-known entrances through the adjacent GM (now Trump-owned) building and from Madison Avenue can possibly gain you quicker access. Otherwise, prepare to wait a little while to get in.

The smiles on your children's faces will make the wait worthwhile—they will be mesmerized!

It's almost impossible to take the kids and leave empty handed, so set a limit of one toy each, and stay in a price range that's comfortable. Sometimes kids (certainly younger children) can surprise you by choosing something that's not high priced.

The story is open 7 days a week (but closed on certain holidays). For store hours, call 212-644-9400.

Lincoln Center for the Performing Arts

Broadway Between 62nd and 66th Streets

The premier performing arts complex in the world, Lincoln Center sits on 16 acres in the Upper West Side of Manhattan. Home to eleven performing arts companies and educational institutions, the renowned multi-building complex attracts over five million visitors annually.

Originally conceived in the 1950s, the complex was the result of a search for new locations by both the New York Philharmonic and the Metropolitan Opera Company. A run-down section of the Upper West Side, in need of revitalization, seemed a perfect location to provide a shot of cultural enhancement. As is often the case with building a facility for arts or entertainment purposes, a battle ensued—some New Yorkers did not agree with the idea of replacing housing with "the arts." By 1959, however, the neighborhood was reassured of the economic benefits that such an upscale complex could bring to the area. The groundbreaking was held in the fall of '59, and by '62, the Philharmonic Hall was completed. On opening night, Leonard Bernstein and the Philharmonic Orchestra played before a live audience of three thousand people plus twenty-six million more watching on television. In didn't take long for the presence of this artistic and cultural complex to transform the Upper West Side into the fine arts center of the city.

The companies that call Lincoln Center home are world renowned. The New York Philharmonic is the nation's oldest orchestra, founded in 1842. They play over 150 concerts annually for over one million people, not including an annual visit to Central Park for a special performance under the stars.

Lincoln Center Address Book

New York City Ballet,
New York State Theater,
20 Lincoln Center Plaza
(212-870-5570)

New York City Opera,
New York State Theater,
20 Lincoln Center Plaza
(212-870-5570)

JVC Jazz Festival,
Avery Fisher Hall, 10 Lincoln Center Plaza and other locations (212-501-1390)

The Chamber Music Society of Lincoln Center,
Alice Tully Hall, 70 Lincoln Center Plaza (212-875-5788)

New York Philharmonic,
Avery Fisher Hall, 10 Lincoln Center Plaza (212-875-5656)

Jazz at Lincoln Center
(212-875-5599)

The Film Society of Lincoln Center
(212-875-5600)

The New York Public Library for the Performing Arts
(212-870-1630)

Jazz at Lincoln Center

For those who think Lincoln Center is just for classical music, opera, and ballet, guess again. Under the artistic leadership of Wynton Marsalis, Lincoln center presents over four hundred concerts, plus lectures, film programs, classes, and workshops for children. Led by the resident Lincoln Center Jazz Orchestra, Lincoln Center now produces more jazz events than any other site in the world.

The Philharmonic schedule also includes Young People's Concerts, Saturday Matinee programs, and other specially scheduled performances. The New York City Ballet, meanwhile, performs for over 5 months, featuring the choreography of founders George Blanching and Jerome Robbins. The annual *Nutcracker* performances through the holiday season are of particular delight to children (if you'd like tickets for this classic ballet, order tickets ahead of time). The Metropolitan Opera performs nearly twenty operas, featuring the world's most acclaimed opera singers and conductors. The Met is the only theater of its kind to have state-of-the-art individual viewing screens available at each seat.

If you are not seeing a performance, which is most often the case on a short visit, then, like millions of visitors every year, check out the buildings of Lincoln Center, most often on a guided tour.

Highlights of the Lincoln Center complex are as follows:

- Avery Fisher hall seats over twenty-seven hundred and is home to the New York Philharmonic, Lincoln Center Festival concerts, and more.
- New York State Theater seats over twenty-seven hundred and is home to the New York City Ballet and New York City Opera.
- The Metropolitan Opera House (the largest structure in the complex) seats over four thousand and is home to the Metropolitan Opera.
- Vivian Beaumont Theater and Mitzi Newhouse Theater seat over a thousand and host the performances of the Lincoln Center Theater Company.
- Alice Tully Hall seats over a thousand, is home to the Chamber Music Society at Lincoln Center, and hosts the Great Performer's series and Lincoln Center Festival events.

Also on the grounds are the small Walter Reade Theater; the Gallery at Lincoln Center, which is both an arts shop and gallery; the Julliard School, complete with the Julliard theater, Paul Recital Hall, and Drama Workshop; Lincoln Center Plaza; and Guggenheim Bandshell at Damrosch Park, which hosts outdoor concerts and events for as many as three thousand people.

While strolling through the grounds, you will see the brilliant murals in the lobby of the Metropolitan Opera House, the architecture and grandeur of these buildings, and the fountains that are the centerpiece. You can buy gifts at the Lincoln Center gift shops. You can dine at Lincoln Center or grab a light snack at Café Vienna, with its Fountain Plaza setting, or enjoy a full sit-down dinner at the Met's Grand Tier Restaurant overlooking Lincoln Center.

Most performances take place between September and May, when the opera season, Great Performance Series, and ballet companies are running. Mostly Mozart takes place during the summer; other events take place throughout the year, from outdoor concerts and meet-the-artist nights to the New York Film Festival. There are events for children of all ages. For group events such as Sea and Symphony, which includes lunch on a yacht and a meet-the-artist program, call the Lincoln Center Visitors Services at 212-875-5370.

Several tours are offered at Lincoln Center. The guided tour covers the Metropolitan Opera House, Avery Fisher Hall, and New York State Theater, taking you backstage where you may get a glimpse of a rehearsal in progress. Tours cost $9.50 and are given 7 days a week. Call 212-875-5350 for tour information. Specialty tours include Tour with a Bite, which includes a light meal at Café Vienna for $18 per person, and the Art and Architecture tour, which features the background and history of how the theaters and performing arts centers originated (this tour is by reservation only).

Lincoln Center is ideal year-round. During the warmer months, in the evenings, you are likely to find outdoor entertainment under the stars, such as the fun-filled Midsummer Night Swing in July, featuring dancers from around the world.

New York Public Library

Fifth Avenue
Between 40th and 42nd Streets

This historic landmark, featuring Beaux Arts architecture, was built in 1911 and is a two-block literary oasis, housing some six million books plus millions of other documents. The library is a research facility, which means that you can't check the books out but that anyone can use it for research. There are eleven reading

The Film Society of Lincoln Center

Films from around the world are the focus of the Walter Reade Theater's ongoing program. The Film Society runs programs ranging from the classic works of Hitchcock and international legendary filmmakers to innovative unknowns and newcomers. Programs also include Movies for Kids and the New York Film Festival.

History and Beer

For those who like old historic taverns, Pete's Tavern at 129 East 18th Street is the oldest bar in the city. Head on down to Union Square and stop in for a drink. Call 212-473-7676.

rooms containing research books. A well-trained staff can locate a book for you in anywhere from a few minutes to nearly an hour (depending on how busy the library is and how far they need to travel to find the book). The stacks extend underground from Fifth to Sixth Avenues. Cardholders can borrow books from any of the city's more traditional libraries, which includes the Mid Manhattan Library, on 40th and Fifth, across the street.

This structure, however, is indeed worth visiting, even if it's for a brief look around. Built for some $2 million originally raised to fund two libraries, this magnificent structure is guarded in the front by two stone lions, Patience and Fortitude. The interior is brilliantly decorated with marble hallways and staircases leading to the recently renovated grand Main Reading Room, with its original chandeliers and oak tables. The library also houses a magnificent art collection.

There are numerous divisions within the building, including the Arts and Architecture Division, the Map Division, the Jewish Division, the Oriental Division, the Current Periodical Division, and so on. Special collections include rare books, photography, and prints. Free tours are offered and advised; they will provide you with a frame of reference. The enormity and grandeur of the building can be intimidating! Tours are available Monday through Saturday, 11 A.M. and 2 P.M.

Lectures, special exhibits, and presentations are offered in the library. You may also stroll behind the building and visit Bryant Park, which is home to fashion shows and other events. For more information regarding the New York Public Library Center for the Humanities, call 212-661-7220 or 212-930-0800. Call ahead for research information; many divisions are closed on Mondays, and hours in the various divisions and collections vary.

New York Stock Exchange

20 Broad Street
At Wall Street

Whether you "play the market" or not, it's certainly worth a visit to the most significant stock exchange in the world. Since 1792 the New York Stock Exchange (NYSE) has seen active trading; it is now the largest stock exchange in the world, wheeling and dealing a trillion shares of stock every day. Selling shares of stock is one manner in which businesses raise capital and build their companies. Thousands of these companies are listed on the New York Stock Exchange, many of which you are quite familiar with, for example, McDonald's, General Electric, the Walt Disney Company, and General Motors. Visiting the NYSE will give you the opportunity to see how stocks are traded.

From the third-floor observatory you can watch the madness as brokers buy and sell on the busy trading floor, using computer technology and a great deal of human energy and persistence. The sheer size and magnitude of the vast trading floor is exciting, particularly when you realize the dramatic implications the activities taking place down below have on economies worldwide.

You need to obtain tickets (which are free), so it's to your advantage to arrive by noon, since this is a popular sight and the market closes daily at 3 P.M. Guided tours run every half hour, from 8:45 to 4:30, but it's more fun to be there before the trading floor closes. A film explaining the hows and whys of stock trading and a presentation on how to read the ticker are part of the learning experience. Computers and videos are available to learn more about the exchange.

No, you do not get any free shares of stock, but it's both educational and enlightening to see the financial world in action and learn the basics of how it works. For a full day of "economic"

Fortunoff, The Source

Located in the heart of Midtown Manhattan, only a few blocks away from Tiffany's and Cartier, Fortunoff offers a wonderful selection of reasonably priced jewelry as well as one floor devoted entirely to silver. They carry crystal by all of the major companies, including Waterford, Orrefors, and Lalique. Fortunoff's is a great place to shop for wedding, engagement or shower gifts. They are located at 681 Fifth Avenue, between 53rd and 54th Streets and are open Monday through Saturday. Call 212-758-6660.

sightseeing, you can hit the Stock Exchange, the World Trade Center, and the World Financial Center on the same day, all in Lower Manhattan. For information call 212-656-5165.

Radio City Music Hall

1260 Avenue of the Americas (Sixth Avenue)
Between 50th and 51st Streets

Billed as the show palace of the nation, Radio City opened in December of 1932 as the largest indoor theater in the world. Some three hundred million people have now enjoyed entertainment at the famed six-thousand-seat theater. The art deco elegance, 24-karat gold leaf grand foyer ceiling, and newly restored 4,178-pipe Wurlitzer organ create a unique ambiance, mixing warmth and excitement that makes the theater a special stop for both tourists and New Yorkers. A 60-by-30-foot mural—called "the Fountain of Youth"— adorns the grand staircase in the main lobby, while the world famous marquee wraps around the front of the building and spans a city block.

The multi-tiered theater has housed concerts, awards shows, television productions, family attractions, film premiers, and more. Although the acoustics and sight lines have always been excellent, a recently completed $122 million renovation to the landmark property has enhanced the theater with state-of-the-art video and audio technology.

Two of the highlights of the Radio City experience have always been the Christmas Spectacular and the Rockettes. The Christmas Spectacular, usually running for nearly 2 months, from November into January, features the "Parade of the Wooden Soldiers" and "Living Nativity" shows. A staple of the hall for decades, the Christmas spectacular is ideal family fare, but you must call and order tickets well in advance. Over one million people annually fill Radio City for the Christmas Spectacular.

The Rockettes were first formed in 1925 as the Missouri Rockets in St. Louis. By 1933, the precision dance team ended up in New York City on the stage of the brand-new Radio City Music Hall. Nearly 70 years later, they are still going strong (no, silly, not the originals). The troop of 150 dancers is famous for its high-kicking chorus line and is now seen both at Radio City and at other

Around the Circle

Located in the middle of a very busy intersection of Central Park South and Broadway, as it meets Eighth Avenue, is Columbus Circle. The circle, not unlike those found in Europe, is home to a marble statue of Columbus amid other monuments. While it's not really a place to stop and visit, it's worth taking a look at as you drive around the circle, or taking note of as you walk by.

events and on television, including the *Late Show with David Letterman*, which is taped nearby.

If you can't see a show at Radio City Music Hall while you are in town, you might want to take a tour of the grand theater. Tours cover the premises from the grand stage to the backstage. The itinerary is subject to change because of rehearsals and pre-show activities. This can, however, get you a free glimpse of the evening's performance. The 1-hour tours are offered Monday to Saturday, 10 A.M. to 5 P.M., and Sunday from 11 A.M. to 5 P.M. The cost is $15 for adults and $9 for children under 12. You may even meet some Rockettes, though you should stand back if they're rehearsing—so they don't kick you.

For Radio City tours, simply show up at the box office. For a listing of upcoming events at Radio City, call 212-247-4777. Event tickets can be purchased at the Radio City box office or through Ticketmaster at 212-307-7171. There is a surcharge per ticket.

Radio City is accessible to people with disabilities; arrangements for wheelchairs can be made by calling 212-632-4039.

Rockefeller Center

Between 48th and 51st Streets
Between Fifth and Sixth Avenues

Since 1934, Rockefeller Center has stood tall in the midst of all the change and growth of the city around it. The nineteen buildings that make up the 11-acre complex house numerous corporations, including some of the leaders in media and communications, and is indeed at the center of the city. Recently renovated, Rockefeller Center remains one of the most popular tourist stops in New York City.

Named for John D. Rockefeller, who initiated the construction of what was originally designed as three office buildings and the Metropolitan Opera, the complex continued to grow. The focal point, and the building most associated with Rockefeller Center, is known as "30 Rock," or, officially, the GE Building, since GE bought the seventy-story skyscraper from RCA in the late '80s.

The towering art deco structure is best known for the many television and radio programs that have emanated from within. *Late*

City within a City

Designed as such, Rockefeller Center is a city within a city, featuring nearly fifty stores, thirty restaurants or eateries, television studios, the great stage at Radio City Music Hall, roof gardens, outdoor skating, and office space totaling nearly 1.5 million square feet. Wow!

The Coffee Shop from *Seinfeld!*

No, Seinfeld was not filmed in New York City. This "New York" show was, in fact, shot in L.A., as evidenced by the back lot outdoor "city" shots. It did however, use several New York exterior shots, none more often than the restaurant in which Jerry, George, Elaine, and Kramer hang out. The restaurant is located at 112th Street and Broadway and is called Tom's Restaurant. The food is basic diner fare and isn't bad. For those who loved the show, it's a great sightseeing stop.

Night with Conan O'Brien, the old *David Letterman Show*, and numerous other programs including talk shows and game shows have been taped in the famed building. A 1-hour NBC studios tour has been a highlight for many years and still provides you with a glimpse of TV past and present. NBC's *Today Show* operates from a storefront glass-enclosed studio across the street from 30 Rock, in another of the many buildings in the complex. If you arrive early, you can watch from the sidewalk as Katie Couric and Matt Lauer do their show every weekday morning.

Tours leave from the main floor of the GE Building every 15 minutes from 9:30 to around 4:30, sometimes later on weekends. Tours cost $10. Children under 6 are not permitted. Call 212-664-7174 for more tour information and scheduling changes.

While touring "30 Rock" and its neighbors, you'll find an abundance of fine art including sculptures, murals, and mosaics. The designers developed a motif for the artwork called "New Frontiers and the March for Modern Civilization," which expressed the vision behind the new venture. Among the great works of art in 30 Rock are two murals, one featuring Abe Lincoln and Ralph Waldo Emerson and one called "Time," depicting the past, present, and future.

Beautifully landscaped roof gardens adorn several of the buildings in Rockefeller Center. Unfortunately, they are only open to employees of the buildings. You can, however, check out the statue of Atlas on Fifth Avenue directly across from St. Patrick's Cathedral. The art deco styled gold statue has been standing tall, holding up the world since 1936, in front of the skyscraper at 650 Fifth Avenue.

Outside the GE Building, take time to stroll the promenade from Fifth Avenue to the Channel Gardens, where nearly twenty thousand varieties of plants can be found. Just before the gardens meet the skyscraper, you'll find the famed ice skating rink, which by summer becomes the outdoor sections of the American Festival Café and Sea Grill restaurant. The Channel Gardens were named by journalists who noted that the promenade was set between the French and English buildings.

Overlooking the skating rink is an 18-foot-tall, 8-ton centerpiece in the form of a massive guilded bronze statue of Prometheus.

The mythical Greek figure sits below a gold leaf and is shown stealing fire from the gods as a gift for man. Annually, since 1936, from early December through early January, the famous Rockefeller Christmas Tree is set up overlooking the rink. The tree lighting ceremony, complete with a bevy of entertainers, draws thousands of onlookers. Thousands more visitors will stop by to see the dazzling tree during the holidays.

Essentially, the entire area is replete with stunning art work and period architecture. Shops are also abundant around the GE Building, as are a few restaurants, including (as previously mentioned) the American Festival Café and Sea Grill Restaurant. High atop 30 Rock sits the famous Rainbow Room restaurant on the sixty-fifth floor. Opened in 1934, the Rainbow Room has long been a fashionable and romantic place for fine food and a spectacular view. A revolving dance floor, fabulous views through large glass windows, and an orchestra add to the ambiance. The exquisite restaurant, featuring a domed ceiling and massive chandelier, is as "New York" as it gets. It is now open to the public on a limited basis—currently Friday dinner and Sunday brunch (call to make reservations at 212-632-5000). A long way down below 30 Rock, underground walkways connect most of the buildings, allowing visitors and the nearly three hundred thousand people who work in Rockefeller Center to stay warm and dry during inclement weather as they head to the maze of subways below.

For a look at the complex as a whole, you can take a walking tour (it commences in the GE Building). Whether you're on an actual tour or strolling the area yourself, Rockefeller Center offers a variety of options, including a look at television history, fine dining, shopping galore, gardens to stroll through, and stunning art and architecture. Bring a camera, take your time, and take in a classic experience in the city—walking around Rockefeller Center. Just watching the skaters and looking at the tree makes for a romantic winter evening.

A Nice Place to Sit

Paley Park, at East 53rd Street, between Fifth and Madison Avenues, was built in memory of Samuel Paley (1875–1963). The small park is surrounded by skyscrapers. A waterfall runs the entire width of the park. A small concession stand offers a light lunch—sandwiches and salads. During the warmer months, it is a great place to sit and relax with a book or a friend and take a brief respite from the hustle and bustle of the city.

Temple Emanu-El

Home to the oldest Reform Jewish Congregation in the city and formed in the mid-nineteenth century, the gray limestone temple was constructed in 1929 and is a massive structure; a religious school building was added in 1963. Standing over 400 feet high and 150 feet long, the ornate interior is most impressive. It's located at 1 East Street at Fifth Avenue and seats 2,500 people.

Saint Patrick's Cathedral

Fifth Avenue
Between 49th and 50th Streets

Designed by renowned architect James Renwick and completed in 1874, this magnificent church sits amid the busy Rockefeller Center area and remains the seat of New York's archdiocese. While holiday masses draw crowds and television cameras to cover the event at Christmas, numerous tourists visit the ornate gothic-style cathedral daily. They stop and look around, awed by the majesty and magnificence of this grand cathedral.

The best-known cathedral in New York City, St. Patrick's is the largest Roman Catholic church in the United States, seating some twenty-four hundred. The statues, the Rose Window, and the sheer size and splendor of St. Patrick's—with the ornate white spires sitting high atop—make this a very special stop for tourists of all faiths.

St. Patrick's Cathedral is but a few steps from Rockefeller Center and Radio City Music Hall, in the heart of Midtown Manhattan, and is open for visitors from 7 A.M. to 8:30 P.M. It is a marvelous place to walk around and enjoy the serenity and majesty of the sights and stores of the area. For additional information, call 212-753-2261.

South Street Seaport

Between the East River and Water Street

Spanning eleven blocks, the Seaport is a combination historic site, shopping mall, and active fish market. Declared a historic landmark in 1967, the Seaport was restored and remodeled over the next several years by the Rouse Corporation (who developed Quincy Market in Boston) to recreate the marvelous shipping port of an era ago. The combination of historic ships and architecture, trendy stores, and spectacular views of the Brooklyn Bridge and the harbor make it a popular attraction for tourists and New Yorkers alike.

Its cobblestone streets are home to quaint shops, fine restaurants, mini-malls, a maritime museum, a fish market, piers, and, of course, sailing vessels. Ships docked along Pier 16 include several sailing vessels from the nineteenth century, some of which still offer rides. The Pioneer, a 102-foot schooner from 1885, sets sail several times daily, starting at 10 A.M. You can purchase tickets at the Pier

Some Other Sights

These are a few other sights in the city you may not want to miss:

- The Cathedral of St. John the Divine is the world's largest Gothic cathedral; it remains unfinished. The cathedral is located at 1047 Amsterdam Avenue by 112th Street.

- The Chrysler Building is a 1930s skyscraper in the art deco style characteristic of the period. It is located at 405 Lexington Avenue near 43rd Street.

- The Flatiron Building is worth checking out, if only from the outside; it's a triangular-shaped building built in 1902. It's located on the corner of Fifth Avenue and 22nd and 23rd Streets. Hard to miss!

- General Grant National Memorial, also known as Grant's Tomb, offers exhibits about the life of the former U.S. general and president. It's at Riverside Drive and 122nd Street.

- The International Center of Photography (ICP), housed in a 1913 building, offers a look at great photography in exceptional exhibits. It's at 1130 Fifth Avenue by 94th Street.

- The Japan Society features exhibits, films, lectures, and examples of performing arts relating to and from Japan. The society is located at 333 East 47th Street between First and Second Avenues.

- Theodore Roosevelt Birthplace features a reconstruction of the first home of the former president. It's located at 28 East 20th Street by Park Avenue.

- Vietnam Veterans Memorial includes letters and diaries of the soldiers who served in Vietnam. It's located at 55 Water Street.

Bowling Green

A historic sight in Lower Manhattan, dating back to 1733, this small park is located at the lower tip of Broadway. The subway station located at the site is one of the oldest, dating back to 1904.

16 ticket booth. Call 212-748-8590 for information or to order tickets by phone from 9:30 A.M. to 5:30 P.M. The 2-hour ride on the Pioneer costs $20 for adults, $12 for children 12 and under, and $15 for seniors or students with an ID. The Pioneer can also be chartered for 2 hours for $925 or $1,050 for a sunset cruise. Call 212-748-5980 for information.

You can also set sail on a Seaport Liberty Cruise for an hour-long ride around the Statue of Liberty or a 2-hour sunset cruise with a DJ or with live music. The Liberty sets sail for 1-hour rides between March and December, and fares start at $12 for adults—$15 with DJ and $20 with live music—$6 for children 12 and under, $10 for seniors, and $11 for college students. Call 212-630-8888 for sailing times. The W. O. Decker can hold up to six people for a unique tugboat ride along the river. Call 212-748-8590 for information.

Other old sailing vessels sit docked along Piers 15 and 16, including the tall sailing ship Peking, at 377 feet, one of the largest sailing ships every built (1911); Wavertree, the largest extant wrought-iron sailing ship (1885); and Ambrose, a 1908 lightship once used to guide ships into New York. Walking tours and special exhibits are also available. Pier 17's fast-food eateries include Cindy's Cinnamon Rolls, Minter's Ice Cream, and the take-out franchise Wok and Roll. It is also home to numerous shops in a seaside mall. There are eateries of the sit-down kind all around the Seaport, including Café Fledermaus for outdoor lunches.

Just inland you will find the Maritime Museum at 207 Fulton Street, Pier 16, founded in 1967. Inside this tribute to the vessels of the sea, you can browse through paintings, prints, and drawings, as well as crafts, sailing gear, shipboard tools, handicrafts, and artifacts from the sailors and fishermen of a bygone era. The museum is also home to thousands of photographs and two million excavation items (some stored at other sites), many of which are also on display. There are three exhibit areas in all, plus a nearby gallery, children's center, and crafts center. There is also a huge maritime reference library and a fully working nineteenth-century printing press, Bowne and Company.

To get the most out of a visit to the Seaport, it's best to plan for a clear day to enjoy strolling and even going for a boat ride.

Unless it's a particularly warm day, it's advisable to have a sweater, jacket, or sweatshirt along, as the East River breezes kick up while you are sailing. You might schedule walking around the seaport to coincide with breakfast or lunch. Remember to give yourself a couple of hours for the museum! The best thing about the Seaport is that it provides a little of everything—history, shopping, activities, entertainment, photo opportunities, and food. It also provides a great place to stroll or sit and relax and watch the people. Give yourself several hours.

The 2, 3, 4, 5, J, or Z subways all go to nearby Fulton Street, as does the M15 bus down Second Avenue.

The museum costs $6 for adults and $3 for children under 12; it's open daily from 10 A.M. to 6 P.M.—8 P.M. on Thursdays, April through September, and from 10 A.M. to 5 P.M., October through march (closed on Tuesday during the fall/winter months). For more information call 212-748-8600.

Statue of Liberty

Liberty Island

What could be more New York than the Statue of Liberty? Along with the Empire State Building, Lady Liberty was the city's premiere tourist attraction of the twentieth century. Officially named Liberty Enlightening the World, the statue was built in France in 1875 and transported in 350 pieces as a gift to the United States. More than 180 cities throughout all of France raised some $250,000 so that Frederic-Auguste Bartholdi could design and construct a statue with a framework by Alexandre Eiffel. It took nearly a decade for New York to get the proper pedestal approved and constructed for Lady Liberty to stand high above the Hudson River. The Statue of Liberty was officially dedicated in 1886. With pedestal, she towers some 305 feet above the waters; she has welcomed ships into the land of liberty for over one hundred years. In 1986, Lady Liberty received a full face-lift and makeover, just in time for her one-hundredth birthday.

The Statue of Liberty stands for freedom and democracy and stands at the gateway to the harbor, just off the tip of Manhattan on Liberty Island, a stone's throw from neighboring Ellis Island.

Schermerhorn Row

Quite the contrast to the skyscrapers that make up the New York skyline, Schermerhorn Row is a row of early nineteenth-century warehouses and courthouses along the south side of Fulton Street (in the South Street Seaport)—which is home to shopping and restaurants. The quaint scenic setting is perfect for photo opportunities featuring Greek Revival cast iron store fronts. The stores themselves are from the modern era and include the Body Shop, Sharper Image, and other popular retailers.

You'll have a tremendous sense of what America, freedom, and democracy are all about after a day at these two sights.

Nearly 4.2 million people visit the statue annually, with the biggest crowds in the summer months—causing a 3-hour wait for the popular, and tiring, climb to the top. An elevator is available to the top of the pedestal, but the rest is by foot—354 steps or 22 stories to the top of the crown (you can't climb up to the torch). The stairway is a narrow climb, but the view from the top is awesome. Besides the opportunity to look out at the harbor, you'll be able to tell your friends you made it to the top of the Statue of Liberty.

At the base of the statue is a museum featuring exhibits chronicling the history of Ms. Liberty and the history of immigration into New York. Admission to the statue is free, but the round-trip ferry costs $7 for adults, $5 for seniors, and $3 for children; it's the only transportation to and from the statue.

The ferry leaves Castle Clinton Monument in Lower Manhattan starting at 9:30 A.M. (9:15 during the summer months). Because it draws huge crowds, it's a good idea to set out for the statue in the morning. Waiting in line can be very hot in the summer, so dress accordingly, bring sunscreen, and wear a hat. If possible, go on a weekday rather than a weekend, when the lines are simply too long.

Liberty Island also has an outdoor café and a large gift shop full of Liberty souvenirs.

Bring your camera for some terrific shots of the statue and of the views from the statue of the city and the harbor. Consider planning to visit both Ellis Island and the Statue of Liberty in the same day.

For more information call 212-363-3200.

The United Nations

First Avenue
Between 42nd and 49th Streets

In October of 1945, following World War II, the United Nations was established. There were 51 countries in the initial formation, and their goal was to join together to maintain peace and provide humanitarian assistance. Over the years, the United Nations has grown to include some 185 countries. Countries joining the United

Nations agree to accept a charter that outlines the basic principles of international relations. While the UN has tried to help maintain world order and promote peace, it is not a lawmaking entity and has taken criticism for not being able to prevent international conflicts. Yet, behind the doors of the United Nations, many conflicts have been averted, and policies and programs have been established to promote harmony between nations and respect for human rights.

The United Nations also has numerous other affiliated organizations involved in other activities, including international air travel, telecommunications, protecting the environment, and improving the quality of life for refugees and people living in poverty. UNICEF is one among many programs that the United Nations has established over the years to help the international community.

The United Nations is made up of six branches, five of which occupy an 18-acre tract of land in New York City. The land, designated as international, was originally donated by David Rockefeller. The five components of the New York headquarters include the General Assembly, the Security Council, the Economic and Social Council, the Trusteeship Council, and the Secretariat (not the racehorse). The sixth body is the International Court of Justice, which is located at the Hague in the Netherlands.

Overlooking the East River, the vast riverside promenade is spectacular, with a rose garden, spectacular landscaping, and sculptures from nations worldwide. There are three primary buildings on the site, including the General Assembly, the tall glass-enclosed Secretariat Building, and the Dag Hammarskjold Library, which was built in 1963. Flags from all member nations flank the buildings and landscape.

The United Nations is best visited on a clear day so that you can stroll through the promenade and enjoy the scenery and the view. Guided tours are available every day, except Thanksgiving, Christmas, New Year's Day, and weekends in January and February. Tours last 45 minutes and run from 9:15 A.M. to 4:15 P.M., leaving the lobby of the General Assembly every 30 minutes. Children must be 5 or older. The tours take you through all the main areas of the United Nations, including inside the General Assembly (unless it is in session) and Security Council Chamber. The numerous exhibits,

UN On-line

There is plenty of information available about the United Nations on-line. By logging on, you can learn all about the United Nations charter, its day-to-day activities, and what the various branches and numerous associated agencies do. Sites include the UN Home Page at www.un.org, a Web site locator at www.unsystem.org, and UNICEF at www.unicef.org. There is also a rather new Web page devoted to humanitarian relief for victims of disasters at www.reliefweb.int.

artwork from around the world, and decor of the buildings are all explained. Tours are given in some twenty languages and cost $7.50 for adults, $5.50 for high school and college students, $3.50 for students in grade school or junior high, and $5.50 for seniors. For information on the tours and tour schedules, call 212-963-7713; you can obtain a brochure about the tours by calling 212-963-4440.

The United Nations Bookshop is open Monday through Friday, 9 A.M. to 5 P.M., and opens a half hour later on weekends. It features a vast assortment of books in many languages, plus marvelous children's books, posters, United Nations calendars, and more. Call 800-553-3210.

The Gift Centre is open from 9:00 A.M. to 5:15 P.M. on the same schedule as the tours (closed weekends in January and February). Unique handcrafted items are available, plus gifts from around the world, as well as flags and the more "typical" souvenirs.

The coffee shop in the public concourse offers light fare; the Delegates Dining Room is available for fine dining. Seating is for lunch only, between 11:30 A.M. and 2 P.M., and reservations are strongly suggested. Proper attire is a must—you may be sitting next to an important delegate from the other side of the world! Be on your best behavior.

There is also a post office on the premises, so you can get those postcards out immediately—with UN stamps.

The World Financial Center

West Street
Between Liberty and Vesey
Battery Park City

This modern four-building complex is home to headquarters of numerous prominent corporations, including American Express, Merrill Lynch, and Dow Jones. Nearly forty thousand people work in the high-rise structures, which are situated on 14 acres of Lower Manhattan, on the East River, overlooking Lady Liberty. For tourists, the stunning Winter Garden, plaza, walkway along the river, restaurants, and Mercantile Exchange Museum are attractions worth checking out.

United Nations Information

The United Nations New York branch employs under five thousand people. (Compare this to the twenty-five thousand who work for Disney World!) Funding for the United Nations has been precarious at best over the years, and the future of the organization depends on raising money for their numerous international humanitarian efforts.

Designed in the early 1980s, the four buildings feature different geometrically designed roofs, built with granite and reflective glass that glistens off the Hudson River in the afternoon sun. Two nine-story gatehouses are located at the entrance to the grounds. Once inside you will find the atrium and the Winter Garden, overlooking the Hudson, surrounded by glass, with marble staircases and 50-foot-high potted palm trees. *(It's the only place in New York City where you will find tall palm trees.)*

Featured within the 300,000 square feet of public space is the Winter Garden and adjoining gallery; since 1988 the gallery has hosted hundreds of exhibits and events ranging from the masks of Mexico to the history, art, and design of the Barbie doll to children's exhibits, jazz festivals, dance companies, and more. Most exhibits and performances are free to the public, and summer events are held outdoors.

The Mercantile Museum celebrates the history of the Mercantile Exchange, the home of commodity trading including precious metals. The exchange is open for the public to watch the busy trading, and the museum provides some background and history about the commodities market. The museum is open from 9 A.M. to 5 P.M. Call 212-299-2499 for information.

Strolling from the Winter Garden, you'll find the scenic yacht basin, outdoor plaza, and first-rate shops, along with a salon and fitness center. If and when you need to settle down for lunch or dinner, the Courtyard stands three stories high and offers eleven restaurants including Coco Marina (providing Italian cuisine), Au Mandarin (combining Chinese and French), the California Burrito Company (serving Mexican), and other eateries that vary in style and pricing.

For performances in the Winter Garden call 212-945-0505. If you give yourself four or five hours, you can enjoy a leisurely stroll along the Hudson, check out the Mercantile Museum, browse the stores, enjoy a fine meal, and see a first-rate performance—all in the World Financial Center. It's more than just a financial office plaza, and with a moderately priced meal included, it can be one of the best values with free entertainment and plenty to see.

UNICEF House

For those who want to learn more about UNICEF's many international programs for children, this multimedia exhibition is open Mondays through Fridays at 3 United Nations Plaza, between First and Second Avenues (by the United Nations). Call 212-824-6275 for more information.

The Trade Center Bombing

The World Trade Center will forever be remembered as the site of a tragic 1993 terrorist bombing. The bomb detonated in a rented van driven into one of the below-ground parking garages. A small memorial on the sidewalk marks the tragedy in memory of the six people who were killed and the hundreds more who were injured in the senseless, horrifying blast that shook the city and the world.

The World Trade Center

West, Vesey, Liberty, and Church Streets
(Just look up!)

If you thought the view from the Empire State Building was spectacular, try the ones from the 107th or 110th floor rooftop observation decks at the World Trade Center. While the World Trade Center may lack some of the charm of smaller skyscrapers, the pair of towers are well worth the visit; simply take in the sheer magnitude of this city within a city and get a look at New York from a mile high. Some forty thousand people work in the two buildings (the third and fourth tallest in the world), and thousands more shop at the sprawling underground mall, descend to the numerous subways passing below, or drop by for lunch in one of a wide variety of restaurants. Visitors ascend to the observation decks, taking the heart-stopping 1-minute elevator ride up 107 floors. The views from the top, on a clear day, can extend some 60 miles.

Also atop the Trade Center is a wild simulated helicopter ride through the streets of the city. There is a 750-building model of Manhattan that you can use to locate the buildings that you see from the windows around you. There are also multilingual communication skyline monitors you can use as guides of the city and a unique kinetic energy wall sculpture. Murals and displays tell the city's story, highlighting neighborhoods throughout the city. A gift shop fashioned after the Great White Way (Broadway) offers a distinctive setting for buying remembrances of your visit. And a subway-style food court sells snacks. The Trade Center has been redesigned in the past few years to provide additional fun, besides the spectacular viewing experience.

The observation decks are open from 9:30 A.M. to 9:30 P.M., September through May, and until 11:30 P.M. in June, July, and August. Admission is $12 and includes the simulated wild helicopter ride and all the trimmings.

If you are looking for a lavish upscale dinner with a fabulous nighttime view, dine at the famous Windows on the World Restaurant, or at least have a cocktail at the bar. The restaurant features several levels for dining and a menu of first-rate culinary delights, including sumptuous desserts. There is also an extensive wine list with nearly seven hundred choices. A recent $25 million renovation has enhanced this already spectacular restaurant.

For those who are satisfied with a hot dog or a sandwich and a soda, you can have lunch in one of the numerous eateries in the massive plaza area below, where there is free entertainment during the spring and summer.

The Trade Center is a modern landmark that accentuates the lower part of the New York City skyline, towering above any buildings in its immediate area. Give yourself some time to walk around the mall, plaza, and atrium and to grab a bite to eat before venturing onto other Lower Manhattan sites.

Shopping in NYC
Barney's New York

This store is full of top-of-the-line men's and women's clothing. The best of the hottest designer's lines can be found at Barney's. Although prices are quite high, Barney's holds an annual sale that is worth watching for. The window displays are fabulous. They change frequently and are an attraction unto themselves. Barney's is located at 600 Madison Avenue near 60th Street (212-826-8900) and in the World Financial Center (212-945-1600); it's open 7 days a week.

Bloomingdale's

Known to New Yorkers affectionately as "Bloomie's," Bloomingdale's occupies an entire city block. Although the main floor is busy with salespeople spraying shoppers with perfume and offering makeovers, if you can see past the glitz and glitter, Bloomingdale's has a tremendous selection of designer clothing for men, women, and children. They run sales regularly, so you can get some bargains. Otherwise, the prices are high. Strolling the wide aisles, you will see a host of the latest in fashions as well as marvelous displays. They also sell linens, furniture, electrical appliances, jewelry, and much more. Personal shoppers are also available. Bloomie's is located at 1000 Third Avenue between 59th and 60th Streets and is open 7 days a week. Call 212-705-2000.

Equal Towers

What's the difference between the two World Trade towers? Besides the fact that One World Trade Center has an antenna, while Two World Trade Center does not, both buildings have something different to see at the top. Number One has the elegant restaurant Windows on the World, for high-priced dining, and Number Two has indoor and outdoor observation decks, for lower-priced views of the city and the world.

Macy's—Herald Square

Macy's is known as "the world's largest department store." Expect to get lost at least twice while navigating your way around this huge place. The main floor is designed in a beautiful marble art deco style, a perfect setting for the fine jewelry and extensive leather departments located on this level. Macy's caters to the mainstream shopper; it carries a variety of reasonably priced clothing, although all the top designers can also be found. Macy's Cellar houses perhaps NY's finest collection of cookware, housewares, and gourmet delicacies. The Cellar is a highlight not to be missed. Macy's also has a restaurant, a hair salon, a post office, and an American Express travel office. The small city of Macy's is located at 151 West 34th Street, from Sixth to Seventh Avenue, and is open 7 days a week. Call 212-736-5151.

Saks Fifth Avenue

Saks Fifth Avenue is one of New York City's most prestigious and most famous department stores. Located across the street from St. Patrick's Cathedral and just east of Rockefeller Center, Saks is very easy to spot: Just look for the flags. Saks is perhaps the most spacious store of its genre in New York City and takes pride in having a luxurious environment and elegant displays. The main floor offers numerous counters filled with accessories. Designer clothing for men, women, and children can be purchased. Saks' own house line, SFA, features more affordable prices. Saks also carries jewelry, cosmetics, and fragrances. In addition, there is a bridal salon, offering the latest in bridal fashion displayed in a gorgeous setting. Cafe SFA serves gourmet lunch and light fare. Saks also offers free hotel delivery to any Manhattan hotel. This is first-rate shopping at its finest. If you're not buying, at least browse. Saks is located at 611 Fifth Avenue at 50th Street. Call 212-753-4000.

Schomburg Center

The Schomburg Center for Research in Black Culture is the largest library and research center for African-American culture in the country. Opened in 1980 and refurbished in 1991, the center hosts exhibitions and lectures and offers a performing arts program. The library itself houses has over five million books, photographs, manuscripts, and artifacts pertaining to African-American culture, including the history of Harlem, where the building is located. At 515 Lenox Avenue and 135th Street, the Shomberg Center is open 7 days a week and is free. Call 212-491-2200 for daily schedules.

Henri Bendel

Here you will encounter the cutting edge of fashion. Bendel features their own in-house lines of clothing as well as some of the more exclusive designer brands. The prices are very high, as is the quality of their offerings. Henri is located at 712 Fifth Avenue between 55th and 56th Streets and is open 7 days a week. Call 212-247-1100.

Tiffany & Company

One of the city's most prestigious stores, Tiffany's was founded in 1837 and was known as Tiffany & Young until 1853. It is considered America's leading house of design and the world's premier jewelry retailer. The store on Fifth Avenue is probably the most famous. The main floor is where Tiffany's finest jewelry can be bought for a hefty price. Just walking around and looking at the showcases is a lot of fun. On the second floor, you will find the silver collection, offering some beautiful pieces at more reasonable prices. On the third floor, one can purchase crystal and fine china; the bridal registry is also located here. Tiffany's offers other classically designed products, such as watches and clocks, flatware, scarves and ties, stationery, pens and pencils, leather goods, and fragrances. Any purchase you make will entitle you to the instantly recognizable Tiffany blue box. A major tourist stop, visitors from around the world enjoy strolling through this famous store. Tiffany's is located in a prime setting at the corner of Fifth Avenue and 57th Street. Call 212-755-8000.

Cross-Cultural Department Store

Takashimaya is a unique, cross-cultural, six-story gift and souvenir boutique. Once you pass into this lovely atmosphere, you are immediately captured by the beautiful aroma of fresh cut flowers. Takashimaya offers a rare and distinctive selection of merchandise. The displays are equally unusual, expressing the sensitivity of Japanese craftsmanship. It is definitely worth a stroll down Fifth Avenue to visit and wander around in this relaxing setting. Takashimaya is located at 693 Fifth Avenue. Call 800-753-2038.

Don't Try This at Home

While many have strolled between the two World Trade Center buildings, a gentleman named Philippe Petit did it by tightrope, hundreds of feet in the air, with crowds below holding their breath. He made the short but daring journey successfully.

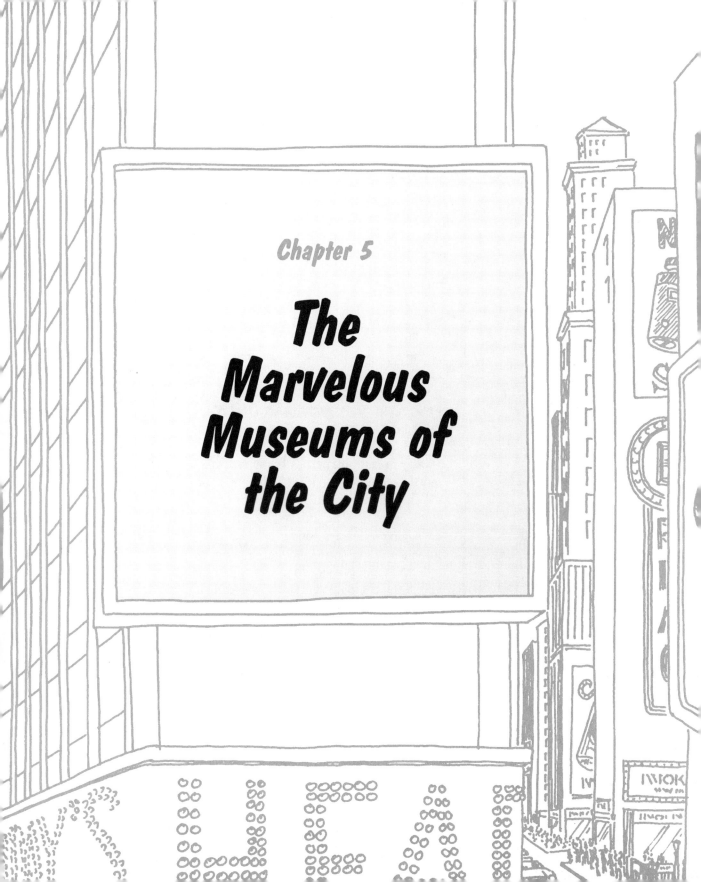

Chapter 5

The Marvelous Museums of the City

When people move out of New York City, their friends inevitably ask them what they miss the most. After a few moments, and perhaps after mentioning Central Park or the ability to find a good bagel, they will quite often say "the culture." Whether New Yorkers attend frequently, or once a year, they are very aware and proud of the vast culture that is captured within New York's famed museums.

There are few cities with as much cultural diversity as New York and few cities, if any, that offer the vast array of museums. Nearly 150 museums grace the five boroughs, ranging from broad themes such as natural history or "art" to specific cultural, ethnic, or historical collections including modern art, Jewish culture, and the city's own transit system.

From the maritime to the moving picture, the city's museums provide an eye-opening educational foray into the past, the present, and, in some cases, the future. And unlike the "boring" class museum trips of years ago, today's museum fuses the knowledge of well-trained guides with modern technology to best present everything from dinosaur bones to airforce fighter jets.

Thanks to benefactors and donations, the city's museums are able to present numerous ongoing and special exhibits. Tours, movies, computer educational centers, gift shops, restaurants, and even performances highlight the busy schedules that are the lifeblood of the city's museums. Anyone visiting the city should plan on seeing at least a couple of these cultural institutions. They offer fun and education for the whole family and usually at a reasonable rate. More importantly, they offer memories. Youngsters will remind you about the dinosaur that towered high above in the Museum of Natural History, the sailing vessels at the Maritime Museum at the South Street Seaport, or the fire engines at the New York City Fire Museum. Adults will talk about the works of Picasso and Cezanne at the Museum of Modern Art, the Currier & Ives lithographs at the Museum of the City of New York, or the Temple of Dendur in the Egyptian Exhibit at the Met.

Several of the city's museums are quite large, built in old mansions that have seen significant expansion over the years. The Upper East Side along Fifth Avenue is known as Museum Row, where several of the city's premier museums are located, including the Metropolitan Museum of Art, the Guggenheim (which also has a SOHO branch), and the Museum of the City of New York.

Admission prices for the museums are "suggested donations"—since the museums operate thanks to benefactors. The suggestion, however, is a strong one, so consider it an admission price. Most are not priced very high, and the money helps keep the museums operational. The only "higher" cost may be for something extra, such as the IMAX films at the Museum of Natural History. To save money, you might take advantage of one of several "free" evenings offered by museums. You won't be able to see a lot, and it may be crowded (who doesn't like a freebie?), but it may give you a glimpse of a museum that you wouldn't otherwise visit.

Museums are for the most part accessible to people with disabilities. Call ahead to find out where the accessible entrance is located and to get information on elevators (which are not always easily found).

Maps will help guide you through your museum of choice, and you'll see many people in the museum lobby planning out their course of action for the day. Remember, in the bigger museums, it's not likely that you'll be able to cover everything in one day, so enjoy what you see and leave the rest for another time. Visiting a museum should be fun for the whole family, not a test of stamina.

Museums, in general, are not always known for fine dining. The food in the museums runs the gamut from sit-down restaurants to your basic hot dogs, sandwiches, and snack foods. Even in the Museum of Natural History, where you can have a sit-down meal with waiter service under the giant whale, you may be better off going to the food court fast-food section. It's cheaper and, for the most part, just as good.

It's hard to imagine a trip to New York City without a visit to at least one museum. They are among the most significant attractions in the city, so much so that New Yorkers frequent an average of at least two a year. Whether you take a tour or stroll through on your own, there's nothing like a museum in New York City.

Note: The museums in this chapter are those found in Manhattan. There are several marvelous museums found in the other boroughs and Long Island (see Chapter 8).

Abigail Adams Smith House Museum

421 East 61st Street
Between First and York Avenues

Surrounded by the high-rise apartment buildings that comprise much of the Upper East Side, this quaint house and garden was made into a museum in 1939 for visitors coming to the World's Fair in Queens. Once part of a much larger property owned by Abigail Adams (daughter of John Adams) and her husband, Colonel William Smith, the museum you see today was originally a carriage house built in 1799. The neighboring mansion became a hotel in the early nineteenth century. However, when the hotel burned down, this carriage house then became a (much smaller) hotel. It would later serve as a private residence before becoming a museum.

The stone structure has been refurbished over the years and houses nine rooms of furnishings from the Federal period. The Colonial Dames of America are responsible for the restoration and upkeep of this city landmark. The gardens around the small museum, when in bloom, are quite beautiful.

Friendly and informed tour guides will fill you in on the background and history of this delightful little museum. A gift shop sells books, posters, and other historic items representing the period.

The museum may not merit a separate trip, but if you are shopping at or just checking out Bloomingdales, or simply visiting the Upper East Side, it's a nice little place to drop by for an hour or so. There's a tranquillity you'll feel as you walk through the gate and step into this little oasis away from the big city.

The Abigail Adams House Museum is open Monday through Friday from noon to 4 P.M. and Sunday from 1 P.M. to 5 P.M., with later hours on Tuesday in the summer. The museum is closed in August and on major holidays. Admission is $3 for adults, $2 for seniors and students, and free for children under 12. For information and to confirm hours (since they are limited), call 212-838-6878.

The museum is a bit of a secret, so it doesn't get too crowded. Don't even think about parking around here, unless you want to find a meter on First Avenue and feed it every hour until 4 P.M. (then move the car or lose it to a tow truck).

American Museum of Natural History

Central Park at West 79th Street

Some thirty-two million specimens and artifacts are on display at this monumental museum that is enjoyed by over three million visitors annually from around the world. Even New Yorkers make return visits to make sure the giant dinosaurs, constructed from bones found on numerous archeological digs, are still in place. Exhibits and educational programs provide visitors with a detailed look at the world around us, featuring the people, the animals, the structures, and the artifacts that have made up civilization for centuries. Scientists, archeologists, historians, and researchers have spent decades unearthing and studying what's displayed here. Children and adults are amazed at the detail of the numerous exhibits.

The American Museum of Natural History first opened in 1869 to enhance the study of natural sciences. The goal—to examine critical scientific issues and increase public knowledge about them—was the basis for the museum. Modern technology has enhanced the presentations, but the goal of studying nature and education remains. Originally in the Arsenal in Central Park (see Chapter 6), the museum settled into its permanent location—on 18 acres just outside the west entrance to the park on 79th Street—in 1874.

Today the museum houses some forty exhibit halls, a planetarium, a natural history library, a teaching facility, and an IMAX theater. There are several gift shops and eateries in the massive structure.

While exhibits change often, a number of permanent exhibits occupy the exhibition halls, including the new Earth Event Wall, which delves into earthquakes, volcanoes, and other natural occurrences that take place on the earth. The exhibit is computer generated and technologically

American Craft Museum

40 West 53rd Street Between Fifth and Sixth Avenues

The nation's premier collection of crafts from the twentieth century, this nearly 45-year-old museum offers a major collection of glass, ceramics, wood, fiber arts, and jewelry. The museum houses a store that sells the work of emerging craft artists. This is not your typical souvenir or book shop; it features high-quality materials, including gold jewelry and items crafted from semiprecious stones. The museum is open Tuesday through Sunday from 10 A.M. to 8 P.M., with an additional 2 hours on Thursday nights. Admission is $5 for adults, and $2.50 for students and seniors; children under 12 are free. It's a unique museum that doesn't take long to see and offers items you wouldn't ordinarily encounter. For more information, call 212-956-3535.

advanced. Another significant exhibit is the museum's Center for Biodiversity and Conservation, which looks at the earth's environmental health and at species that are facing extinction. Other halls include African Mammals, Primitive Mammals, Human Biology and Evolution, Fossils—including two dinosaur halls, Reptiles and Amphibians—Gems, and a section of a rain forest. Several exhibitions feature the people of the world, including the Hall of African People, Margaret Mead Hall of Pacific Peoples, and the Asian and South American Peoples Halls.

Besides the museum exhibits, you should catch one of the IMAX films. These much-larger-than-life films capture many aspects of nature, from African elephants to a trip down the Amazon River, on four-story high screens. Give yourself plenty of time before the showing of the film for which you've purchased tickets. You'll have to find the theater (don't hesitate to ask directions—the staff is very helpful) and wait in line, usually for about 20 minutes prior to show time. The massive screen is easily viewed from all seat locations.

Also, the brand-new Rose Center for Earth and Space features the Hayden Planetarium, housing the Space Theater and the "Big Bang Theater." Here, beneath the domed, 87-foot-diameter ceiling, visitors can see a recreation of the formation of the earth. Numerous other exhibits are found within this dramatic new, state-of-the-art interactive, high-tech facility.

If all this seems like a lot to see, it is, and chances are you won't cover it all unless you move very quickly. The museum gets crowded, especially on weekends; if possible, visit on a weekday. Take public transportation; parking is next to impossible.

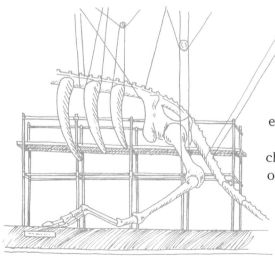

The museum is open from Sunday through Thursday from 10 a.m. to 5:45 P.M. and Friday and Saturday from 10 A.M. to 8:45 P.M. It is open year-round, except Thanksgiving and Christmas.

Admission to the museum is $8 for adults, $4.50 for children, and $6 for seniors and students. Packages include one IMAX show plus admission to the museum at $13 for adults, $9 for seniors and students with an ID, and $7 for children ages 2 through 12. You can see two different IMAX films by paying your $16 per adult, $12 for seniors and students with an ID, and $9 for children 2 through 12. There are also dinner packages available. As of the writing of the book, the admission for the new Rose Center and packages had not been established.

Call 212-769-5100 for recorded information. Call 212-769-5000 to talk to an operator.

You can also take a tour of the museum. Free tours feature various themes, such as dinosaurs, insects, or a look behind the scenes. Tours are given in several languages. For group tours and group package tours, call 212-769-5200.

Children's Museum of Manhattan

Tisch Building
212 West 83rd Street

A marvelous place to spend an afternoon with the kids, the Children's Museum has hands-on exhibits providing fun (and learning too, sssssh!) for kids from 2 to 10 years of age. Founded in 1973, the museum is designed to enhance learning in five key areas, including literacy, the arts, media and communication, the environment, and early childhood education.

A quarter of a million children visit annually to take part in the various interactive exhibits. In the Body Odyssey, for children five and over, visitors follow a walking tour through a 4,000-foot reenactment of the human body, including the blood tunnel, digestive tracts, and so on. An exhibit for the under five set, Wordplay, has a tiny word-filled town and other activities that will enhance little ones' language acquisition while allowing them to play. SEUSS!!, and the SEUSS Interactive Theater are delightful and educational tributes to *The Cat in the Hat*, and an urban treehouse (open May through September) teaches children about their environment.

On the higher floors, you'll find various activity rooms featuring arts and crafts, climbing, and a small theater where puppet shows, storytelling, and other performances are given. The Time Warner Center for the Media allows children to take part in their own television shows on CMOM-TV, with real cameras and a state-of-the-art production center. The museum also provides workshops, classes, and several outreach programs to children and families of the community.

One of the nicest aspects of the museum is that it avoids video and computer-generated activities, allowing children to see, hear, and discover the real sights and sounds around them as they play. This is a museum for children—not about them—designed to pique their interest. You will enjoy seeing it all through their eyes. Get a schedule when you enter, and you'll know what shows or workshops or story readings are taking place that day. And, when you're done, wash your children's hands, since hundreds of eager youngsters enjoy the hands-on museum every day.

There is a small gift shop with children's items, including toys and books, that emphasize learning. There is no restaurant on the premises.

The museum is open Wednesday through Sunday and on public school holidays from 10 A.M. to 5 P.M. Admission is $6 for children and adults, $3 for seniors, and free for children under a year old.

Strollers are not allowed, so you'll have to check them when you come in. Call 212-721-1234 for information or 212-721-1223 to talk to a staff member.

The Cloisters Museum

Fort Tryon Park
191st Street in Manhattan

Perched high above the Hudson River and tucked away in Fort Tryon Park is the marvelous Cloisters Museum, dedicated to medieval art and architecture. The Cloisters has one of the most extensive collections in the world of art and artifacts from the period between the twelfth and sixteenth centuries. Byzantine, Early Christian, Romanesque, and Gothic works are all represented in this site, run by the Metropolitan Museum of Art.

Silver, enamels, stained glass, metalwork, ivories, jewelry, and fifteenth-century manuscripts are all on exhibit. One, among many, highlights are the renowned fifteenth- and sixteenth-century unicorn tapestries. From the galleries, you can stroll out into the lavish gardens, with their rich and varied plant life. The building, which opened in 1938, is architecturally unique in that it was built to represent several different medieval architectural styles, including

French, Spanish, and other cloisters (places devoted to religious seclusion, such as a monastery).

The setting and exhibits compliment one another, creating an atmosphere of medieval times; sometimes medieval concerts are held to enhance the experience. Special programs, gallery talks, and other presentations are held on Saturdays.

After your journey to the past, you will want to explore the grounds surrounding the sprawling structure, Fort Tryon Park. Bring a picnic lunch, visit the museum, and enjoy the marvelous views of the Hudson River below. The Cloisters is Upper Manhattan's foremost sight and worth the trip. There's even parking.

The museum is open Tuesday through Sunday from 9:30 A.M. to 5:15 P.M. from March through October and until 4:15 P.M. from November through February. Tours are free. Admission is $8 for adults, and $4 for students and seniors, and free for children.

Cooper-Hewitt National Design Museum

2 East 91st Street
Corner of Fifth Avenue

The former estate of Andrew Carnegie is now part of the Smithsonian Institution. Exhibits include an extensive collection by a host of designers of outstanding decorative objects in the form of textiles, jewelry, drawings, prints, woodwork, and even wallpaper. In short, if you can think of anything that has been "designed," you might find it here. The museum initially housed the collections of industrialist Peter Cooper and his granddaughters, Amy, Sarah, and Eleanor Hewitt. Exhibits from the massive collection change every few months, as the Cooper-Hewitt facility is not as large as some of the city's other museums. Exhibits from 2000 through 2002 include the first National Design Triennial and one hundred masterpieces from the Vitra Museum, featuring concepts, styles, and materials central to furniture in the modern era that have been created since the 1820s. An exhibit called Landscape and Wallcoverings traces the history of wallpaper, with examples from the nineteenth century throughout much of 2001.

New Museum of Contemporary Art

583 Broadway
Between Houston and Prince Streets
Established in 1977, this Lower Manhattan museum is dedicated to "emerging artists and experimental ideas." There are permanent exhibits, but most notable are new exhibits, which are constantly being featured in this gallery-esque setting. Exhibits vary greatly, but all are contemporary works by living American and international artists. The museum houses a bookstore. Hours are Wednesday through Sunday from noon to 6 P.M. and Thursday through Saturday from noon until 8 P.M. Admission is $5 for adults, students, and seniors and $3 for artists (a professional courtesy) and free for those under 18. Admission fees are waived on Thursday from 6 P.M. to 8 P.M. For more information about current exhibits, call 212-219-1222.

A library houses numerous seventeenth- and eighteenth-century books on design and architecture. There is a gift shop on the premises that sells designed objects, books, and gift items. A recent multimillion-dollar renovation has given Cooper-Hewitt a new look.

Cooper-Hewitt is open Sunday from noon to 5 P.M., Tuesday from 10 A.M. to 9 P.M., and Wednesday through Saturday from 10 A.M. to 5 P.M. It is closed on Monday. There is no restaurant on the premises. Admission is $5 for adults $3 for seniors and students, and free for children. For more information call 212-849-8420.

Parking in the area is not easy to find, making public transportation your best bet.

The Frick Collection

1 East 70th Street
Corner of Fifth Avenue

You've seen them in numerous art history books; now you can see them in person. They're the paintings by the old masters, appropriately housed in a 1913 mansion that was transformed into a museum in 1935. The mansion was built by Henry Clay Frick, former Pittsburgh steel giant, who wanted a Manhattan home to house his family and the art collection.

Upon entering the Frick, you'll feel as if you are entering an elegant private mansion. You will head straight for the prime attractions in the living room and foyer. There you'll find great works of art, including Rembrant's self-portrait and so-called *Polish Rider*, along with works by El Greco, Piero della Francesca, Vermeer, Whistler, Goya, and other legendary painters of the fifteenth and sixteenth centuries. The Frick sells a guide to its paintings and offers prerecorded self-guided tours with lively, fascinating commentary about each work.

The collection is so vast that paintings hang by the staircase, in the east wing, which was added in 1977, and even in the garden, where you'll find Manet's *Bull Fight* (1864). The garden, meanwhile, designed by landscape architect Russell Page, is a marvelous glass-enclosed courtyard that provides a sanctuary from the rest of the city and the rest of world.

The museum is not as enormous as some of the others along museum row (Fifth Avenue), but what it lacks in size it more than makes up for in quality; it features a truly priceless collection of awe inspiring artwork. Lectures and chamber music concerts are also given on occasion. The Frick Library, in an adjacent building, contains hundreds of thousands of photos of the artwork and a quarter of a million publications. The library is open to scholars, students, and artists.

A gift shop sells posters, books, and reproductions of the great works. There is no restaurant. Free lectures and chamber music concerts are occasionally held.

The museum is open Tuesday through Saturday from 10 A.M. to 6 P.M. and Sunday from 1 P.M. to 6 P.M. and is closed on Monday and major holidays. Admission is $5 for adults, $3 for students and seniors; children under 10 are not admitted. Parking is very difficult. Although the museum can be covered in a couple of hours, you may want to enjoy a leisurely stroll through the garden. For more information, call the Frick at 212-288-0700.

The Guggenheim Museum

1071 Fifth Avenue
Between 88th and 89th Streets

The giant spiraling washing-machine shape is hard to miss. The distinctive architecture is the work of Frank Lloyd Wright and features both permanent and special exhibits.

Built in the late 1950s, the Guggenheim was designed to display the vast collection of modern works of Solomon R. Guggenheim. Although Frank Lloyd Wright died before completion of the building, it was his final masterpiece, allowing the patrons to wind their way down six stories, slowly, in a sprawling circular structure, while viewing great works of art. An additional tower gallery was opened in 1992 to house the growing collection of permanent features.

Inside the Guggenheim, visitors can enjoy the works of French Impressionists, Cubists, Surrealists, and Abstract Expressionists. Picasso, Chagall, Klee, Kandinsky, Degas, Manet, Toulouse-Lautrec, and van Gogh are all represented in a seemingly priceless collec-

New Century Artists Gallery

168 Mercer Street Between Prince and Houston Streets
New Century Artists Gallery is comprised of two galleries which feature exhibits ranging from fine art to photography. The work is from a diverse cross section of talent including many minority artists, seniors and even children. The gallery is open Tuesday through Saturday from 11 A.M. to 6 P.M. For more information call 212-431-5353.

tion. In 1990 the museum acquired over two hundred works of American minimalist art from the '60s and '70s, and in 1993, two hundred photographs by Robert Mapplethorpe introduced photography into the permanent collection.

The Guggenheim suggested donation is $12 for adults, $7 for students and senior citizens, and free for children under 12. The price includes admission to the downtown **Guggenheim SoHo Branch,** which opened in 1992; it's located at 575 Broadway by Prince Street and houses 30,000 square feet of exhibits in six additional galleries. Hours for the Guggenheim are Monday through Wednesday from 10 A.M. to 6 P.M. and Friday through Sunday from 10 A.M. to 8 P.M. The museum is closed on Thursday. Call 212-423-3500 for more information. Call 212-423-3878 for information about the SoHo branch.

On the premises, you will find a museum store featuring books on contemporary and modern art, plus gifts, jewelry, toys, and various other unique items. The museum café is a casual place to grab a snack.

Intrepid Sea-Air-Space Museum

Intrepid Square
Pier 86 at Twelfth Avenue and 46th Street, Hudson River

What can you do with a retired 900-foot-long aircraft carrier? Turn it into a museum. Actually the USS *Intrepid* itself is only one of several parts of this museum floating in the Hudson River, just west of Times Square. The strategic missile submarine *Growler* and the destroyer *Edson* are also part of this tribute to the American navy and its technology.

The *Intrepid* itself was used by the U.S. Navy from 1942 into the early 1970s and saw action in World War II, Korea, and Vietnam. At its peak, the great ship housed over three thousand sailors and carried over a hundred airplanes and helicopters on the massive deck. The ship, weighing in at nearly 42,000 tons when loaded, is virtually a full military installation at sea, and fighter planes are still perched on deck for viewing. Most of the planes featured on the *Intrepid*, however, were not carried by the ship but demonstrate a variety of aircraft used for various purposes. The A-12 Blackbird, for example, is still among the fastest, highest flying planes ever built. The titanium built plane was used by the CIA to watch the activities on the other side of the Berlin Wall during the Cold War. In contrast, a detailed reproduction of a World War I biplane, complete with propeller, is also found on one of the lower decks.

The unique seaside museum also explores the undersea world, both on the *Growler* and through special exhibitions about submarines and underwater study. A past exhibit featured the *Titanic* and a current exhibit features the history of submarines. Within the museum, you'll also find Pioneers Hall, which looks back at the planes of the early years of the twentieth century, and Technologies Hall, which highlights modern technology, including weaponry. Detailed descriptions and some hands-on features accompany the exhibits.

Onboard the ships of the Intrepid Museum, you'll climb narrow staircases and squeeze through more tight corridors than you would at the Guggenheim or the Met. Consequently, your youngsters may have a better time exploring the contents of this museum. A great deal of history is packed into this unique museum, and it makes one recognize the sheer might of the navy and the history of how they have protected U.S. interests at sea. There is also a tribute to the space program, featuring one of the space capsules retrieved at sea prior to the smooth ground landings of more recent space shuttles.

There is a lot to see here, and the museum draws a crowd, so plan to stay awhile. It's preferable to go in the warmer months. The museum is open weekdays from 10 A.M. to 5 P.M. and weekends from 10 A.M. to 6 P.M. from April through September, and from 10 A.M. to 5 P.M. and closed on Monday from October through March. Admission is $10 for adults, $7.50 for students over 12, seniors, and veterans, $5 for ages 6 through 11, $1 for ages 2 through 5, and free for children under 2.

Self-guided tours of the USS *Intrepid*, USS *Edson*, and USS *Growler* are free with admission. The museum has a very popular gift shop featuring *Intrepid* baseball caps, T-shirts, water glasses, playing cards, beer steins, mugs, and anything else they can put a logo on.

A cafeteria onboard the *Intrepid* features much better fare than the sailors ate, including a full menu of sandwiches and hot items. For more information call 212-245-0072.

Museum of Chinese in the Americas

Founded in 1980 as the New York Chinatown History Project, the museum was chartered in 1992 and is currently the only museum in the United States dedicated to documenting and interpreting the history and culture of Chinese Americans. In the heart of Chinatown, at 70 Mulberry Street, the galleries reflect through art the Chinese American experience in America. Included are photos, documents, sound recordings, textiles, and more. There is a gift shop with exhibition posters, children's books, and other gift items. Admission is $3 for adults, $1 for students and seniors, and free for children under 12. Call 212-619-4720 for more information.

Jewish Museum

1109 Fifth Avenue
At 92nd Street

The Jewish Museum is housed in a mansion that was built at the start of the twentieth century. The history presented within these walls dates back thousands of years, recounting the story of the Jewish people. The lower two floors of the four-story structure are set up for ongoing special exhibitions; the top two floors house the permanent Culture and Continuity: The Jewish Journey exhibit.

In the permanent collection, you'll find artifacts (such as those from the ancient Dura Europos Synagogue, built many centuries ago), along with photographs and texts. From the exodus out of Egypt to the festival of Hanukkah, the drama and significance of the stories is evident. There is also a section dedicated to rituals and Jewish tradition, featuring ancient prayer shawls, menorahs, wedding cups, and other items, plus a film explaining some of the longtime traditions.

Another section is devoted to the Holocaust. Although this is not the focus of the museum as a whole, it is included as part of a much larger history. There is also a section of the museum dedicated to looking at anti-Semitism. Representative work by Jewish artists is included in the various sections. A film and artwork reflecting Jewish culture in the contemporary world plus a children's gallery round out the substantial museum. In fact, with the expansion in the early 1990s, this is now the largest Jewish museum devoted to culture and history outside of Israel.

The exhibitions, the films, and computers (providing information and even asking philosophical questions from the Talmud) can take several hours to experience fully. There is often a wait to get in, so plan early and, as with most of the city's museums, try for a weekday. The museum, which is also home to renowned Jewish artists such as Marc Chagall, provides a sense of culture through art and artifacts and offers a marvelous learning experience.

A gift shop offers books and other items relating to Jewish Culture. You'll also find a café on the premises.

The museum is open Sunday, Monday, Wednesday, and Thursday from 11 A.M. to 5:45 P.M. and on Tuesday from 11 A.M. to

8 P.M. It is closed on Saturday. Admission is $7 for adults, $5 for seniors, and free for children under 12. On Tuesday evenings from 5 to 8 P.M., the museum is free for everyone—and very busy. Call 212-423-3200 for more information.

Lower East Side Tenement Museum

90 Orchard Street
Corner of Broome Street

Housed in an actual tenement that was home to over seven thousand immigrants between 1863 and 1935, the museum recounts, in photos, artifacts, and furnished rooms, the experience of the immigrants who lived there and throughout the lower portion of Manhattan known as the Lower East Side.

The museum, chartered in 1988, is small in stature (compared to the massive museums of Upper Manhattan), and exemplifies urban dwelling and the immigrant experience. The highlight of a visit is the tour in which one of several first-rate tour guides recount the stories of several families who lived in the tenement and describe the possessions that were donated to the museum.

Across the street, at the visitor center, visitors can view a film featuring interviews with historians and former residents of the classic tenement. A slide show called Urban Pioneers describes the history of the tenement. Free outdoor exhibits are also featured. A gift shop sells books and other materials relating to the Lower East Side. Walking tours and other special tours highlight aspects of the surrounding neighborhood.

This museum will greatly appeal to anyone whose family first settled in the Lower East Side after stepping off a ship onto Ellis Island. It's truly inspiring to learn how so many people managed to survive and even prosper in this neighborhood of poor immigrants.

The museum is accessible by guided tours only. Visits take about an hour. Tours begin in the visitor center Tuesday through Friday every hour from 1 to 4 P.M. and Saturday and Sunday from 11 A.M. to 4:30 P.M. There is free parking in a lot on Broome Street, between Norfolk and Suffolk, for up to 4 hours. For more information, call 212-431-0233.

Outside the Museum Walls

Many of the city's museums, such as the Museum of the City of New York and the Lower East Side Tenement Museum, offer walking tours that take visitors around the neighborhoods of the city. Call and ask whether they offer such tours. Guides are generally very knowledgeable, and such tours can be enlightening and fun.

Metropolitan Museum of Art

1000 Fifth Avenue
At 82nd Street

While the Upper West Side of Central Park has the American Museum of Natural History, the Upper East Side has the Metropolitan Museum of Art, one of the world's largest museums, with over three million works of art. Needless to say, no matter how hard you try, you cannot see it all in one visit, or two for that matter. It's huge. You can, however, select areas of interest and tour specific galleries displaying any type of art you desire, from prehistoric times to modern and from any culture worldwide. And it's not just paintings and sculptures!

As you enter and head to the ticket area in the Great Hall, you will notice the marble stairway leading up to the famed European Collection of nineteenth-century classics. To your left will be Greek and Roman art and to your right Egyptian art. You will soon realize that wherever you turn, you will be enveloped in art and artifacts, many priceless, from the history of another part of the world.

The famous collection of armor includes European armor, firearms, and swords, as well as Japanese arms and armor. Weapons from Europe, the Middle East, Asia, and America are on display. Walking through a hall filled with knights in shining armor is almost like being in King Arthur's court. The vast American Wing provides a look at fourteen thousand paintings, sculptures, and decorative art objects acquired by the museum since its establishment in 1879. The works span American history from the eighteenth through the twentieth centuries, with American domestic architecture including everything from eighteenth-century cabinetmakers to a Frank Lloyd Wright living room from 1915. A glass collection (including American stained glass), textiles, quilts, and silver are all part of this extensive look into Americana.

The first floor is home to arts of Africa, Oceania, and the Americas, featuring sixteen hundred objects spanning 3000 years in the Michael C. Rockefeller wing. Works from New Guinea, Melanesia, and Polynesia and stone objects from pre-Columbian cultures of Mexico and Central and South America highlight this vast and very rare collection. The first floor is also home to European sculpture and decorative arts, medieval art, twentieth-century art, and more. The Egyptian art display, established in 1906, features some thirty-five thousand objects dating back to 3000 B.C. and includes jewelry, artistic and archeological findings that represent daily life, and religious articles from centuries ago. The Temple of Dendur, an Egyptian monument from the early Roman period (15 B.C.) was a gift from the Egyptian government in recognition of the American contribution to the international campaign to save the ancient Nubian monuments and has been rebuilt to resemble the temple on the banks of the Nile. A reflecting pool has been built to represent the Nile.

On the second floor, along with the European paintings and the American wing, you'll find musical instruments, Japanese art, Asian art, Chinese art, Greek art, and Romantic art, drawings, prints, photographs, and more.

Suffice to say, there's far too much in the museum to even attempt to describe it all. Even the photography collection now has more than fifteen thousand works acquired over the past 70 years. The museum has information desks in the Great Hall and the Uris Center for Education. The staff, many of whom are volunteers, are glad to help you find your way. Tours and assistance can also be found at the international visitors desk in the Great Hall, where several languages are spoken, including Chinese, French, German, Italian, Japanese, and Spanish.

The museum is open Sunday and Tuesday through Thursday from 9:30 A.M. to 5:15 P.M. and Friday and Saturday from 9:30 A.M. to 8:45 P.M. It is closed on Monday, Thanksgiving, Christmas, and New Year's Day. Admission is $10 for adults, $5 for students and senior citizens, and free for children under 12 accompanied by an adult. Tours are offered in several languages and are free with your admission. The information desk will provide you with a tour schedule. Very important: get a map when you enter.

There are group tours available but advance reservations are required. Call 212-570-3711 for information. There are also a wide variety of educational programs, should you be in town for a while.

The museum has parking for a discounted fee (enter on the 80th Street side) when you validate your ticket at the Uris Center information desk. Parking is limited, so it is best to use public transportation.

Museum Of American Folk Art

2 Lincoln Plaza Columbus Avenue Between 65th and 66th Streets

Easy to miss with restaurants and stores all around it and Lincoln Center across the street, this little museum houses folk art from the eighteenth century to the present. Included are textiles, sculptures, paintings, quilts, carvings, pottery, and a giant Indian chief weathervane. Lectures and workshops in folk art are given, and the neighboring gift shop is a nice place to buy books and craft items. The museum is open Tuesday through Sunday from 11:30 A.M. to 7:30 P.M. and costs $3. Call 212-977-7298 for more information. This is a pleasant place to spend time, prior to or after visiting Lincoln Center, while exploring the sights and sounds of the Upper West Side.

Unlike the Museum of Natural History, you won't stumble on gift shops at every turn. The gift shop, two floors in all, is located just off the Great Hall (the main entrance). Books and publications, reproductions, and other items are available.

Eateries include a cafeteria, café, and restaurant on the premises. The restaurant requires reservations (212-570-3964). You will also find the Great Hall balcony bar located on the Twentieth-Century Sculpture Roof Garden; it overlooks Central Park and is a delightful, even romantic, place to stroll during the summer. Beverages are served from May through October, and there is generally music from 5 to 8 P.M. The roof garden, with its statues and tranquillity, is a truly delightful corner of the city.

If you're planning to visit the museum, and you should, start early and take your time. Young children may not be as fascinated as they will be in the Museum of Natural History, so make sure to hit the room full of knights and armor (some young children might be scared). If your children get restless after a while, you can always go back another time. Meanwhile, take your time and enjoy this great cultural institution.

The Museum of Modern Art

11 East 53rd Street
Between Fifth and Sixth Avenues

Some one hundred thousand paintings, sculptures, drawings, photographs, architectural models, drawings, and design objects are part of what is the largest collection of modern art in the world. You may find yourself standing and staring at an eclectic work and wondering exactly how or why it is considered art and then turn around and look at a work that you find to be sheer brilliance. The idea that everyone's perception of art is different is no more apparent than in this spectacular museum. You'll love some of it and hate some of it, but you'll want to see as much as you can.

Some 1.5 million people visit the museum annually to check out special exhibits as well as the vast permanent collection that occupies 67,000 square feet of the 87,000 square feet available. The permanent collection includes all major artists and movements since the late nineteenth century. Van Gogh's *Starry Night* and Rousseau's

Sleeping Gypsy are among many classics on display, and scores of works by Matisse, Picasso, Cézanne, Miró, Mondrian, Brancusi, and Pollock, among others, fill the exhibit halls. A massive architecture collection features drawings and models of buildings. More than twenty-five thousand photographs span over 150 years, and a film library, founded in 1935, 6 years after the opening of the museum, houses some thirteen thousand films and four million film stills—no, they are not all on display at one time. The collection includes the works of Charlie Chaplin, Buster Keaton, Walt Disney, John Ford, Frank Capra, Fritz Lang, Ingmar Bergman, innovative Russian director Sergei Eisenstein, and many others. There is an extensive collection of drawings and even a video collection. Can a CD or computer disk collection be far off?

Unlike many museums that just display culture, the Museum of Modern Art has long played a role in building and legitimizing culture, displaying avant-garde works that have sometimes met with criticism. They have helped nontraditional forms of art to flourish by putting photography, drawings, and architecture on display. The six-floor museum allows you to indulge yourself in culture, primarily of the twentieth century, from household items to prints and textiles to sculpture and painting. You will see the progression of artistic styles as you stroll through the second-floor galleries and work your way up to the third-floor drawings and on to the fourth floor, which even has a helicopter hanging from the rafters.

MOMA, as it is known, is open Saturday through Tuesday and Thursday from 10:30 to 5:45 and Friday from 10:30 to 8:15. The museum is closed on Wednesday, Thanksgiving, and Christmas. Admission is $9.50 for adults, $6.50 for full-time students and seniors, and free for teens or children under 16 accompanied by an adult. On Fridays from 4:30 to 8:15, it's "pay as you wish."

Gallery talks, tours including family programs, family tours, and educational programs are all offered. Talks begin in the garden, which, by the way, is a lovely place to stroll or to sit and relax. The museum also has two theaters showing foreign films, classics, and independent features, plus a bookstore and design store. The bookstore is open Saturday through Thursday from 10 A.M. to 7 P.M. and Friday from 10 A.M. to 9 P.M. The Design Store is open Saturday through Thursday from 10 A.M. to 6:30 P.M. and Friday from 10 A.M. to 8 P.M. For information, call 212-708-9480.

The Sette MOMA is an Italian restaurant open for lunch every day (except Wednesday) from noon to 3 P.M. and for dinner everyday (except Wednesday and Sunday) from 5 to 10:30 P.M. The Garden Café is open every day (except Wednesday) from 11 A.M. to 5 P.M. For group sales information, call 212-708-9685

Museum of Television and Radio

25 West 52nd Street
Between Fifth and Sixth Avenues

Established in 1965 by William Paley and later moved to this sleek Midtown location, the Museum of Television and Radio is essentially a place to watch old television programs or listen to radio programs. Special tributes and galleries highlight the early years of television. Old television shows on display include Edward R. Murrow broadcasts and the Beatles' first appearance on *The Ed Sullivan Show* (the most watched program at the museum). Vintage commercials provide a fascinating, whimsical glimpse of the past 5 decades and illustrate how society has changed.

With the advent and availability of home video collections and so many channels showing syndicated programs, this museum has less one-of-a-kind appeal than those museums whose collections of tangible items and artifacts of the past cannot show up at your local video store or on *Nick at Nite*. Two theaters and a screening room, however, are used for interesting seminars and special evenings dedicated to television luminaries. They are worth checking out on the schedule.

The museum has free tours on Tuesday and is open Tuesday, Wednesday, Friday, Saturday, and Sunday from noon to 6 P.M. and Thursday from noon to 8 P.M. Admission is $6. There's a small gift shop in the lobby. For more information, call 212-661-6600.

The Museum of the City of New York

1220 Fifth Avenue
At 103rd Street

If you're visiting New York City, why not learn firsthand about its history? Along with the New York Historical Society, this is one of two museums devoted to the history of the city it calls home. With an enormous wealth of materials of all types, this is, perhaps, the more "fun" of the two galleries paying homage to NYC.

Set in a massive mansion looking out on the northern portion of Central Park, the Museum of the City of New York offers provocative special exhibitions along with a wide range of permanent exhibits celebrating different aspects of the city. It's a good idea to choose your favorites, as you'll never get to all of it in 1 day.

Major exhibits found in the vast museum include the prints and photography collection featuring thousands of photographs tracing the history of New York City along with the largest known collection of Currier & Ives lithographs.

You don't have to be a theater afficionado to appreciate the stunning theater collection celebrating the Great White Way, Broadway, and American theater. Costumes and memorabilia, set designs, posters, paintings, and photographs recount the legends of the Broadway stage as well as Yiddish theater, which thrived in New York in the early twentieth century.

A decorative arts collection includes precious metals and other rare items. The highlight is a look at New York's furniture from 1790 through 1890, some of which is built better than furniture made in 1990.

New York Toy Stories is a tribute to toys that the children of the city have played with, dating back to the 1800s. Cast iron toys, wooden soldiers, mechanical toys, rare dolls, boats, and renowned doll houses are on display in this unique exhibit that all ages can enjoy.

Start early and know when to quit. From a wealth of paintings to a giant head of Andrew Jackson to a New York "Hall of Fame" honoring some of the city's remarkable achievers, this is a very well-packed museum. You can also sit and watch documentaries and films of the city.

The museum is open Wednesday through Saturday from 10 A.M. to 5 P.M. Tuesday is for tour groups only. On Monday and all legal holidays, the museum is closed. For group tours—Tuesday through Friday—call 212-534-1672, ext. 206. Fees vary depending on the length of the tour and the program.

Admission to the museum is $5 for adults, $4 for seniors, students, and children, and $10 for families.

The Museum Shop sells items relating to the exhibits and to the city of New York, including books, videos, and toys (not the ones on display, but some good reproductions). You can buy New York City photo reproductions or reproductions of Currier & Ives prints that provide a nice reminder of your trip (and are better than postcards).

The museum does not having parking and it's not an easy area in which to find a space, so take public transportation. Also, there is no restaurant in the museum and few choices on the surrounding blocks, so eat before or after your visit.

The New York City Fire Museum

278 Spring Street
Between Hudson and Varick

No, it's not the Metropolitan Museum of Art, but to a 5-year-old, it's probably a lot more fun. Set in a 1904 firehouse, the museum provides a walk through the history of fire fighting, from horse-drawn carriages to modern "jaws of life" rescue equipment. But the museum is more than a display of fire-fighting equipment. For those who want to learn a bit more about "New York's Bravest," there is information about aspects of fire-fighting skills and equipment, including the hose, hydrant, ladders, and so on. You'll even learn about animals that helped fight fires, including the Dalmatian, which became the mascot of firefighters everywhere.

Basically, if it's fire fighting related, it's in the museum. Exhibits range from toy fire trucks to very real shields, uniforms, and fireboat equipment. In contrast to other museums, you might find this one less crowded on the weekends when the class trips aren't visiting. Although they probably won't appreciate the historical aspects, it's a great place to stop by with the kids for a couple of hours, particu-

A Few More Museums

The American Numismatic Society, located at Broadway and 155th Street, features coins of the world. Call 212-234-3130.

The Americas Society, located at 680 Park Avenue and 68th Street, has exhibits about Central, South, and North America, including the Caribbean and Canada. Call 212-249-8950.

The Children's Museum of Arts, located at 182 Lafayette Street, between Broome and Grand, is a great place for children of all ages. Call 212-274-0986.

The Dahesh Museum, located at 601 Fifth Avenue and 48th Street, has two thousand works of nineteenth- and twentieth-century European art. Call 212-759-0606.

The Dykman Farmhouse Museum is Manhattan's only remaining Dutch farmhouse. It's located on West 204th Street. Call 212-304-9422.

Old Merchant's House Museum, located on East 4th Street, is an intact Greek Revival house from 1832.

The Morris-Jumel Mansion Museum, located at 160th Street in Roger Morris Park, is the oldest extant residence in Manhattan. It was built in 1765 and was once George Washington's headquarters. Call 212-923-8008.

The El Museo Del Barrio, located at 1230 Fifth Avenue near 105th Street, features exhibitions pertaining to Puerto Rico and Latin America. Call 212-831-7272.

The Museum of American Financial History, located at 28 Broadway by Bowling Green Park, recounts the rise of Wall Street and Lower Manhattan to the financial capital of the nation. Call 212-908-4519.

The Museum of Jewish Heritage, a living memorial to the Holocaust, located at 18 First Place, features personal accounts of the Holocaust. Call 212-945-0039.

The Museum of the American Piano, located at 211 West 58th Street, presents the history of keyboards to 1820. Call 212-246-4646.

The National Museum of the American Indian, Smithsonian Institution, located at 1 Bowling Green, is an enormous collection of art and artifacts devoted to American Indian culture. Call 212-514-3700.

The Police Academy Museum, located at 235 East 20th Street, displays police memorabilia. Call 212-477-9753.

larly if you are planning a day at other Lower Manhattan sights, such as the Stock Exchange, which may be less interesting to a 6-year-old.

The museum is open Tuesday through Sunday from 10 A.M. to 4 P.M. Admission is $4 for adults, $2 for students or seniors, and $1 for children under 12.

The museum gift shop sells toys, books, and T-shirts. There are no restaurants but plenty of places to eat in the area. As for parking, some spaces are available in front, but as usual it's probably best to take public transportation. For information, call 212-691-1303.

New-York Historical Society

2 West 77th Street
At Central Park West

Founded in 1804, when New York was hyphenated, the museum houses literally millions of examples of Americana, including books, newspapers, maps, manuscripts, photographs, silverware, antique toys, posters, political cartoons, architectural drawings, carriages, furniture, and much much more. The second oldest historical society in the country, the society's goal is to preserve all kinds of materials related to the city of New York. From George Washington's inaugural chair to the world's largest collection of Tiffany lamps, there is a wealth of cultural history represented here. Furniture is displayed chronologically so that you can take notice of the changes in design and style through the centuries. A gallery of 1830s paintings from the collection of Luman Reed and 432 watercolors by John James Audubon for his book *Birds of America* are two artistic highlights of this museum that you should not miss. There are also changing exhibits featuring items from the collection.

The Historical Society has a gift shop but no restaurant on the premises. Also found here is one of the most extensive American history research libraries you'll ever encounter. The library is open Tuesday through Saturday from 11 A.M. to 5 P.M., and children must be accompanied by an adult. The museum is open daily from 11 A.M. to 5 P.M. You can probably cover the museum in 4 to 5 hours at a leisurely pace. Admission is only $5 for adults and $3 for students, seniors, and children. Guided tours are at 1 and 3 P.M. and generally focus on certain sections of the museum, so ask if they cover the area(s) of interest to you.

Parking is difficult, so unless you want to pay for a neighborhood garage (if they have room), take public transportation.

The Studio Museum in Harlem

144 West 125th Street

The Studio Museum opened in 1968 as an exhibition space. It has grown over 32 years into a full-fledged museum, with galleries, workshops, and even a sculpture garden.

New permanent galleries (under construction as of this writing) will add an additional 72,000 square feet of exhibit space to the current galleries. The current collection includes nineteenth- and twentieth-century African-American paintings, sculptures, twentieth century Caribbean art, and traditional and contemporary art and artifacts from Africa. Featured exhibitions in 2000 include African-American Artists and American Modernism, which will feature the work of at least a dozen artists and Beads, Body, and Soul: Art and Light in the Yoruba Universe, which will feature Yoruba beaded art.

Some one hundred thousand visitors yearly browse the galleries that make up Harlem's premier museum. It's open Wednesday through Friday from 10 A.M. to 5 P.M. and Saturday and Sunday from 1 to 6 P.M. A museum shop in the lobby sells books and gift items relating to the exhibits of the museum. Admission is $5. For more information, call 212-864-4500.

The museum should not disappoint anyone interested in African-American art. Public transportation is the best way to get there.

Whitney Museum of American Art

120 Park Avenue
At 42nd Street

Founded in 1930, the Whitney now houses more then twelve thousand works of art by nearly two thousand artists. The museum features twentieth-century and contemporary American art, including paintings, sculpture, photography, and more. Works from the estate

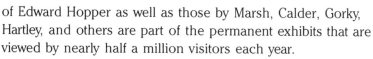

of Edward Hopper as well as those by Marsh, Calder, Gorky, Hartley, and others are part of the permanent exhibits that are viewed by nearly half a million visitors each year.

The current building, which was recently expanded by 7,600 square feet, is actually the third to house the collection and was built in 1966. The oddly shaped building is a work of art itself, surrounded by a sculpture garden and walls.

Quite entrenched in the American Century exhibit for over a year, the museum is now slowly returning to the business at hand, including a biennial celebration of the best in contemporary art over the previous 2 years. Other special exhibits are also planned.

If you enjoy a look at contemporary art, the Whitney has plenty to offer. The special exhibits are worth a visit; they tend to promote these more heavily than they do their permanent collections.

Sarabeth's Restaurant is open for lunch and brunch within the Whitney. The Whitney Museum Store and Museum Bookstore offer gift ideas and books primarily about American art.

The museum is open Tuesday, Wednesday, and Friday through Sunday from 11 A.M. to 6 P.M. and Thursday from 1 to 8 P.M. and is closed on Monday. Admission is $12.50 for adults, $10.50 for seniors and students with a valid ID, and free for children under 12 For more information, call 877-WHITNEY. Take public transportation; this is a very busy area, not known for street parking.

Chapter 6

Central Park

Activities and Family Things to Do

Central Park, an 843-acre oasis in the middle of the busiest city in the world. The initial idea to set aside space for a public park came from William Cullen Bryant as early as 1844. Over a decade later, Frederick Law Olmsted and Calvert Vaux began designing the rolling lawns and picturesque vistas that would make up the vast park.

The first landscaped park in the country, the vast acreage was constructed over 20 years, from 1857 until 1877. Building the park was not an easy task; the land was primarily swamps, bluffs, and rocky outcroppings. Thousands of workers moved soil and blasted through rock, then planted trees and grass in their place. Some six bodies of water, three dozen bridges, and miles of irrigation pipes were part of the undertaking. Workers planted over four hundred varieties of trees and nearly a thousand types of shrubs. A significant number of residents living in shantytowns on the site were displaced. Slowly the park emerged, stretching from 59th Street on the south end up to 110th Street on the north. From Fifth Avenue across to the equivalent of Eighth Avenue, known as Central Park West, the marvelous park became the crown jewel of the city, with fancy carriages and well-dressed New Yorkers parading along the paths within the vast acreage. Since its completion, the park has been a refuge for New Yorkers and visitors looking for a respite from the busy city streets for a little while.

Today, Central Park is a haven for bicycling, rollerblading, jogging, boating, ice skating, strolling, or taking a ride in a horse-drawn carriage. You'll find people playing Frisbee, softball, football, tennis, chess, and checkers, as well as people flying kites. There are great rocks for climbing, horses for riding, and places to sit and listen to concerts under the stars. From sunbathing to folk dancing, Central Park is the ultimate resort, and with the exception of some sites and activities that charge an admission, it's all free.

On a spring, summer, or even warm fall or winter day, the park will give you the opportunity to step into another world within the city itself. The view of the high-rise buildings flanks the outskirts of the great park. As you venture further into the park, you'll lose the sounds of traffic and the fast pace that is New York City. Everything in Central Park moves at a slower pace, except perhaps the rollerbladers. Strolling through, you'll find yourself stopping to enjoy street performers, including musicians, jugglers, mimes, dancers, and clowns. Buy a pretzel, climb the side of a giant rock formation, or simply toss down a blanket and lie on the grass. Designated "quiet areas" prohibit loud radios to disturb your escape from the world.

Completely manmade, Central Park is full of sights, statues, lakes, ponds, bridges, and the second most popular zoo in the city. Many of the best-known sights and landmarks within the park have been there since the nineteenth or early twentieth century.

Nearly twenty million visitors enjoy the riches of the park annually; more than fifty groups or organizations, including running clubs and bird watching groups, hold their gatherings in the park. A private not-for-profit group, the Central Park Conservancy, handles the park's financial activities through private donations from foundations, corporations, and individuals.

The Central Park Wildlife Center

Also known as the **Central Park Zoo**, the center is one of the best bargains you'll find in the city. The zoo is small—but large on smiles from the millions of children who visit every year. The country's oldest public zoo, it was remodeled in the early '90s; the neighboring children's zoo reopened in 1997.

The main zoo does not have "large" animals, such as lions and tigers, but it does have a large sea lion pool as the centerpiece. (Feeding time is a fun activity to watch.) To cool off, you might want to stop in the Polar Circle, an indoor enclosed exhibit featuring more penguins than you can count. The tuxedoed waddlers frolic in a recreated wintry arctic setting, complete with mini-glaciers and icy waters. Arctic foxes and tufted puffins also live in the Polar Circle.

Venturing through the zoo, you will find a large land and water home for New York City's popular polar bear, who, after several weeks of sulking, at one point actually inspired the city to hire an animal psychologist to visit. There are actually three bears, and they have plenty of room to play and are fun to watch, when they're not taking an extended nap. Nearby, you'll find Monkey

Filmed in Central Park!

Numerous movies and television shows have ventured into the friendly confines of Central Park. Among the many feature films with scenes shot in and around the park are:

- *An Affair to Remember*
- *Ghostbusters*
- *Annie Hall*
- *Wall Street*
- *When Harry Met Sally*
- *Tootsie*
- *Hannah and Her Sisters*
- *Kramer vs. Kramer*
- *Zelig*
- *Love Story*
- *Barefoot in the Park*
- *Balto*

Island, home to numerous Japanese Snow monkeys among other varieties of monkey.

A large, indoor (and hot) tropical rain forest exhibit is complete with tall trees, waterfalls, and other vegetation; it is home to numerous birds, Colobus monkeys, insects, and other living things. Following along the trail, you'll find yourself smack in the middle of the Amazon, right in the middle of New York City!

All in all, the beautifully landscaped zoo takes about an hour to visit at a leisurely pace. There is a restaurant, the Café; it serves primarily snack foods, hot dogs, and sandwiches. There's also a gift shop with all kinds of "zoovineers."

The zoo is open year-round from 10 A.M. to 4:30 or 5:30 P.M., depending on the time of year. The winter months may be a bit brisk for strolling. Admission is $3.50 for adults, $1.25 for seniors, $.50 for children ages 3 through 12, and free for children under 3. The zoo is accessible to people with disabilities.

Buying a ticket also entitles you to visit the neighboring Tisch Children's Zoo, where children can visit and pet goats, pigs, sheep, and other children-friendly animals. The small well-planned zoo is fun for the little ones. Summer days can produce long lines on weekends, but the lines generally move quickly along.

The famous Delacorte Clock is located just outside the zoo. It was constructed on top of an archway early in the century. It consists of four bronze animals on a small carousel that rotates at the hour, with the animals moving as the chimes are heard.

Wollman Memorial Rink

By winter, Wollman Rink is a mid-city paradise for ice skaters, and by summer, it's home to rollerskaters and inliners. A terrace above offers, to those who enjoy watching, a lovely perch on which to stand and look down at the skaters. Ice skating prevails from November to March and rollerskating from March into November. It costs $4 to rollerskate for adults and $3.50 for children under 12 and seniors. You can rent inline skates for $6 (which includes skates and safety gear). You can also rent just safety gear for $3. Children under 14 must wear helmets (by New York State law). If you want to skate around the park, skate rental is $15 plus a $100

New Yorkers and Their Park!

New Yorkers care deeply for Central Park; in fact, the park has received the bulk of its money over the years from contributions by wealthy benefactors. Beyond just money, the people of New York have spoken out when it comes to protecting and taking care of their park. In the 1950s, when a well-known developer, Robert Moses, wanted to build a parking lot for the Tavern on the Green Restaurant on the west side of the park by 68th Street, mothers who took their young children to that serene corner took up a letter-writing campaign. They won their battle. Residents complained when Disney held their *Pocahontas* opening night extravaganza in the park, and Disney promised not only to give money to the park but also to leave the park exactly as they found it.

More Sights in Central Park

If you enter the park by a horse-drawn hansom cab, you'll come in from the southwest corner, where you'll soon see Wollman Rink and the Zoo. Then you have choices of whether to head north to the Pond or veer west to the Sheep Meadow in the direction of Tavern on the Green. No matter how you experience Central Park, you'll have a host of sights to check out, including these:

- Alice in Wonderland (a statue)
- The Arsenal
- Balto (a statue)
- Belvedere Castle
- Bethesda Fountain and Terrace
  (Don't miss it, on 72th Street, almost central in the park!)
- The Conservatory Garden
- The Dairy
- Dana Discovery Center
- Delacorte Theater
- The Great Lawn
- The Harlem Meer
- Loeb Boathouse
- The Mall (with its main path, Literary Walk)
- The Pond
- Sheep Meadow
- Strawberry Fields
- Swedish Cottage (an imported schoolhouse from 1876)
- Tavern on the Green
- Wildlife Center (the zoo) and Children's Zoo
- Wollman Rink

deposit. Ice skating is $7 for adults and $3.50 for children under 17 and seniors. Skate rental is $3. You can also skate in the winter at Lasker Rink and Pool at 106th Street, mid-park; it is the only public swimming facility in the park during the summer months. Call 212-396-1010 for more information on Wollman or Lasker.

Playgrounds

Playgrounds can be found all throughout the park in different configurations. Some twenty-one playgrounds offer different themes and styles centered around fun activities, including the largest sliding board in Manhattan at the East 67th Street's Billy Johnson Playground. Other playgrounds include the Timber-style Diana Ross Playground at West 81th Street, built for the singer who played a concert in the park and later donated money for the facility, and the Wild West Playground, sporting a western theme with a small stream running through it.

Playgrounds also can be found at East 67th Street, East 72th Street, and around the Great Lawn at East 77th, 79th, and 85th, and West 81th, 84th, 85th, and 86th Streets. Playgrounds around the reservoir are at East 96th Street, West 91th, 93th, and 96th Streets. North end playgrounds are at East 100th and 108th Streets, 110th and Lennox Avenue, and on the west side at 100th and 110th Streets.

The park's playgrounds are generally well kept and fenced in. Remember to be attentive to your children and to keep the playgrounds (and the park for that matter) clean.

The Carousel

The carousel in Central Park is over 90 years old, but it is not the park's original. The first carousel in the park was built in 1871 and turned by "horsepower" (and not the horsepower that you find in your car). It was later destroyed in a fire and rebuilt, only to be destroyed by fire for a second time. In 1953 the park acquired a 50-year-old carousel from Coney Island and refurbished it; this is the carousel that is in the park today. Adults and children can sit atop one of the many hand-carved horses and go for a spin on this antique treasure. The Carousel is located mid-park by 64th Street.

The Charles A. Dana Discovery Center

The Dana Discovery Center (at the Harlem Meer) is one of the newest points of interest and education for children—and grown ups too. The center, in a chateau at the northeast corner of the park (Fifth Avenue and 110th Street), offers environmental studies on an 11-acre section of the recently restored Harlem Meer. Various exhibits and workshops focusing on ecology, orienteering, and nature, as well as walking tours and performances, are all found at the new center; during the week, it's a haven for class trips.

The Swedish Cottage Marionette Theater

This is a fun-filled place to find entertainment for the little ones. The cottage, located at the 79th Street Transverse, is originally from the nineteenth century and has since been renovated. The puppet shows are performed Tuesday through Friday at 10:30 A.M. and noon and Saturday at 11 A.M., 1 P.M., and 3 P.M. Call for a reservation at 212-988-9093.

The Loeb Boathouse and the Lake

The boathouse and lake can be found on the west side of the park between 72th and 77th Streets. The second biggest body of water in the park at 18 acres, the lake is home to plenty of boating activity and makes for a scenic, romantic place to stroll around. Call 212-861-4137 to rent a boat. Boats rent at $10 per hour. They are primarily rowboats. There is one gondola for those who haven't been to Italy for a while.

Tennis, Anyone?

Tennis players can enjoy swinging away on some thirty courts from April through November. For those who will be staying in the

Central Park Statues

There are numerous statues throughout the great park, including a number of famed monuments to leaders from nations around the world. Among the many famous statues in the park are these:

Hans Christian Andersen
(as he sits reading one of his fables)

Balto
(in memory of the dog sleds of Alaska that brought medicine to ill children)

The Civil War Statue
(commemorating the 107th Union Regiment)

The Angel of Waters
(the multi-tiered statue within the Bethesda Fountain)

Still Hunt
(the statue of a panther perched on a ledge watching over one of the many trails)

Hansom Cabs

In the 1880s, the horse and carriage was the only way to travel. Over the years, the hansom cab rides through Central Park have become a tradition. The clip-clop of hooves and the old-fashioned appeal is fun for kids and romantic for adults. Perched along Central Park South, most notably from the southeast corner of the park at Fifth Avenue (by the Plaza Hotel), the carriage rides cost $34 for 20 minutes plus $10 for each additional 15 minutes. And you should tip the driver.

city for a while or visiting often and want to take advantage of the few courts available in Manhattan (most of the others are in membership clubs), you can buy a season-long permit at the Arsenal on 64th Street and Fifth Avenue in the park (permit information is at 212-255-8036). Permits cost $50 for adults, $20 for seniors, and $10 for children under 17. For those who are visiting the park on a short stay in the city and only want to play once, you can purchase a single-day permit for $5 per person. These can be purchased at the courts on 96th Street toward the west side of the park, by the reservoir. Call 212-360-8134 for information.

Other Activities

Anyone with a remote control or scale model sailboat can put their vehicle to the test in the Conservatory Water just north of 72th Street by Fifth Avenue. Horseback riding is also one of the park's numerous activities. You can take a horse out from the Claremont Stables at 175 West 89th Street if you want to ride English saddle style along one of several bridle paths through the park. Call 212-724-5100 for information. Riding costs $38 per half hour and is for experienced riders only.

Bicycle riding is also a very popular park activity. Bike paths designate where you can ride. You can rent a bike during the months of March through November from 10 A.M. to 6 P.M. The fee is $10 per hour plus a deposit or slightly more for bicycles for two.

If you'd prefer more sedentary activities, you can hit the Chess and Checker House near West 64th Street. There are numerous places throughout the park to sit and play these or other board games.

Sights in the Park

The Arsenal

The Arsenal was built on the property in 1851, prior to the construction of the park. While the building is now predominantly home to the Parks and Recreation Department offices, it served briefly (in the late nineteenth century) as the American Museum of

Natural History. It also housed Civil War troops for a short period. Today, the historic structure, on Fifth Avenue just inside the 62th Street entrance, is filled with offices.

Bethesda Terrace

Bethesda Terrace is home to the multilevel Bethesda Fountain, dedicated in 1873 and named for a pool in Jerusalem, with the "Angel of the Waters" sculpture sitting high atop and overlooking the European-esque terrace. A stone staircase leads down to the three-tier fountain that sits near the mall with a backdrop on the lake. The view is spectacular from the top of the stairs, with row-boats in the background below lush trees with their branches and green leaves hanging over the waters. The boathouse can be seen to the right. The terrace surrounding the fountain is a busy stopping point for the numerous visitors who stroll by and stop to enjoy the beauty of the scene. Street performers including jugglers, magicians, and musicians delight the kids—and their parents too for that matter. Bethesda Terrace is by 72th Street, toward the east side (or Fifth Avenue side) of the park.

The Dairy

The dairy was originally just that, a nineteenth-century dairy. Today, the small Victorian building is a museum and visitor center housing books and information about the park. Just north of the Wollman Rink, the Dairy is a place to get maps, buy books about the park, and find out about park events and park history. The Dairy is open Tuesday through Sunday from 10 A.M. to 4 P.M., and admission is free.

The Harlem Meer

The meer is an 11-acre lake (*meer* is Dutch for *lake*) that sits on the northeast corner of the park (by Fifth Avenue) at the foot of Harlem. It was redesigned, relandscaped, and reopened in 1993 and features numerous plants, shrubs, trees, and winding paths through nature around the lake. There are walking tours offered for those

And Then Came Garth

Some 30 years after New York's own Barbra Streisand took center stage in front of a quarter of a million fans in Central Park, country star Garth Brooks hit the North Meadow with what has been billed as the biggest park concert to date. Although attendance numbers could not be confirmed, concerts by popular superstars including Elton John, James Taylor, Diana Ross, and Placido Domingo have also drawn hundreds of thousands and spawned cable specials and, in some cases, albums.

The Garth Brooks performance was indeed of epic proportions, taking some five hundred staffers 12 days to build and dismantle the stage, video screens, and technical equipment. The free concert drew half a million people and brought in $16 million in revenue to the city. Perhaps most impressive and even surprising to some was the drawing power of a country music star in New York City.

Shakespeare in the Park

Shakespeare's plays come to life every summer, thanks to the Joseph Papp Shakespeare Theater Company, who perform two plays annually from June until Labor Day. Admission is free. The Delacorte Theater, located just south of the Great Lawn and next to the Belvedere Castle (a short walk inward from the West 81th Street entrance), seats two thousand. Tickets are given out at 1 P.M. on the day of the performance (two per person) at the theater. Get in line a few hours in advance. Bring your lunch and sunscreen. For information on the season's performances, call 212-539-8750. Tickets are also available at the Joseph Papp Public Theater and in the boroughs. Call the above number, and you can pick up tickets in the boroughs, possibly without the wait you'll have in the park.

who want to look more closely at and learn about the plant life. You can also find a newly created block of land called Duck Island.

The Harlem Meer is one of the few places in Manhattan that you can actually drop a fishing line into the water and fish. Stocked with fifty thousand minnows, largemouth bass, catfish, golden shiners, and bluegills, the meer is Central Park's "Fishing Hole." Bamboo poles are available free of charge at the Dana Discovery Center, adjacent to the meer (bait is free). Fish must be thrown back to maintain the careful ecological balance of life. Poles are available with a photo ID on a first-come basis Tuesday through Sunday from 11 A.M. to 4 P.M. Groups of up to twenty can reserve poles by calling (212) 860-1370.

Woodlands, meadows, and even battlegrounds from the War of 1812 can be found within a short walk from the Meer. Although many people still don't know about the Meer, you will find some one hundred people a day fishing in nice weather.

Belvedere Castle

This is the only "castle" on park grounds. Located in the middle of the park at 79th Street, the massive stone structure was built in 1872 and has seen a few renovations since, including replacement of several of the massive columns in 1995. The highest point in the park, the castle is the place to go to get a great view of the acreage around it, including the Great Lawn and the Delacorte Theater, home to Shakespeare in the Park during the summer months. Inside the castle you'll find the Henry Luce Nature Observatory (which looks at nature through microscopes and telescopes), various displays, programs for the kids, and workshops. The Castle is also home to the park's weather department. For over 80 years, meteorological instruments have provided New Yorkers with the temperature in Central Park.

The Reservoir

The Reservoir is a 106-acre body of water, built in 1862 smack in the middle of the northern part of the park above 86th Street. It was renamed the Jacqueline Kennedy Onassis Reservoir in 1995.

The path surrounding the reservoir, just over 1.5 miles in length, is now the park's most popular jogging track, home to thousands of runners in training for races. Although the reservoir is no longer used for drinking water by the city, it still remains the largest of several bodies of water in the park. The view across the reservoir is stunning, and the trees, including cherry trees, and numerous birds make for great scenery. A reconstruction of the landscape is just being completed.

Lawns, Gardens, and Wide-Open Spaces

Yes, You Can Picnic in Manhattan

Many New Yorkers, particularly those in the city, live in modern apartments that are not as spacious as they would like. The park offers some elbow room—places to lie on the grass and enjoy the wide-open spaces. Of course, on a warm spring or summer day, those places can get crowded, but the serenity of the park can almost always be found if you look carefully. Off-the-beaten-path locations are often just down the road or over a large rock from the path you're on.

A truly awe inspiring experience is lying in Central Park and looking up and out at the tall buildings standing high and flanking the peaceful setting. The city is so close, yet so far away; the park is a refuge unto itself.

Two of the most notable "wide-open spaces" in the vast park are the **Great Lawn** and the **Sheep Meadow.** The Great Lawn, a reservoir until the 1930s, was replanted, re-sodded, and redone in recent years to once again be one of the prime locations for out-door fun in the park. Frisbees fly by, as do softballs and hardballs from countless games played all spring and summer on baseball dia-monds, of which there are over two dozen in the park. The lawn has also seen massive crowds (with estimates of anywhere from two hundred thousand to nearly one million people) for concerts from Paul Simon, Elton John, Diana Ross, Garth Brooks, Sheryl Crow, and others. Even the pope spoke to throngs of people on the Great

Bird Watching

Over two hundred species of birds have been spotted by bird enthusiasts in the park, primarily in an area known as "the Ramble," a 37-acre wooded area with wildly growing bushes, waterfalls, and even a brook. The area, near the East 79th Street entrance, can be somewhat desert-ed, so it may be best explored with others.

Lawn. The lawn spans some 14 acres of open air and has been the central gathering point for the largest crowds in the city.

The Sheep Meadow, meanwhile, was just that, a sheep meadow into the mid-1930s. Actually it was a large flat piece of land used by the national guard and the military as a parade ground, to practice marching for competitions. After some concern that the marching and the crowds that gathered to watch would turn the area into a dustbowl, the area was redesigned for grazing, and the sheep replaced the military. Today, the sheep are long gone and the 15-acre meadow is a haven for sunbathing on the west side of the park. There is less activity here than in the Great Lawn, with no ball playing or loud radios allowed. You may look up and see a kite overhead, however; in fact, a kite flying jamboree is held every spring. Essentially, though, the Sheep Meadow is reserved for sedentary pleasures such as relaxing and picnicking.

Just north of the Sheep Meadow is the Lawn Sports Center, which is home to croquet players and lawn bowlers.

Among the numerous gardens that highlight the park are the **Shakespeare Garden, Strawberry Fields,** and the **Conservatory Garden**. The Shakespeare Garden is tucked between the Swedish Cottage and the Belvedere Castle. The little-known garden, dedicated to the great writer, was established in 1912 and restored in 1988. The nearby Delacorte Theater features the immortal Bard's plays performed by the Joseph Papp Shakespeare Theater Company. Plaques around the garden contain quotes from the works of Shakespeare, and the flowers within are those found in his works, including thyme, sage, savory, rosemary, chamomile, and several varieties of seasonal flowers.

Strawberry Fields, meanwhile, is dedicated to a writer, singer, and legend of a different era, John Lennon. The 2.5-acre west side garden is the result of a $1 million gift to the park by Yoko Ono. The couple visited the garden often when they lived across the street in the Dakota apartment building.

A serene setting, the romantic garden is home to tree clusters, outcroppings, and a marble mosaic, a gift from the city of Naples, Italy, with the word *Imagine* imprinted in it; fans gather there each year on the anniversary of the tragic death of Lennon. The garden, home to gifts from countries around the world, has twenty-five hundred strawberry plants in keeping with the name.

The Conservatory Garden is a three-garden structure on 3 acres on Fifth Avenue near 105th Street, just south of the Harlem Meer. Originally opened in 1937, the outdoor gardens replaced greenhouses that occupied the site from 1899. A 1982 restoration and landscaping brought back these gardens that have been home to weddings and other festive occasions.

The North Garden is a French-style design surrounding a large bronze fountain known as "Three Dancing Maidens." The flower beds around the centerpiece display twenty thousand tulips in the spring and twenty-five hundred Korean chrysanthemums in the fall. The Central Garden features an Italian design with a large manicured lawn leading to a central fountain with large surrounding hedges. Pink and white blossoms and trees surround the garden. The South Garden is English in style. A lily pond and large bronze fountain dedicated to the children's story *The Secret Garden* are surrounded by the trees, shrubs, and flowers that outline this third garden within the conservatory.

Free tours are given rain or shine on Saturday mornings at 11 A.M.

Fine Dining

By day, fine dining in Central Park consists of whatever you pack for your picnic. By night, or for a fancy brunch, you might want to stop at the premiere eatery in the park and one of the best-known restaurants in the city—**Tavern on the Green**. The structure, called a classic example of mid-Victorian architecture, was originally built in the late nineteenth century (just off the entrance at West 67th Street) as a sheepfold to hold the park's resident flock. Today, thousands of tourists and New Yorkers flock to the upscale, sprawling, dazzling restaurant. From floor to ceiling and wall to wall, the restaurant's decor is stunning. Stained glass, exquisite chandeliers, ornate gold trim, flowers, statues, outdoor dining—it's all part of the experience.

Go Fetch, Spot

If you've got a dog and a Frisbee, you can play. Besides playing Frisbee catch with your favorite canine just for the fun of it, you can also enter the annual June tournament, which gives prizes for the most athletic mutt. This fun event takes place around 66th and 67th Streets on the west side of the park. For information, call 212-777-2297.

Summer Stage

Just southeast of Bethesda Fountain, music fills the air throughout the summer as the sounds of jazz, blues, pop, country, Latin, African, and Calypso music emanate from the amphitheater. For a schedule and information, call 212-360-2777.

With its expansive glass-enclosed Crystal Room looking out over the park, and sparking lights lining the trees around the structure, Tavern on the Green provides a wonderful dining experience. During the holiday season, the lights and seasonal display are spectacular. Tavern on the Green offers jazz in the Chestnut Room and dining outdoors (in the warmer weather) in their outdoor garden. It is also the only place in the park to legally buy alcoholic beverages, and with that in mind, they have a very extensive wine list. As for the food, although it's met with some criticism, the response is usually favorable, particularly the better-known choices and the fine desserts. Reservations are a good idea but not mandatory.

The Loeb Boathouse, at East Drive between Terrace Drive and the 79th Street Transverse, is also home to **The Boathouse Café**, serving light fare at reasonable prices. The café dining experience can be either indoor or outdoor on the terrace overlooking the lake. And if you can't find the Boathouse Café, a trolley will pick you up at 72th Street and Fifth Avenue and take you there.

While there are no other significant eateries in the park, there are other places to grab a bite, including the the **Ballplayers House**, the **Ice Cream Café**, **Mineral Springs Pavilion**, and the **Zoo Café**. All are easily accessible and busy during the summer months.

You can also stop at one of a wide range of vendors, who are licensed to sell food in the park from carts. Or do as many New Yorkers do and bring your own bag lunch or picnic lunch and settle down for a meal under the trees, surrounded by the skyline.

Other Manhattan Parks
Battery Park

This 23-acre park is at the southern tip of Manhattan, where colonial New Amsterdam was first established. The park is home to a rose garden planted in honor of the many who have died from the AIDS virus. There are also memorials in this historic park for World War II veterans and those who fought in the Korean War.

Fort Tryon Park

On the northwest side of Manhattan, bordering on Broadway and the Henry Hudson Parkway at Dyckman Street, this park has 60 acres of wooded hills surrounding the Cloisters Museum, with a marvelous view of the Hudson River. Originally a fort in the Revolutionary War, this park's country atmosphere allows you to forget you are in Manhattan.

Riverside Park

Located between Riverside Drive and the Hudson River, from 72th Street all the way up to 158th Street, this 4-mile long park is a popular place for strolling, dog walking, bird watching, and more, including sleighing and cross-country skiing in the winter. Designed by Central Park co-landscaper Fredrick Law Olmsted and opened in 1910, the long waterside park features a bird sanctuary, community garden, a marina, and an adjacent rotunda. From posh Upper West Siders to Columbia University students to numerous joggers, the park has a wide variety of daily visitors.

Carl Schurz Park

Running along the East River between 84th and 90th Streets, this park was once a fortification for the Continental Army in the Revolutionary War and was later taken over by the British. Today it is taken over primarily by Upper East Siders. The park is on several levels, with marble stairways and beautiful paths. Playgrounds, basketball courts, and dog runs are part of this secret little gem. Tucked away in a cozy east side corner of the city, the park is bordered on the upper tip by the mayor's house, Gracie Mansion. The most noteworthy aspect of this inviting little park is the John Finley Walk, a wide riverside walkway with spectacular views of Roosevelt Island, Queens, and the boat traffic along the East River. The serenity and tranquillity make for a delightful afternoon.

Tours

The Dairy, Belvedere Castle, and the Dana Center at the Harlem Meers are the places to catch free guided tours that will familiarize visitors with the park today and yesterday. Experienced tour guides will lead the way and fill you in on the nitty-gritty about the world's premiere park. Most tours are given on the weekends, but there are some weekday tours as well. For tour information, call the tour hot line at 212-360-2727.

Union Square Park

Between 14th and 18th Streets, and Broadway and Park Avenue, this small park is home to a giant green market (featuring fresh fruits and vegetables) and a flea market selling a variety of craft items. The popular 14th Street Union Square subway line deposits many travelers on the park's borders, as the park remains the centerpiece of Union Square. The surrounding area has been refurbished in the past several years, with cafés and trendy restaurants now highlighting the increasingly popular neighborhood.

Washington Square Park

At the foot of Fifth Avenue in Greenwich Village, Washington Square Park is home to a giant white marble arc built in 1892, along with two statues of George Washington that were added in the early part of the twentieth century. The nearly 10-acre park, used in the early nineteenth century for military parade drills and public hangings, is nestled between brownstones and New York University and has been for decades a favorite stomping ground for an eclectic variety of locals. Hippies, yuppies, punks, poets, artists, bohemians, Frisbee players, chess players, students, panhandlers, and a variety of street performers all come to enjoy themselves here. Visiting the park is a "let your hair down" experience and has been for many years. Outdoor art shows are very popular before and after the summer.

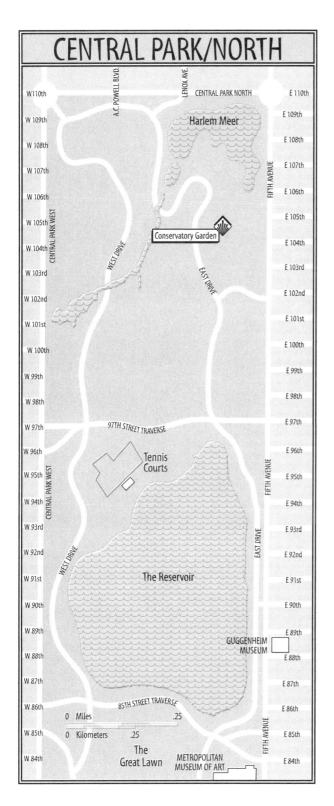

CENTRAL PARK/NORTH

W110th · CENTRAL PARK NORTH · E 110th
W 109th · E 109th
Harlem Meer
W 108th · E 108th
W 107th · E 107th
W 106th · E 106th
W 105th · E 105th
W 104th · Conservatory Garden · E 104th
W 103rd · E 103rd
W 102nd · E 102nd
W 101st · E 101st
W 100th · E 100th
W 99th · E 99th
W 98th · E 98th
W 97th · 97TH STREET TRAVERSE · E 97th
W 96th · E 96th
W 95th · Tennis Courts · E 95th
W 94th · E 94th
W 93rd · E 93rd
W 92nd · E 92nd
W 91st · The Reservoir · E 91st
W 90th · E 90th
W 89th · GUGGENHEIM MUSEUM · E 89th
W 88th · E 88th
W 87th · E 87th
W 86th · 85TH STREET TRAVERSE · E 86th
W 85th · E 85th

0 Miles .25
0 Kilometers .25

W 84th · The Great Lawn · METROPOLITAN MUSEUM OF ART · E 84th

A.C. POWELL BLVD. · LENOX AVE. · FIFTH AVENUE
CENTRAL PARK WEST · WEST DRIVE · EAST DRIVE

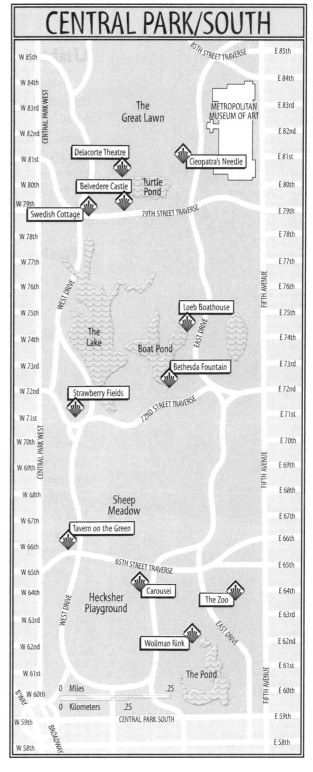

CENTRAL PARK/SOUTH

W 85th · 85TH STREET TRAVERSE · E 85th
W 84th · E 84th
W 83rd · The Great Lawn · METROPOLITAN MUSEUM OF ART · E 83rd
W 82nd · E 82nd
W 81st · Delacorte Theatre · Cleopatra's Needle · E 81st
W 80th · Belvedere Castle · Turtle Pond · E 80th
W 79th · Swedish Cottage · 79TH STREET TRAVERSE · E 79th
W 78th · E 78th
W 77th · E 77th
W 76th · E 76th
W 75th · Loeb Boathouse · E 75th
W 74th · The Lake · E 74th
W 73rd · Boat Pond · Bethesda Fountain · E 73rd
W 72nd · Strawberry Fields · E 72nd
W 71st · 72ND STREET TRAVERSE · E 71st
W 70th · E 70th
W 69th · E 69th
W 68th · Sheep Meadow · E 68th
W 67th · E 67th
W 66th · Tavern on the Green · E 66th
W 65th · 65TH STREET TRAVERSE · E 65th
W 64th · Carousel · The Zoo · E 64th
W 63rd · Hecksher Playground · E 63rd
W 62nd · Wollman Rink · E 62nd
W 61st · The Pond · E 61st
W 60th · E 60th
W 59th · CENTRAL PARK SOUTH · E 59th
W 58th · E 58th

0 Miles .25
0 Kilometers .25

CENTRAL PARK WEST · WEST DRIVE · EAST DRIVE · FIFTH AVENUE
B'WAY · BROADWAY

Chapter 7

The Neighborhoods of Manhattan

When you look at Manhattan from across the Hudson or the East Rivers, you see a spectacular skyline view of skyscrapers, including the World Trade Center towering over Lower Manhattan, the Empire State Building, standing a head above its neighbors in the lower part of Midtown, and the slanted roof of the Citicorp building in the East 50s. From a distance, it's a sea of office buildings and high-rise apartments, co-ops, and condominiums.

Walking, driving, or touring the streets of Manhattan, however, you'll discover that it's a blend of distinctive neighborhoods with their own characteristics. You'll see the nooks and crannies, the parks, the playgrounds, and the architecture. You'll encounter the local merchants, read the signs, and see the storefronts that characterize the overall flavor of each neighborhood. There's a definite pulse to the city found in the subcultures that coexist from one part of town to another. Even the pace changes slightly from the frantic pace of Chinatown to the slower saunter of Bleecker Street in the Village. With the exception of parts of Midtown, you'll find residential buildings including brownstones, old brick apartment buildings, and sleek modern glass high-rise buildings. Historical sights, special events, and the people you'll pass on the street will confirm what part of town you are in.

The diverse mixture of people and places is like no other city. Buildings from different eras share the same block, and a ten-block stroll can take you into an entirely different socioeconomic and ethnic neighborhood. You'll also find a variety of manufacturing centers throughout parts of Lower and Midtown Manhattan. The upper West 20s, for example, is called the flower district; it leads to the fur district, around 30th Street and Seventh Avenue. The West 30s is home to the garment industry, and in the West 40s, you'll find electronics on one block and jewelry on another, in the "diamond district." And these areas aren't subtle; you'll see a row of jewelry stores lining a city block on West 47th Street between Fifth and Sixth Avenues.

Here's a rundown of Manhattan neighborhoods from north to south: Washington Heights, Morningside Heights, Harlem, the Upper East and Upper West Sides (divided by Central Park), Midtown (including the theater district of the West 40s and Hell's Kitchen), Murray Hill, Chelsea, Gramercy Park, Union Square, Greenwich

Village and the East Village, SoHo, Tribeca, Chinatown, Little Italy, the Lower East Side, and Lower Manhattan.

In the following pages, we'll take a look at a few of these busy, distinctive neighborhoods.

The Lower East Side

It is hard to find a neighborhood more diverse in culture than Manhattan's Lower East Side. The first settlement for millions of immigrants who came to Ellis Island from Europe, the Lower East Side has been, for more than a century, home to tenement housing with sparsely furnished apartments.

From 1892 to 1934, over twenty-five million men, women, and children took their first steps onto American soil at Ellis Island. The next stop from the tiny island for a great number of these immigrants was the small pocket of land near the Brooklyn Bridge along the East River, Manhattan's Lower East Side. In the early 1900s, the neighborhood was the most overcrowded in America. On what had been farmlands, builders started erecting three- and four-story row houses that barely fit on the narrow strips of land that had been sectioned off for single-family dwellings. These Lower East Side tenements were quickly filled and then over-crowded with more people than they were designed for. Many ethnic groups lived together in the area, including an enormous Jewish population, immigrants from Eastern Europe, and large contingencies from Ireland and Italy.

While the neighborhood to this day has never developed much beyond the poor, tenement-style housing, many New York celebrities grew up on the Lower East Side. Robert DeNiro, Zero Mostel, James Cagney, George Burns, and Jimmy Durante were among those born in the neighborhood, and the Marx Brothers, George Gershwin, and others honed their skills in the burlesque houses, Yiddish theaters, and (in later years) the settlement houses there. One of New York's most famous gangsters of the 1930s, "Lucky" Luciano, and one of the city's most renowned mayors, the multi-ethnic Fiorello LaGuardia (who would later put Luciano behind bars), were also born in the neighborhood.

Today, the population of the neighborhood is very much Latino, but still mixed with various ethnic groups. There is still a Jewish influence present, with Katz's and Ratner's Delicatessens and various stores. Trendy shops are now sprinkled in with old storefronts in what was, for a long time, a very depressed run-down area. There are definite signs of improvement, and the local population has made it very clear that they take pride in the Lower East Side.

A visit to the Lower East Side should include the following:

- Stroll along Orchid Street and along Delancey Street for some great bargains. From vintage clothing to hip-hop wear and designer clothes, plus shoes and inexpensive packs of underwear, you can pick up plenty of good bargains here. For many years, vendors took their wares out to the streets on Sunday along these popular shopping locales. Some still do so today.
- Visit the Lower East Side Tenement Museum for a guided tour through an 1863 tenement at 97 Orchid Street. The furnishings depict the lifestyles of but a few examples of the thousands of immigrants who lived there. The unique museum is a tribute to urban housing (see Chapter 5).
- Get a bite to eat at either Ratner's Restaurant or Katz's Delicatessen where the portions are big, the decor isn't fancy, and the traditional Jewish-style food is still first rate.
- Stop by the Elderage Street Synagogue for a look at the city's first Orthodox synagogue, built in 1887.
- For those who like kosher wine, visit Shapiro's House of Kosher and Sacramental Wines on Rivington Street; it has a winery you can visit on Sunday. It's a family-run business where they still make wine in the cellar.

There's nothing flashy about the Lower East Side. There are new clubs and night spots such as the club Torch and the dance club Baby Jupiter, but the area retains the spirit of another time, when immigrants flooded the city with hopes and dreams. Many have fulfilled those dreams that began in this old, significant melting pot neighborhood of Manhattan.

Chinatown and Little Italy

Two of Manhattan's most obviously ethnic areas are located just blocks from the city's courthouses, City Hall, the municipal buildings of Lower Manhattan, and the Lower East Side.

For years, Chinatown has been *the* place to go for New York's best Chinese food. But it is much more than a neighborhood of restaurants. It is a full-blown, hustling and bustling community and home to well over a hundred thousand of New York City's Chinese population. Since the early settlers came to the neighborhood from China in the 1870s, the area has been growing and has extended beyond the boundaries into Little Italy and even across Canal Street. For years, immigrants worked in factories, restaurants, and local shops. Many locals still do.

The neighborhood houses garment factories and numerous shops. Many of the shops sell food and feature roasted ducks hanging in the window. Noodles, seafood, and vegetables are abundant inside and outside the jam-packed little shops that line the tiny streets. Clothing, electronics, souvenirs, and all sorts of goods are for sale here beneath Chinese signs. You'll even see a few pagoda-style roofs. But the area is not a tribute to Chinese culture; it is an authentic and very busy neighborhood that moves at a frantic pace. If you stroll the main business streets, Canal and Mott, you'll find yourself smack in the height of the frenzy.

A visit to Chinatown should include the following:

- Stop at the Museum of Chinese in the Americas on Mulberry Street (see Chapter 5).
- Shop or at least stroll along the stores on Mott Street, including a stop at Quong Yuen Shing & Company, a classic neighborhood retailer for over 100 years.
- Have lunch and/or dinner at one of three hundred restaurants in the neighborhood including these:
  - Bo Ky on Bayard Street between Mott and Mulberry
  - Canton on Division Street between Bowery and Market
  - Hunan Garden on Mott by Worth

Home of Dim Sum

If you like Dim Sum, check out the Golden Unicorn on East Broadway by Catherine Street.

- Jim Fong on Elizabeth between Bayard and Canal
- Mandarin Court on Mott between Bayard and Canal
- Nam Wah Tea Parlor on Doyers between Bowery and Pell
- Oriental Garden on Elizabeth by Bayard
- Peking Duck House on Mott between Park Row and Pell Street
- Sweet 'n Tart Café on Mott by Canal
- Wong Kee on Mott between Canal and Hester
- Stop at Fung Wong's on Mott Street to buy rice cakes, roast pork buns, egg rolls, and other delights to take back to your hotel
- Visit the Chinatown Ice Cream Factory on Bayard Street by Mott for a taste of lychee, papaya, or some other exotic ice cream flavor

While there aren't many traditional "sights" found in Chinatown, beyond the museum, the neighborhood is worth a visit. And if you love Chinese food, as mentioned above, it is *the* place to go!

Little Italy, meanwhile, is a smaller, slightly less bustling area than Chinatown, with narrow streets, some still cobblestone, and turn-of-the-century buildings with restaurants and shops below. It was for many years the settling neighborhood for numerous Italian immigrants. In the early twentieth century, many of the half million Italian immigrants to the city lived in this area extending from the Lower East Side. In the past 40 years, however, neighborhoods in the other boroughs, such as Bensonhurst and Belmont (in the Bronx), have the lion's share of Italian-Americans.

Today Little Italy is a small area condensed somewhat by the expansion of Chinatown and the exodus to other parts of the city by many who grew up in the area. The neighborhood is home to a bevy of first-rate old-fashioned Italian restaurants and bakeries, along with some trendy newer shops mixed in. E. Rossi & Company is still at Grand and Mulberry, selling everything from Italian cookbooks to embroidered postcards to pasta makers and bocci balls. Also in the area you'll find Old St. Patrick's Cathedral on Mulberry Street and San Gennaro Church on Baxter Street. San Gennaro Church hosts one of the premier festivals you'll ever

encounter in New York City, the annual Feast of San Gennaro. If you happen to be in town during the second week of September, you might enjoy the festival excitement that lines Mulberry Street from Canal to Grand. Tons of food, outdoor games, music, and fun fill the *very* crowded streets. It's an experience. (Do not drive there!)

A visit to Little Italy should include the following:

- Stop at Ferrara's to buy incredible pastries on Grand Street between Mott and Mulberry.
- Have lunch or dinner at one of a number of local favorites including the following:
  - Angelo's of Mulberry Street between Grand and Hester
  - DaNico on Mulberry between Grand and Broome
  - Il Cortile on Mulberry by Canal
  - Taormina of Mulberry Street near Grand
  - Umberto's Clam House on Mulberry

Greenwich Village

The Dutch settlers of New Amsterdam ventured north in the early 1600s and discovered a large portion of land on which to plant crops. The land, to that time, had been inhabited by Native Americans. When the English took over in the latter 1600s, the neighborhood became a country setting—a suburbs of sorts. By the 1700s, the West Village by the Hudson River would become a major area for fishing and for produce. An area in the center of the city, now Washington Square Park, would be set aside as a place for public gallows.

As the 1800s began, more and more settlers moved north to escape the epidemics—smallpox, yellow fever, and cholera—that plagued the city. They moved primarily to the area below Houston Street. The Village began to grow with farms, shops, markets, and various businesses. Finer, more fashionable homes were built, particularly at the foot of Fifth Avenue around Washington Square Park.

Big Celebration!

The Chinese New Year is celebrated in grand style in Chinatown, with parades and all sorts of festivities. It's very crowded, but if you're in town in late January or early February, when the Chinese New Year falls, you might head on down and check out the excitement.

Note: Although the city has curbed fire-cracker use (which is illegal), be careful; they are very popular in Chinatown around this time of year.

The nineteenth century also saw the birth of New York University and the emergence of galleries and establishments where the literary community gathered. An upscale community throughout much of the nineteenth century, the neighborhood evolved slowly toward the turn of the century as the elite moved further north and a more bohemian culture settled into the area. Small theaters and galleries sprang up and diverse local magazines were published, along with irreverent books by small local publishers.

The Village blossomed into New York City's home of up-and-coming writers and musicians. Edgar Allan Poe, Walt Whitman, and Mark Twain lived in Greenwich Village in the 1800s, and Sinclair Lewis, Eugene O'Neill, Jackson Pollock, and Norman Rockwell were among the many to be part of the Village in the twentieth century. The beat poets of the '50s gave way to the folk singers of the early '60s, including Bob Dylan, Arlo Guthrie, and Peter, Paul & Mary. By the late '70s, the East Village was home to the punk rockers.

Whatever the artistic trend, the Village captured it in art and music. Outdoor art shows flank the park twice a year, and clubs like the Bottom Line present the hottest up-and-coming, and established, performers. Off-Broadway and avant-garde theater became part of the local artists, own brand of self-expression many years ago and remain a significant part of Village culture today. Stores and galleries have displayed the latest trendy paraphernalia of each new generation, and the fads and fashions are evident in the area around Washington Square Park. Movements and social causes have also been an important part of Village life, from the antiwar protests of the '60s to activities championing the rights of gays and lesbians in recent decades. The Village has become a place where the gay and lesbian community can thrive and flourish.

Little has actually changed aesthetically in the past 25 years in Greenwich Village. The redbrick townhouses with cozy little courtyards still line the streets. Restaurants, shops, and galleries are still busy at night; only the latest merchandise changes with the times. The neighborhood still serves as a cultural barometer for the 18 to 25 set. If you want to know the latest concerns and fashion choices of a 21-year-old, visit Greenwich Village. In essence, there is always a street musician or poet in Washington Square Park; only the clothes and the lyrics (or verses) have changed to reflect the times.

The neighboring East Village, which became a drug infested, seamy neighborhood in the '70s, has seen an economic and social resurgence, with trendy clothing shops, boutiques, and popular restaurants. Over a dozen relatively inexpensive Indian restaurants can be found on East 6th Street (between First and Second Avenues); several theaters featuring rising talent are busy on East 4th Street; and trendy shops are in vogue on St. Marks. The East Village has emerged as the alternative to the alternative, for those looking to escape the more commercialized Greenwich Village. Don't be fooled, however—some of the East Village Shops have Fifth Avenue prices.

If you're planning to meander around the village, it's best to get down there by public transportation. Greenwich Village is very popular, and parking is at a premium.

A visit to Greenwich Village should include some of the following:

- Stroll through Washington Square Park. Note the Memorial Arch built in 1889 to celebrate the one-hundredth anniversary of the inauguration of George Washington. Also, people-watch (but don't be obvious about it!) or watch street performers, chess and checker players, and artists drawing or sketching (see Chapter 6).
- Go for a shopping spree on Eighth Street in the more popular mainstream stores, on Bleecker Street for more trendy shopping, or on St. Mark's Place in the East Village for even *more* trendy shopping. You can also get great gourmet food at Balducci's on Sixth Avenue by 10th Street or the absolute best in pastries and deserts at Veniero's on 11th Street between First and Second Avenues. If you want first-rate tea or coffee, try McNulty's Tea & Coffee Company on Christopher by Bleecker.

- See a play at the Actor's Playhouse, Cherry Lane Theater on Commerce Street, The Minetta Lane Theater, or Astor Place Theater on Lafayette (East Village); or see *The Fantasticks*, at the Sullivan Street Playhouse, where it's been playing for over 40 years. Or find out what is playing at the Joseph Papp Public Theater on Lafayette Street between 4th Street and Astor Place, where plays such as *Hair* and *A Chorus Line* had their first performances (see Chapter 9). Call the theaters listed in the theater section in advance for details about buying tickets and current productions. Check *The Village Voice* or *New York Magazine* for current theater listings.

- Take in a concert at the Bottom Line on West 4th Street, where local heroes Bruce Springsteen and Billy Joel and even newcomers from abroad such as Elton John played the Village in their early years. There's also the longtime home of folk music, the Bitter End, on Bleecker. You can also find plenty of jazz you if you visit legendary clubs like Blue Note, Village Vanguard, or Visions. Perhaps you'll drop by the former punk haven CBGBs in the East Village, where you'll still hear hot new bands (see Chapter 9).

- Check out the nineteenth-century houses of Grove Court between Bedford and Hudson Streets or Gay Street between Waverly and Christopher. You might also look at 75½ Bedford Street (*go slowly so you don't miss it*)—it's only 9.5 feet wide and was build in 1873—and 77 Bedford Street, which is now some two hundred years old.

- Browse the Forbes Magazine Galleries, featuring items from Forbes' personal collections, including hundreds of toy boats, thousands of toy soldiers, old Monopoly games, rare Fabergé eggs, plus numerous trophies and awards. There are also changing exhibits at the gallery on 62 Fifth Avenue in the Forbes Building.

- Have a drink, or at least a look, at White Horse Tavern on Hudson Street at Eleventh Avenue. The 120-year-old saloon was the drinking home of poet Dylan Thomas, among other writers, poets, and artists.

- Stroll down narrow Minetta Lane or stopping in the former speakeasy Minetta Tavern at Minetta and MacDougal. You might also stop at a great people-watching locale and long-time favorite Village hangout, La Figaro Café, on the corner of Bleecker and MacDougal.
- Admire the Gothic Revival architecture of the Grace Church (1846) or the Church of the Ascension (1841), or the Romanesque architecture of Judson Memorial Church (1892) or the more recent copper-domed St. George's Ukrainian Catholic Church (1970s).
- Have dinner at one of the many village restaurants including the following:
  - Café Loup on West 13th Street between Sixth and Seventh Avenues
  - Ennio & Michael on LaGuardia between Bleecker and West 3rd Street
  - James Beard House on 12th Street between Sixth and Seventh Avenues
  - Il Mulino on 3rd Street between Thompson and Sullivan
  - La Ripaille on Hudson between Bethune and West 12th Street
  - Mesopotamia (serving Belgian food in the East Village) on Avenue B between Sixth and Seventh Avenues
  - Pearl Oyster Bar on Cornelia between Bleecker and West 4th Street.

The spring and fall art shows are enjoyable, but the Village always has so much activity that it's hard not to get caught up in the atmosphere that makes this New York City's most eclectic, yet earthy, neighborhood. Anything goes in the village.

Times Square and 42nd Street

Just as brownstones, narrow streets, bohemian coffee shops, blue jeans, and a quiet subtlety have characterized much of Greenwich Village for years, less than 2 miles north, bright neon lights, mega hotels, and anything-but-subtle tourist shops and restaurants define

Times Square. Like the billboards that look down from the rooftops above, everything is grand and bright in the lights of Times Square.

From as far back as the early part of the twentieth century, the area around Times Square has been home to numerous theaters. It was the place to go for entertainment, and as the city grew with housing up and down the East and West Sides, it became a central focal point. All Manhattan subways stopped at 42nd Street, Grand Central Station (since 1913). The Port Authority bus terminal brought visitors to the city, and passenger ships docked at piers on the West Side of town. In short, it was the first stop for numerous visitors to the city. A focal gathering point, advertisers saw it as a place for grand-style billboards, and theater owners made sure to have dazzling marquees. By 1904 it had become known as "the Crossroads of the World." It was the place the ball was dropped on New Years Eve, with large crowds flooding the streets below, a tradition that began early in the twentieth century.

Times Square and 42nd Street went largely unregulated in many respects. Primarily a nonresidential neighborhood, the area around West 42nd Street became a haven for anyone who could do business with the visitors coming into the city, from merchants to prostitutes. Always a home for the latest trend in cinema, 42nd Street movie houses would run into competition as theaters were built in neighborhoods throughout the boroughs after World War II. This would eventually cause the neighborhood to sell out to sleaze merchants who made it home to the porno theaters, porn shops, and peep shows that filled the once popular old theaters. For years the city simply shrugged its shoulders and looked away as 42nd Street declined. Broadway theaters still operated north of 42nd Street while the gang-ridden, dangerous Hell's Kitchen remained, for many years, home to anyone daring enough to actually live there. Theatergoers would see a Broadway show and then jump into a cab or limo and get out of the neighborhood.

Finally in the early 1990s, the drugs, prostitution, and porn became more than the city could tolerate, and a cleanup of Times Square commenced, with Disney leading the charge. The neighborhood was radically overhauled with new stores, and many of the old theaters were revamped. There are still some stores selling

X-rated videos and numerous trashy "tourist" souvenir stores selling junk, but the Times Square area is the most turned-around neighborhood in the city. In fact, some New Yorkers even think it's been overly transformed and overly Disney-fied, and they miss a little of its old character.

Walking around Times Square and 42nd Street today, you'll see the usual big, bright, and brassy giant neon lights—"the lights of Broadway." Don't stop and look up without stepping into an alcove, or you might get knocked over, as the streets are very crowded. Thousands of people work in the large office buildings around the area, including much of the media—from the *New York Times* (the reason it's called Times Square) to HBO, *Billboard*, and MTV.

Times Square itself is where Broadway and Seventh Avenues cross as Broadway slants its way down the city from the West Side toward the East Side. Standing in the actual Square (really a triangle), you can see a bevy of massive billboards, huge storefronts, major hotels, marquees, fast-food eateries, and hordes of people, not to mention constant traffic.

If you are heading into the area, do not drive. All major transportation goes to Times Square and cabs are plentiful, but parking is not. Be forewarned that many of the nonfamiliar, nonfranchise stores sell overpriced junk; don't get suckered. And while the neighborhood has been cleaned up, once it gets late (after the theaters let out at 10:30 or 11 P.M.), there is still a seedy element that emerges, so be alert. There are also many street vendors. You can buy from them, but "buyer beware"—meaning buy a book, an umbrella, or a drawing, but don't spend $90 on a "designer" watch.

Times Square and 42nd Street are always full of activity. A visit to the Times Square/42nd Street area should include the following:

- Look at One Times Square Plaza on Seventh Avenue between 42nd and 43rd Streets. Originally opened in 1904, the building has been refurbished and taken over by Warner Brothers. The flagpole on the roof is where the famed ball is dropped every New Years Eve, to the delight of hundreds of thousands in the streets below.

- Stop at the actual Times Square between 42nd and 47th Streets, and Broadway and Seventh Avenues, to look up at the myriad immense billboards, some of which move.

- Look at the new Times Square Studio on 44th Street and Broadway, with its glass windows behind which *Good Morning America* is broadcast live every weekday morning. If you get there early enough, you can watch them do the show.

- Take in a Broadway show. From 42nd to 54th Streets, you'll find nearly thirty shows at spectacular old theaters. You can stop at the TKTS booth on 47th Street and Broadway. They sell tickets at half price (plus a service charge) for many of the Broadway shows, as posted on a board behind the ticket window (see Chapter 9).

- Check out some of the remodeled, reopened theaters such as the New Amsterdam on West 42nd Street. (Forget about getting tickets to *The Lion King* unless you call many months in advance.) The 1903 theater was the original home of the Ziegfeld Follies and was remodeled and reopened by Disney in 1997. The art deco facade was added in the 1940s and remains on this architecturally stunning theater. The New Victory Theater, dating back to 1900, was restored a few years earlier. This was a former home to numerous productions in the early part of the twentieth century, before becoming a popular burlesque house in the 1930s. For many years, these theaters remained unattended to and deteriorating amid the decadence that was 42nd Street. Today they are worth seeing at least from the outside, unless you are fortunate enough to get tickets for a show within. The New Victory Theater hosts many types of shows, often for kids, including acrobatic acts and other fun events (see Chapter 9).

- Stop by the New Ford Center for the Performing Arts, which opened in 1998 with the hit show *Ragtime*. Built to reflect the architectural elements of two New York landmark theaters, the Lyric and the Apollo, this is one of the most dazzling and one of the largest theaters in the city. (Tours are available; call 212-556-4750.)

- ❦ Test your gamesmanship at the multilevel entertainment complex, XS New York, on Broadway between 41st and 42nd, featuring state-of-the-art video games and virtual reality. You can also check out similar space-age games at Lazar Park on West 46th Street by Seventh Avenue.
- ❦ Shop at one of the many huge stores including Disney and the Virgin mega-store (for tapes and CDs).
- ❦ Dine at the theater crowd's longtime favorite, Sardi's, on 44th between Broadway and Eighth Avenue.
- ❦ Head west and check out the Intrepid Sea-Air-Space Museum, off Pier 86 in the Hudson (see Chapter 5).
- ❦ Head east to Fifth Avenue and visiting the incredible New York Public Library, between 40th and 42nd Streets (see Chapter 4).
- ❦ Take a stroll through Bryant Park. Formerly a dangerous, drug-infested eyesore, this little 7-acre park was completely renovated in recent years and now sports lovely gardens, interesting statues, plenty of chairs for outdoor concerts or fashion shows, and a grill. The park is situated behind the library (and over stacks of thousands of books stored underground) on Sixth Avenue between 40th and 42nd Streets.
- ❦ Stroll down West 46th Street between Eighth and Ninth Avenues and check out Restaurant Row, with its wide selection of first-rate dining (and entertainment in several of the establishments).
- ❦ Check out some of the incredible hotels in the area, including the Marriott Marquis, Millenium Broadway, brand-new Time Hotel, or classic Algonquin (see Chapter 1).

There's never a "dull" moment at Times Square and 42nd Street.

Harlem

North of 110th Street, the neighborhood of Harlem covers some 6 square miles and has been one of America's pre-eminent African-American communities for decades. Divided by Fifth Avenue into Harlem and East Harlem, the overall neighborhood, which also includes Spanish Harlem, has a long history that has seen its share of both high and low points.

Originally a Dutch settlement called Nieuw Haarlem back in 1658, the area would grow into an affluent section of the city in the 1800s, with estates, farms, and even plantations. Many immigrants from the Lower East Side would, if they were successful, move north to this rapidly growing section of the city.

It was thought that the new subway lines of the early 1900s would further the growth of this area by making Harlem more easily accessible to the rest of the city. With that in mind, developers began constructing more apartment buildings throughout the neighborhood. The buildings, however, did not fill up. A developer named Phillip Payton bought up many of these empty properties and began turning them over to hundreds of black families, hard pressed for housing in the city. By 1915 nearly a quarter of a million black families had moved in, and an equal number of white families had moved out.

By the 1920s, Harlem was the largest black community in the United States. It was at that time that the Harlem Renaissance began. Harlem was filled with popular nightspots, including the famous Cotton Club, and jazz greats could be seen and heard performing all over the neighborhood. White audiences traveled north to hear the likes of Count Basie, Duke Ellington, and Cab Calloway. Literary legends like Langston Hughes and James Baldwin would also grow up in this thriving, exciting community.

The Depression, however, caused the bottom to drop out economically for Harlem, but for several more years the sounds of jazz flourished. But by the '40s, Harlem was in trouble; it had not received any significant help from the city and was not able to bounce back from the Depression. The '50s brought much-needed housing developments, but jobs were still hard to come by for many residents of Harlem. The '60s brought civil unrest as events rocked the area. Malcolm X, one of the most prominent civil rights leaders, was assassinated at the Audubon Ballroom. Riots broke out; the residents of Harlem were tired of being ignored by the city as landlords turned their backs on the properties, allowing the area to deteriorate even further. Fires left shells of buildings; storefronts were boarded up and empty.

It would, unfortunately, take some 20 more years before the rebirth of Harlem would begin. The famed Apollo Theater returned, and restaurants, clubs, parks, and new housing would finally begin to emerge again in Harlem in the 1990s. And while the area is still in the throes of re-establishing itself, there is definitely a sense that Harlem is "back!" Today, Harlem is a busy developing community once again.

A visit to Harlem should include the following:

- Stop at the classic Apollo Theater on 125th Street between Seventh and Eighth Avenues. It's one of the neighborhood's greatest landmarks and has seen a long list of legendary performers in its nearly 90-year history. Catch a show (particularly on Amateur night) or take the tour (see Chapter 4).
- Browse the Studio Museum; it features a history of Harlem on Lennox Avenue between 125th and 126th Streets.
- Stop at the Schomburg Center for Research in Black Culture on Lennox Avenue at 135th Street.
- See a production at the National Black Theater on Fifth Avenue between 125th and 126th Streets.
- Have a weekend gospel brunch at the new rendition of the old Cotton Club on West 125th Street, or enjoy the finest soul food in town at Sylvia's, on Lennox and 126th Streets.
- Take a trip west to Riverside Drive at 120th Street and visit Riverside Church, with its 400-foot carillon tower and a spectacular view looking out over the Hudson River.
- Take a tour featuring the gospel music of Harlem. (There are now, after many years, a significantly growing number of points of interest highlighting the neighborhood, starting with the Dana Discovery Center.)

These are but a few of the neighborhoods of Manhattan. Sit with a native New Yorker, preferably one over 50, and he or she can tell you so much more about the neighborhood in which he or she grew up. Big Apple Greeters (see Chapter 2) offers volunteer guides from a particular neighborhood to show you around and tell you about life in their various sections of the big city.

Chapter 8

The Boroughs and Long Island

For many, "the city" refers to Manhattan only. Even residents of Queens or Brooklyn will say, "We're going to the city for the evening," without considering that they are already in the city. New York City consists of five boroughs, which were united in 1898. The boroughs, along with the New Amsterdam Settlement of Lower Manhattan, grew in population through the eighteenth and nineteenth centuries and established themselves as independent communities of their own. Although officially united as a city in 1898, the subway system of the early 1900s made commuting between four of the five boroughs much easier and allowed the diverse populations of the city to expand into the Bronx, Brooklyn, and Queens. Subway connections made the boroughs outside of Manhattan far more easily accessible.

Much of the land in the boroughs was once farmland. Today, you'll be hard pressed to find many farms, as all four "other" boroughs are vibrant centers of activity, with private homes and apartments complemented by numerous small businesses, office buildings, parks, and even beaches. Millions of New Yorkers commute into Manhattan everyday for work; many others work within the boroughs.

Most vacationers to New York City will likely spend the bulk of their trip in Manhattan, unless they have a particular reason (such as visiting family or friends) to spend much time in the other four boroughs. There is, however, a lot to see and do in the Bronx, Queens, Brooklyn, and Staten Island. Each borough has its own charm. From seafood at Sheepshead Bay in Brooklyn to the hot dogs at Yankee Stadium in the Bronx, there are a host of flavors that characterize each borough and a large multicultural population to match. Brooklyn, home to over four million New Yorkers, is large enough to qualify as the fourth largest city in America. Staten Island, meanwhile, is the least populated of the boroughs, with only four hundred thousand residents.

Although runners in the New York City Marathon (which takes place in November) actually manage to make their way through all five boroughs, beginning in the morning in Staten Island and ending in the afternoon in Manhattan (it finishes in Central Park), for most of us, it's more enjoyable to explore the boroughs on separate trips.

Traffic can be difficult on major roadways at peak, but in general driving is a preferred way of getting around in the four "other" boroughs, especially if you have an "itinerary" of several sights planned. Bus service is not as frequent as in Manhattan, subways only go to certain destinations in each borough, and taxis are not easily found, unless you call for one. Parking is easier than in Manhattan in many areas, although in some highly residential neighborhoods such as Forest Hills in Queens it can still be very tough.

Ask about the parking and traffic and whether or not a subway or express bus (the city has privately run express bus service to and from many prime locations in the boroughs) goes to your destination.

While the boroughs are united in many ways, all under the services of the city of New York, and all sharing the 718 area code (except Manhattan, which is 212), they are primarily separated by water (except Brooklyn and Queens). Bridges will get you from one borough to the other. For example, the Verrazano Bridge connects Staten Island and Brooklyn, the Whitestone Bridge and Throggs Neck Bridge connect Queens and the Bronx, and so on. Local streets such as Atlantic Avenue as well as major roadways like the Jackie Robinson Parkway and the Brooklyn Queens Expressway will take you from Brooklyn to Queens or vice versa.

Each borough has a rich history and several key points of interest. The following pages offer a little local flavor along with some key sights you may want to visit in Queens, Brooklyn, Staten Island, the Bronx, and Long Island (which is not a part of New York City but is attached to Queens and Brooklyn).

Brooklyn

Ebbets Field and the Brooklyn Dodgers, the Cyclone at Coney Island, Jackie Gleason and *The Honeymooners* are all part of the rich culture that characterizes New York City's second most visited borough.

The onetime home of Woody Allen, Mae West, Neil Diamond, Mel Brooks, Barbra Streisand, and numerous other celebrities, Brooklyn is the composite of numerous distinctively ethnic neighborhoods including Brighton Beach, with its large Ukrainian and Russian population, the Italian community of Bensonhurst, and the numerous

Brooklyn Children's Museum

This Crown Heights museum, built in 1976, was designed as an interactive play center utilizing twenty thousand cultural artifacts and natural history specimens as part of the fun.

Interactive exhibits will have children petting animals, visiting a greenhouse, checking out their five senses in a model of the human head, and much more. It's a fun/learning experience for kids under 10. The museum also offers films, workshops, storytelling, and often smaller crowds than the Manhattan Children's Museum. The museum is open Wednesday through Friday from 2 P.M. to 5 P.M. and Saturday and Sunday from noon to 5 P.M. Admission is $3. For more information, call 718-735-4432.

Orthodox Jews that make up Borough Park. There's no doubt as you drive or walk through different sections of Brooklyn that the neighborhoods take on their own identities. Park Slope, for example, is a trendy outgrowth of Manhattan, with fashionable shops and cafés. Sheepshead Bay is home to seafood fresh from the fishing boats that dock at the marina. Brooklyn Heights, sitting high on a hill overlooking Manhattan, is still a posh neighborhood, founded in the early nineteenth century as a suburban alternative to "city life." Bensonhurst is an older Italian-American neighborhood, rich with tradition. Row houses and redbrick buildings characterize the various residential neighborhoods, stores line the busy streets, and municipal buildings make up the downtown section of the busy borough.

There is plenty to enjoy while visiting Brooklyn, including Manhattan Beach and Coney Island, a wealth of activities in Prospect Park (which houses the borough's only zoo), the aquarium, the children's museum, and various historical sights. You can stroll through the galleries of Williamsburg or along the Brooklyn Heights Promenade, or you can stop at a bistro in Park Slope. A seafood dinner in Sheepshead Bay can be topped off with an evening at New York's oldest comedy club, Pips, or you might drop by a hot dance club, such as Brooklyn Mod, in Fort Greene. A ride along the Belt Parkway will take you along the shoreline around the borough.

While Brooklyn is home to a lot of small, tight-knit neighborhoods, the overall borough is one in which residents take great pride. It truly is a city within a city.

The New York City Transit Museum

Boerum Place and Schermerhorn Street

What better place to house a transit museum than in an old subway station from the 1930s. Yes, the subways of New York can be crowded, and the stations can be roasting hot during the summer months. But there is a rich history to the subways that lurk below the city streets. The museum, which opened in 1976 in a station that had been closed some 30 years earlier, houses some four thousand artifacts, including scale models of historic trains, mosaics, a bus and trolley exhibit, an assortment of turnstiles, tools, artwork, a working signal, and more. Drawings, posters, and photographs show the transition of the city through its subways, but the most representative examples are eighteen restored subway cars.

Some 113,000 visitors visit the Transit Museum annually to get a glimpse of what New York's underground has looked like over the past century. Lectures, excursions, walking tours, and other programs explore the transportation facilities and their impact on the city. Special events include art exhibition openings, demonstrations of emergency rescues, an annual bus festival with vintage city busses, and more.

The museum store and annex opened in 1999 in Manhattan, in Grand Central Terminal, selling and displaying other items relating to the transit system, including "token" watches, strap-hanger ties, and more.

The New York Transit Museum is open Tuesday through Friday, 10 A.M. to 4 P.M. Admission is $3. For more information, call 718-330-3060.

The New York Aquarium

Surf Avenue and Eighth Street
Coney Island

The city's only full-scale aquarium has been in Coney Island since the mid-1950s and attracts thousands of visitors annually. On 14 acres off the Boardwalk, the New York Aquarium has operated longer than any similar type of facility in the country. There are temporary exhibits and special events on occasion, but the permanent attractions are the major crowd pleasers. Such popular exhibits include Sea Cliffs, with walruses, penguins, and seals in a recreation of their native habitat, and the Aquatheater, where the dolphins perform (from May to October) much as they do at Sea World.

From Beluga whales to thousands of varieties of fish in a host of massive tanks, the aquarium is packed with delights of the underwater world. A 90,000-gallon shark tank will put you eye-to-eye with 400-pound sandtiger sharks while stingrays whiz by. Computer enhanced over the years, the aquarium also offers a wealth of information available to learn more about the creatures of the sea.

Prospect Park Wildlife Center

The small zoo/wildlife center is designed to teach children about wildlife through special programs and indoor and outdoor exhibits. The Wildlife Center features a sea lion pool and is home to mostly smaller animals. Children can meet prairie dogs, pet farm animals, and even hatch from a giant goose egg. The zoo is open 365 days a year from 10 A.M. to 4:30 or 5:30 P.M., depending on the season. The cost is $2.50 for adults, $1.25 for seniors, $.50 for children 3 through 12, and free for little ones under 3. There is free parking on Flatbush Avenue and food available at the cafeteria. The zoo is under the auspices of the Wildlife Conservation Society, which also runs the much larger Bronx Zoo. For more information, call 718-399-7339.

The aquarium is fun for both children and their parents. It's an enjoyable place to spend a few hours after a stroll on the Boardwalk. It can, on summer weekends, get overly crowded, with long lines to see everything, so it's best to arrive early on a weekday if possible.

There is an indoor cafeteria and an outdoor snack bar with tables on the deck overlooking the Boardwalk.

Open 365 days a year, the aquarium can be visited Monday through Friday from 10 A.M. to 4 P.M. and weekends and holidays (during the summer months) from 10 A.M. to 6 P.M. Admission is $8.75 for adults, $4.50 for children 2 through 12, and free for children under 2. Children under sixteen must be accompanied by an adult. Parking is available for $6, but lots fill up quickly on weekends, so get there early.

Coney Island

Surf Avenue
Between 37th Street and Ocean Parkway

In the movie *Annie Hall*, Woody Allen claimed he grew up in a house under the roller coaster in Coney Island. The house, once a residence and now an office, is real. It is under the old Thunderbolt roller coaster, which closed many years ago, when the famed Cyclone took the neighborhood by storm.

Coney Island—which is the English spelling for the Dutch name *Konijn* meaning *Rabbit Island* (for the many rabbits that were once found in the area)—is not actually an island but a neighborhood that was once the hotspot of the borough, billed as the "World's Largest Playground." It its heyday, the early 1900s, an elephant-shaped hotel, a replica of Bagdad called Luna Park, and a popular nightspot called Dreamland drew large crowds, along with the always popular beach, amusement park, and 2.5 mile boardwalk.

Today, a stroll on the boardwalk is the perfect way to take in the sea air, and the beach is the place for sun and relaxation in the summer heat. Nathan's has been serving their world famous hot dogs since 1916, and you can still "relish" the experience. The

amusement park, Astroland, has seen its share of wear and tear, but it is still home to the breathtaking (literally) Cyclone roller coaster. The screams of the other thrill rides still echo through the park all summer long. Dante's Inferno, the haunted house, is scary even from the outside, and the Ferris wheel will give you a view of all of Coney Island and much of Brooklyn. New and old rides for all ages are part of the Astroland experience, which, along with Rye Playland, just north of the Bronx in Westchester, and Adventureland, on Long Island, are among the few amusement parks around New York City.

Many people are nostalgic about Coney Island; you can experience that feeling yourself just by looking at the old Parachute Jump ride, which is now simply "the tower" and hasn't been operative for over 30 years. You can also see the history of Coney Island at a small Coney Island museum. The Sideshows by the Seashore and Museum are home to an old-fashioned circus sideshow with a fire eater, sword swallower, and other entertainers, as well as a museum with memorabilia from the neighborhood's illustrious past. The museum and sideshow are at West 12th Street and Surf Avenue. Call 718-372-5159 for information.

The boardwalk also leads to the New York Aquarium (mentioned earlier). The Coney Island season kicks off in May with the Mermaid Parade, a nearly 20-year-old tradition in which a parade of women, and some men, dress up in their mermaid best to parade along the boardwalk.

In the off-season, October through April, the neighborhood is relatively deserted, except for a visit by the Polar Bear club, which is made up of a bunch of "zanies" who make the news every January by putting on their bathing suits and heading into the ocean for a really chilling experience.

If you're heading to Coney Island, prepare to spend the day—a warm late spring or summer day. Bring your blanket, sunscreen, and some patience—parking is not easy. You can take the B or F trains, but it's a long ride from Manhattan. Coney Island can still provide, after all these years, some good outdoor family fun in an old-time landmark neighborhood that is a staple of Brooklyn's historic past.

Prospect Park

Brooklyn's largest park is one of the city's finest. Started shortly after the completion of Central Park and designed by the same landscape architects, the park has the same wide variety of characteristics, including large open meadows, winding paths, hills, wooded areas, a lake, and even a zoo. Yes, there is even a Wollman Rink (like the one in Central Park) for skaters. Activities abound throughout the park, including special and structured events and impromptu ballgames, kite flying, skateboarding, or simply picnicking.

A 1910 Tennis House, Flower Garden, Oriental Pavilion, and band shell are among the attractions in Prospect Park.

During the summer, there are many free concerts in the park, ranging from African rhythms to the Brooklyn Philharmonic Orchestra. Call 718-965-8999, the park hot line, for more information.

The Brooklyn Botanic Gardens

1000 Washington Avenue
South side of the Brooklyn Museum

Smack in the middle of Brooklyn are 52 of the most lavishly beautiful acres New York City has to offer. Over 750,000 people visit this spectacular tribute to Mother Nature annually. It's located among the redbrick buildings, row houses, storefronts, and municipal buildings that characterize much of the borough.

Consisting of several gardens, greenhouses, and exhibits, all in one sprawling location, the gardens offer a visual mirage of colors and a host of pleasing fragrances. Included on the grounds are the Shakespeare Garden, Cranford Rose Garden, Japanese Garden, Fragrance Garden, Children's Garden, Osbourne Garden, Steinhardt Conservatory, C.V. Bonsai Museum, Celebrity Path, Visitor Center, Garden Gift Shop, Terrace Café, Palm House, and three large pavilions.

The Cranford Rose Garden features tens of thousands of rose bushes of numerous varieties in formal beds and over arches and onto the accompanying pavilion. The Rose Garden opened in 1928 and comprises just one of the acres of this massive outdoor flower gallery.

The Children's Garden, first opened in 1914, is a place where children can learn about plants by enjoying the hands–on experience of planting and gardening. Instructors teach children of all ages about the plants, insects, and animals. It's both fun and educational. Thirty-minute Children's Garden family tours (free with your admission) are offered on Tuesday afternoons at 2 P.M. in June, July, and August. The tour covers activities and displays and gives children a chance to care for and harvest flowers and vegetables. Some twenty-five thousand youngsters have tended this garden over the years.

"Get Your Plants Here!"

If you happen to visit the Brooklyn Botanic Garden in early May, you might just stumble upon their annual plant sale. Plants are relatively inexpensive. Remember, however, that if you are traveling far, you'll need to get plants that will travel well.

The Japanese Hill-and-Pond Garden is brilliantly landscaped and features bridges, waterfalls, a pond, a viewing pavilion, a waiting house, and shrubs carefully designed and shaped.

The Fragrance Garden, built in the 1950s, is designed for people who are visually impaired. It features raised flower beds, various aromas, and textured foliage. Enjoyed by the sighted as well, it is the only garden of its kind.

The Shakespeare Garden, like its Central Park counterpart, features flowers mentioned in the works of William Shakespeare in a setting modeled after an English cottage garden.

The Steinhart Conservatory, built in the late 1980s, is a modern $25 million complex featuring greenhouses that display the thousands of indoor plants that are part of the Botanic Gardens.

The Terrace Café offers gourmet lunches and beverages with outdoor dining in the warmer months; the Palm House, a catering facility, offers luncheons and parties.

Osbourne Garden is a formal setting, complete with fountain, seating, and columns found in traditional Italian gardens. Within the 3-acre garden is a 30,000-square-foot center lawn surrounded by flowering trees and shrubs.

The garden is open Tuesday through Friday from 8 A.M. to 6 P.M. and weekends from 10 A.M. to 6 P.M., April through September, and Tuesday through Friday from 8 A.M. to 4:30 P.M. and weekends from 10 A.M. to 4:30 P.M., October through March. The garden is closed on Thanksgiving, Christmas, and New Years Day. Admission is free to the public on Tuesday (except holidays) and Saturday mornings until noon; otherwise it is $3 for adults over 16, $1.50 for seniors and students with IDs, and free for teens and children 16 and under.

Guided tours are free and feature seasonal highlights. They are offered at 1 P.M. on weekends, except major holiday weekends. Group tours and lunch tours can also be set up (for a fee) by calling 718-623-7220. The visitor center is staffed by volunteers who will fill you in on programs, courses, seminars, and events. For a schedule, call 718-623-7263. Parking is available for a fee.

Honoring Brooklynites

A walkway known as Celebrity Path can be found as you walk through the Brooklyn Botanic Gardens; it features stones engraved with Brooklyn-born celebrities, including Woody Allen, Mel Brooks, Mae West, Mary Tyler Moore, and many others.

Shea Stadium

Flushing

Every baseball fan wants to visit the ballparks of the other teams in the major leagues. Shea has been the home of the Mets since 1964, named for William Shea, one of the principals behind bringing a National League team back to New York after the departure of the Giants and Dodgers in '57. Besides the Mets and two world championships, the ballpark has seen the Beatles in concert, the pope, the Yankees play there for 2 years during the remodeling of Yankee Stadium, and New York Jets football, until their departure to New Jersey. Planes fly overhead en route to LaGuardia Airport, trains pass by from Flushing en route to Manhattan, and fans flock into the ballpark for eighty-one home games annually. It is now, at 36 years, one of the league's older ballparks, but it's still a great place to see a game.

Brooklyn Museum of Art

200 Eastern Parkway

Second in size (in New York City) only to the Met, this is a substantial museum with numerous exhibits featuring historic works from around the world as well as classic American art. Set inside a massive 1893 structure, the museum houses over one million paintings, artifacts, drawings, photographs, and more.

One of the world's most renowned collections of Egyptian art covers the third floor with a chronological display dating back to 1350 b.c. Jewelry, ivory, gold, and other invaluable objects can be found. A separate exhibit entitled Temples, Tombs, and the Egyptian Universe houses nearly two hundred more Egyptian artifacts.

Carved ivory and numerous items including masks and shields from Central Africa and arts of the Pacific from Polynesia, Malaysia, and Indonesia are also found in the huge building. There is a large collection of pan-American art including a fifteenth-century Aztec stone jaguar, plus textiles, ceramics, and gold objects. You'll even find portraits of the kings of the Inca empire, painted in Peru. An extensive collection of Asian art includes works from Cambodia, China, India, Iran, Japan, Thailand, Tibet, and Turkey, as well as Korea.

Some twenty-eight period rooms are also displayed, ranging from a seventeenth-century Brooklyn Dutch farmhouse to a twentieth-century art deco library. A walk through the rooms offers a look at a chronology of styles of decor in America spanning more than two centuries. Paintings and sculptures from American and European artists also span some five centuries. You'll note there are classic painters represented, including Monet and Degas, in this large, often overlooked museum.

While the museum may not dazzle the younger set, it does provide a great cultural history for visitors from around the world. A sculpture garden is ideal for a pleasant stroll outdoors; inside the museum you'll find shops and a café. The museum is open Wednesday through Friday from 10 A.M. to 5 P.M.; Saturday from 11 A.M. to 6 P.M.; the first Saturday of the month from 11 A.M. to 11 P.M.; and Sunday from 11 A.M. to 6 P.M. Admission is $4 for adults, $2 for students with a valid ID, and free for children under 12. For more information, call 718-638-5000.

Queens

The home of two world's fairs, the city's two major airports, the Mets, Queens College (its heralded alumni include Jerry Seinfeld, Paul Simon, Marvin Hamlish, and the author of this book), and more, Queens is a far-reaching borough in the center of it all. It connects to Manhattan and the Bronx by bridge and to Brooklyn and Long Island by land.

Not unlike Brooklyn, Queens has its share of ethnically diverse neighborhoods. In fact, over 120 languages are spoken by Queens residents. In the middle of this multilingual borough is the Unisphere, a giant metal sculpture of the globe, in Flushing Meadow Park. Once a garbage dump, the park was transformed into the fairgrounds to host the 1939 and later the 1964 World's Fairs.

Numerous architectural styles typify the various neighborhoods, including old redbrick buildings, rowhouses, and attached houses of the '50s and '60s. There are large estates in the aptly named area of Jamaica Estates, and a quaint old-fashioned, wall-enclosed residential community called Forest Hills Gardens. You will also find some modern office buildings springing up—along with movie studios—in Long Island City. Named for Queen Catherine, the wife of King Charles II of England, and colonized in 1683, the sprawling Queens combines a taste of the suburbs with an urban flavor. There are a host of major highways zigzagging their way through the borough connecting with Long Island and New York's two major international airports. The mass of roads were developed because of the two world's fairs.

Queens is often the first part of New York that visitors will see if flying into the city. Once out of baggage claim, you are likely to be on either the Van Wyck or Grand Central Expressways en route to Manhattan. A return trip for a visit, however, can take you to one of a few historical sights, a ballgame at Shea Stadium, tennis at the U.S. Open, or a film or science museum. The borough is home to the Kaufman Astoria and Silvercup film studios, just a stone's throw from Manhattan. The studios are once again thriving. In fact, Queens was host to a great number of classic films made by screen stars of the '20s and '30s, including Edward G. Robinson, Marlene Dietrich, the Marx Brothers, and many others. It is hoped

Flushing Meadow Park

First developed into a park in 1939 for the World's Fair, Flushing Meadow is a nice place for a picnic, a round of golf on the small "Pitch and Putt" course, or a game of tennis on championship courts at the USTA Tennis Center (home of the U.S. Open).

The Hall of Science, the Queens Art Museum, and the wildlife center are all located in the vast park. The park offers a day of fun-filled activities, boating, and even culture, all in one place.

Queens Wildlife Center

Flushing Meadow Park
Essentially, the word to sum it up is zoo. Redesigned and remodeled in 1992, you can interact with animals in the bird and garden center. The larger animals on the grounds include elk, bison, a mountain lion, bears, and, like most New York City zoos, a sea lion pool. Open year-round, the zoo is just $2.50 for adults, $.50 for children 3 through 12, and free for youngsters under 3. For more information, call 718-271-1500.

that at least one of the studios will add guided tours and provide another fun stop for tourists and New Yorkers to visit.

American Museum of the Moving Image

36-01 35th Avenue (in Astoria)

Although you can't tour the studios, you can get a great glimpse at movie making history. Just over the bridge from Manhattan, and within close proximity to the Silvercup and the old, still very busy Kaufman Astoria Studios, this unique museum pays tribute to the powerful and influential media that are motion pictures and television. From the early days of film in Queens to the digital media, there is a lot represented in these archives.

The 50,000-square-foot museum, opened in 1988, is housed in part of the historic old studio built by Paramount in 1920. Three floors of exhibit space feature attractions such as *Behind the Screen*, a look at the history of the cinema, complete with movie memorabilia and photos from studios local and worldwide. Television is not neglected either; memorabilia include the diner set from *Seinfeld*.

Also featured in the museum are fourteen interactive exhibits. Visitors learn sound editing, and music editing, and can make their own animated cartoon or a video flip book. You can even dub your own voice on a movie scene. The charming, whimsical Tut Fever Movie Palace is a mini-theater built like the movie palaces of the 1930s, showing classic images and serials like *Flash Gordon*, *Buck Rogers*, and *The Lone Ranger*. Ongoing film programs are featured on weekends at 2 and 4 P.M.

A computer space exhibit of classic video arcade games and new home computer games brings the museum into the twenty-first century.

A store sells movie books, toys, posters, postcards, and other objects with movie and TV themes. There is also a café for light dining and snacks.

More of an actual "museum" than its "video library" counterpart (The Radio and Television Museum in Manhattan), this one is off the beaten path but worth the short ride to visit. One mile from Queensboro Bridge, the "R" train to Steinway Avenue is one quick way to get there. Or you can drive and park without much trouble on the weekend.

The American Museum of the Moving Image is open Tuesday through Friday from noon to 5 P.M. and Saturday and Sunday from 11 A.M. to 6 P.M. Admission is $8.50 for adults, $5.50 for seniors and college students with a valid ID, and $4.50 for children. For more information, call 718-784-0077 or 718-784-4520.

Hall of Science

11th Street in Flushing Meadow Park

Part of the 1964–65 World's Fair, this museum closed in the 1970s and reopened in the late 1980s. An interactive hands-on museum, the Hall of Science features over two hundred exhibits for youngsters and parents to explore, play with, and learn from, including a high-powered telescope. Microbiology, quantum physics, geology, audio technology. and other subjects are covered in a fun way; kids can learn while enjoying themselves.

A 30,000-square-foot outdoor science playground adjacent to the museum features an oversized seesaw, a giant pinball machine, and other activities to climb in, climb on, run through, and explore. Designed to show the principles of physics while providing a good time, the playground/science park is open for children 6 and over.

The museum has a gift shop with a wide range of science-related items, from inexpensive gadgets to toys, books, and even telescopes. There is no restaurant, but you can buy snacks and sandwiches from a vending machine or bring your own food for a bite in the dining area.

The hall is open Monday through Wednesday from 9:30 A.M. to 2 P.M.; Thursday, Saturday, and Sunday from 9:30 A.M. to 5 P.M.; and Friday from 2 P.M. to 5 P.M. Admission is $6 for adults, $4 for children, and free on Thursday. Parking isn't hard with some six hundred available spaces on the 22-acre site. Call for summer hours. For more information, call 718-699-0005.

Sculptures Growing in Queens!

If you like sculpture gardens, two have sprouted in the Long Island City area just over the 59th Street Bridge from Manhattan. The Socrates Sculpture Garden on Vernon Street in Astoria features modern sculpture that looks as though it was made to salvage the last remnants of a scrap heap. For more information, call 718-956-1819. The Isamu Noguchi Garden Museum on Vernon Boulevard near 33rd Street has a dozen galleries housing the works of this famous sculptor who utilized wood and marble. There is a garden in the back. For more information, call 718-204-7088.

Queens Museum of Art

Flushing Meadow Park

The third of three very distinctive museums in Queens features the history of the two major world's fairs held in Flushing Meadow Park, complete with memorabilia. But that's not the exciting part of this 1939 building, known as the New York City exhibit in the '39 and '64 fairs. The reason to visit the museum is the 9,000-square-foot miniature replica of New York City. It represents the entire city, block by block, house by house, with changes made from time to time to replicate new buildings replacing older ones. The scale is 1 inch per 100 feet, and the detail is awesome. Much safer than a helicopter ride over the city, you could stand and look at the buildings, the bridges, and the neighborhoods for hours (if they're not crowded). It's truly remarkable!

Also in the museum you'll find an extensive Tiffany lamp exhibition, plus an exhibit about the building itself. There is also an adjoining ice skating rink, if you want to take a spin on the ice during the winter months.

A gift shop sells world's fair momentos. There is no restaurant.

Just outside the museum is the giant metal Unisphere, a throwback to the great world's fair days. The museum is open Wednesday through Friday from 10 A.M. to 5 P.M. and Saturday and Sunday from noon to 5 P.M. Admission is $4 for adults, and $2 for seniors and students. For more information, call 718-592-9700.

The Bronx

The Bronx Bombers, or the Yankees as they're also known, the famed Bronx Zoo, a spectacular botanical garden, Edgar Allan Poe's house, one of the oldest golf courses in the country, and a small seafood island are all found in the Bronx.

The borough was named after Jonas Bronck, a Swedish sailor who built a farm on the land in the seventeenth century. By the nineteenth century, fashionable estates, parks, the Botanical Gardens, and other marvelously landscaped areas set the tone. Homes were spread out and life was grand along the "Grand Concourse," *the* major street of the borough. It wasn't until the twentieth century, and post–World

War II in particular, that the Bronx started to reflect the poverty and despair that has plagued much of the borough over the past 25 years.

Yet, while areas like the South Bronx epitomize urban decay with tenements, burned out buildings, and boarded up storefronts, parts of the Bronx have survived and others have seen growth. Apartment complexes like the massive Co-op City brought affordable housing to many in need in the housing crunch of the '60s and '70s. Fordham University, meanwhile, continued to be a leading educational institution, and longtime landmark sights remained, keeping the Bronx a viable location for visitors. Parks like Van Cortlandt, spanning 1,146 acres, with numerous attractions including the oldest municipal golf course in the country, and mansions like Wave Hill in the fashionable section of Riverdale, maintain the long-standing history of the only borough attached to the mainland.

Like most of the city, the Bronx has a wonderful diversity of ethnic neighborhoods including the Caribbean section of Williamsbridge and Woodlawn and the Italian-based Belmont, with its local shops, bakeries, and old-time New York flavor.

While much of the Bronx is in need of a face-lift, there are still a number of prime attractions that won't disappoint.

The New York Botanical Garden

Kazimiroff Boulevard and 200th Street

The most beautiful 250 acres you'll find in the Bronx, and possibly in all of New York City, are in the Botanical Garden. A serene refuge from the big city, the garden is worth the trip to the Bronx, especially if you also visit the neighboring Bronx Zoo.

The site was selected back in 1891 and developed as a place for the public to enjoy the beautifully landscaped outdoors. Today, the facility incorporates dramatic rock outcroppings, wetlands, ponds, a waterfall, and a 40-acre forest, along with sixteen specialty gardens, including a rose garden and a rock garden. A glasshouse has been home to indoor plants since 1902, and there is a museum building and stone cottage. The garden is also in the scientific research game, with their new Plant Studies Center and a new plant studies library, one of the biggest in the country, with over 1.26 million print and nonprint items.

Where the Pros Play

No, you can't play ball at Shea Stadium, but across the street, Roosevelt Avenue, you can play tennis at Arthur Ashe Stadium, where the U.S. Open is held every August. There are thirty-six indoor and outdoor courts available. Courts are $33 per hour indoor and $23 per hour outdoor. Call 718-760-6200 for more information or to book a court.

Included among the gardens, you'll find the Peggy Rockefeller Rose Garden, with a central iron gazebo and thousands of varieties of roses. Along with a 2.5-acre rock garden, you'll enjoy a native plant garden with nine different habitats displaying plants indigenous to the northeastern United States. Over 150 herbs are found in the Nancy Bryan Luce Herb Garden, and the Demonstration Gardens offer a variety of gardens that visitors can recreate in their backyards, including fragrance, country, and cutting gardens. There's even a children's garden, where youngsters can learn about tending to plants.

From bulbs to daffodils to daylilies to chrysanthemums, if it's a plant or part of a garden, it's most likely found in the Botanical Garden. There is even a forest with birds and wildlife in one of the oldest tracts of uncut nature remaining in the city.

The garden shop is open for buying anything you need for a garden, from seeds to watering cans; it also has a great selection of gardening books. You'll find a children's shop in the Everett Children's Adventure Garden.

The New York Botanical Garden is open Tuesday through Sunday from 10 A.M. to 6 P.M., April through October, and 10 A.M. to 5 P.M. from November through March. Admission is $3 for adults, $2 for seniors and students, and $1 for children 2 through 12.

There are special events and several tours are offered, including a tram tour for $1 ($.50 for children), a golf cart tour (no putting allowed), and walking tours of the gardens or the forest. The Garden Café and picnic tables are available. A visitor center will provide maps as you enter, and you will need one to find your way around. For more information, call 718-817-8700.

The Bronx Zoo

International Wildlife Conservation Center
Fordham Road and Bronx River Parkway

Just past celebrating its one-hundredth birthday, the Bronx Zoo has for a century been a marvelous adventure for children and adults alike. The zoo, now known as the International Wildlife Conservation Center, is home to over four thousand

animals in a variety of settings designed to recreate the natural habitats for the six hundred species that reside here.

For families, it can be a full day of activities, with numerous exhibits including the recently added Gorilla forest, which covers more than 6 acres and recreates an African rain forest with over three hundred animals.

Other exhibits include the following:

- Jungle World is another rain forest. This one is an indoor tropical exhibit, complete with Asian Gibbons and numerous other fascinating creatures.
- The Bengali Express is a monorail ride through (or over) the recreated forests and meadows of Asia. It's complete with all the creatures of those nature documentaries on PBS, including elephants, deer, antelope, and, of course, Bengal tigers. The Bengali Express guided monorail tour is open from May to November and costs $2 extra.
- Baboon Reserve is a simulated archeological dig tracing the evolution of the Gelada baboons, complete with numerous baboons playing on the side of the mini-mountain range.
- World of Darkness gives you a glimpse into the nocturnal creatures of the night, including various bats and rats. It's not for the squeamish.
- The Himalayan Highlands exhibit features red pandas, endangered snow leopards, and other animals of the Himalayas.
- The Children's Zoo allows the kids to meet, greet, and feed a variety of animals and to have fun with various kid-friendly activities. Closed during winter months, the Children's Zoo costs a few dollars more.
- Still other exhibits include Mousehouse, Skyfari, World of Birds, African Plains, and much more.

There is also a gift shop plus snack stands, the Lakeside Café, the African Market, and other eateries. Several rides are also open in the summer. Zoo rides cost extra, including the Skyfari ($2), Camel rides ($3), and the Zoo Shuttle ($2).

Bronx Zoo Tips

1. Decide what you want to see. Unless you get there early, you probably won't cover everything in a day.
2. Avoid holidays unless you are comfortable with big crowds.
3. Take precautions for the sun in the hot summer months. There is not a lot of shade, so sunscreen, hats, sun glasses, and cool clothing are advised.
4. Wear comfortable shoes; the exhibits are spread out over 265 acres.
5. The zoo is accessible to people with disabilities. Call ahead for information regarding the best entrances and how to best plan your day. Call 718-220-5100.
6. Take note of where you park in the lot or of where your subway entrance or bus stop is located.

The Bronx Zoo is open 365 days a year, although several exhibits close down during the winter months. The hours are 10 A.M. to 5 P.M. (4:30 in the winter). Admission is $7.75 for adults and $4 for seniors and children 2 through 12. Prices are lower between November and March. Most of the year, Wednesday is free. Call 1-718-220-5100 for more information.

Parking at the zoo is $6 for cars and $8 for busses.

Tickets are sold up until an hour before the zoo closes, but you should allow yourself at least 3 hours to see some of the massive zoo. Also, check the weather before you plan a day at the zoo.

City Island

Long Island Sound

A small bridge connects this 230-acre, four-block-wide island with the mainland, which is the Bronx. An attractively laid out miniature golf course, Turtle Cove, is located next to a golf driving range where you can stop to play along the way as you head to City Island Bridge. Once over the bridge, the smell of fresh seafood will remind you of New England. Essentially, City Island has all the great seafood as can be found on the shores of Maine and Massachusetts. The tiny island is also chock full of boats, and you can rent one and take a ride.

Fishing, sailing, and boat building have been more than just a pastime of the island since its founding days in the eighteenth century. A little museum called the Northwind Undersea Museum can be found in the old sea captain's house at 610 City Island Avenue. The museum is devoted to the maritime and deep-sea fishing and costs $3. It is open March through November. For information, call 718-885-0701.

As you drive along the one main road on the island, you'll smell the sea air as you encounter a slew of restaurants. With names like Crab Shanty, King Lobster, Lobster Box, Lobster House, Sammy's Fish Box, and Sea View, you'll immediately get the idea that it's time to don a bib and prepare for some great seafood. Portions in most of these eateries are large, the food is fresh, and the dining experience at most of the twenty plus restaurants is first rate.

Bronx River Art Center and Gallery

On East Tremont Avenue at 177th Street, an art center and gallery overlooks the Bronx River. Housed in an old 1920s dress factory, the gallery displays the works of contemporary artists, with exhibits changing several times throughout the year. The Center and Gallery are open Tuesday through Thursday 3 P.M. to 6 P.M. and Saturday noon to 6 P.M.

Less than an hour from Manhattan by car, City Island is a worthwhile excursion that even some longtime New Yorkers don't know about. It's quaint, it's fun, and if you love seafood, bring your appetite. While you could get there by subway or bus, or by boat, the best way to get there is by car. April through October are the months to visit.

Besides those listed above, other restaurants on the small island include Artie's of City Island, Café Rio, City Island Diner, Fran's Place, Laura's Café & Deli, Johnny's Famous Reef, JP's, Lazy Susan's, Lido, Scotto's, Portofino, and Tito Puente's.

Yankee Stadium

East 161 Street and River Avenue
Off the Major Deegan

Built in 1923, the year the Babe hit his first home run, and remodeled in 1976 (during the less notable Bobby Mercer era), Yankee Stadium is home to the winningest baseball franchise in major league history. The Yankees have fans nationwide and world-wide and a roster of hall of famers matched by no other team, including Babe Ruth, Lou Gehrig, Joe DiMaggio, Mickey Mantle, Whitey Ford, and Yogi Berra.

The stadium itself sits on 11.6 acres and was actually the third home of the Yankees, who played in the Polo Grounds in Upper Manhattan (1913 to 1922) and before that in Hilltop Park (1903 to 1912), also in Upper Manhattan.

With very little foul territory, seats are as close to the field as you'll find anywhere. The ambiance is still that of "real baseball," without artificial turf, skyboxes, waterfalls, or massive electronic score-boards overshadowing the game itself. If you arrive early, you can visit Monument Park, just over the centerfield fence, featuring monuments and plaques for great Yankees including the hall of famers already mentioned plus Bill Dickey, Phil Rizzuto, Roger Maris, Thurman Munson, Elston Howard, Casey Stengel, and others. A special walkway honors those players whose uniforms have been retired.

The stadium holds 57,545, but getting a ticket is not easy when the Yankees are playing well, so plan in advance. For ticket information and a schedule of games call 718-293-6000. The season runs from early April to the end of September, and usually a few weeks longer for the Yankees. Tickets can be purchased at Ticketmaster (212-307-1212) locations throughout the city and at the Yankee Stadium Box Office (718-293-6000). For stadium tour information, call 718-579-5431.

For day games, the subway is quick and gets you right to the stadium. If you'd prefer not to travel the subways at night, you can park in any of several lots around the ballpark, (Avoid the ones that say valet parking; they cost more and you're kept waiting in line to get your car after the game). Self park in a lot and walk with the crowds. This is not a neighborhood for seeking out street parking or wandering away from the stadium area.

Staten Island

The Rodney Dangerfield of the boroughs, Staten Island gets no respect. It's the only borough that has never had a major league baseball team, and it still remains separated from the subways that connect the other four boroughs. Until 1964, and the opening of the Verrazano Bridge, Staten Island was even more separated from the rest of the city. To many New Yorkers, Staten Island is still an enigma. Ask a resident of the other four boroughs to name a neighborhood in Staten Island, and most won't be able to do so.

Staten Island's inclusion as part of the city came as a prize in a sailing contest in 1687, when the Duke of York gave the island to Manhattan. Residents of the borough today, in response to being the "fifth wheel," sometimes talk of separating from the rest of New York City. In fact, in 1993 they voted to do so, but obviously it has never happened. In time, the borough may well become a separate city.

While it remains part of New York City, Staten Island is a suburban, sprawling setting, rich with its own ethnic and cultural diversity. The island is an enjoyable 25-minute ferry ride from Manhattan. Less densely settled than the other boroughs, it has several large open spaces, including the Greenbelt, La Tourette Park, Willowbrook Park, William T. Davis Wildlife Refuge, and various significant attractions, including Historic Richmond Town and the Snug Harbor

Free Staten Island Info!

The Whitehall Staten Island Ferry Terminal in Lower Manhattan offers tourist information, maps, and more at kiosks. While waiting for the ferry, check out things to see and do across the Hudson when you reach Staten Island.

Cultural Center. Other cultural attractions include the Garibaldi-Meucci Museum, housed in a converted farmhouse, and the Jacques Marchais Museum of Tibetan Art, housed in a building designed to look like a Tibetan Temple. A day trip to Staten Island can cover the sights and sounds of this often overlooked but very pleasant borough. And you'll be able to tell friends (and many New Yorkers) about an area they haven't yet taken the time to visit.

Historic Richmond Town

La Tourette Park
441 Clarke Avenue

You'll find twenty-seven buildings on 100 acres, making up the Historic Richmond Town, which represents three centuries of Staten Island life. The village saw its first buildings in 1690 and expanded over the centuries. These structures withstood the Revolutionary War and the modernization of the city around them. A museum was added and is open to the public, along with fourteen of the twenty-seven historical structures.

Included in the historic town, you'll find the oldest surviving elementary school, the Voorlezer House, from 1695, a stately Greek Revival courthouse from 1837 (which has been transformed into a visitors center), a 1740s farmhouse, and an 1860s general store museum. Located in the former county clerk's office, the museum's exhibits feature items made in Staten Island and a "Toys!" exhibit.

Other exhibits within the quaint setting include early American crafts and feature demonstrations of quilting, carpentry, spinning and weaving, fireplace cooking, and other aspects of colonial life. Along with guided tours of the buildings, the unique historical setting is host to a fair every Labor Day weekend, flea markets, an annual summer re-enactment of the Civil War battles, a nineteenth century outdoor dinner, complete with plates and utensils of a bygone era, Saturday night concerts, an autumn celebration, and Christmas festivities.

There is a museum store that sells reproductions, handmade items by the craftspeople in the village, and books on Staten Island history. A Victorian-style full-service restaurant offers casual dining.

And They're Off!

For those who watch the annual event on television (and for those who like to run), Fort Wadsworth is the annual starting point for the New York City Marathon, which attracts over thirty thousand runners from around the globe!

As close as you'll find to Colonial Williamsburg in New York City, the historic town provides a fun afternoon as you step into the past. Admission is $4 for adults and $2.50 for seniors and children 6 through 18. Historic Richmond Town is open Wednesday through Sunday from 1 to 5 P.M. and closed on major holidays. And there's plenty of free parking! For information, call 718-351-1611.

Fort Wadsworth

Wadsworth Avenue and Bay Street

From 1795 through 1945, this was a navy-run fort that protected New York harbor. Today, the 226-acre site is run by the New York Park Service and is home to Coast Guard personnel and the Army Reserve. Fourteen historic defense structures remain overlooking the harbor and the neighboring Verrazano Bridge. Views are outstanding!

Admission is free, and the park is open from dawn to dusk. The visitor's center is open Wednesday through Sunday from 10 A.M. to 5 P.M. The center has a film on the history of the fort, plus other exhibits. You can buy books and other items in a gift shop. Ranger-led tours are also available. Within the park itself, you can fish, hike, or follow a trail by foot or by bike. Special events include lantern tour nights, living history re-enactments of rifle or musket demonstrations, special hikes, and more.

A deli on the grounds is open every day except Sunday, or you can pack a picnic lunch and enjoy a day of history and fun in the great outdoors. Bring a camera for shots of New York harbor. For more information, call 718-354-4576.

Snug Harbor Cultural Center

1000 Richmond Terrace

A small historical city within a city, Snug Harbor houses some twenty-eight historical structures and acres of public parkland, with meadows, wetlands, and gardens. Greek Revival and Victorian architecture characterize many of the buildings, which include a music hall built in the late nineteenth century and a main hall dating back to 1833. Five Victorian artists cottages and a Veterans

Memorial hall from 1856 are also among the classic structures you'll find here. While Historic Richmond Town has a greater focus on history, Snug Harbor is a home for culture and the arts.

Just a 10-minute bus ride from the Staten Island Ferry, Snug Harbor has a variety of attractions for varying interests. Included, you'll find the John A. Noble Collection of Maritime Art and the Visual Arts/Newhouse Galleries, featuring cutting-edge contemporary art creatively displayed in vivid contrast to the nineteenth-century main hall in which it stands. All in all, the structures house some 15,000 square feet of exhibit space, forty visual and performing arts studios, three dance studios, and three assembly halls.

The Staten Island Botanical Garden is also part of Snug Harbor. The complex is home to several smaller gardens, including a "White Garden" with white flowers, a bird and butterfly observatory, a fragrance garden, a rose garden, an herb garden, a greenhouse, and the English Garden. A Chinese Scholar's Garden and operating vineyard are also on the premises. The Botanical Garden serves as a living, working, growing scientific and educational center. The gardens are free. Call 718-273-8200 for hours and information.

The Staten Island Children's Museum, also found in the Snug Harbor Cultural Center, offers kids under 12 a variety of hands-on exhibitions in five interactive galleries, along with storytelling, workshops, and performances. There is a gift shop with books and souvenirs. Admission is $4 per person (free for children under 2). Call 718-273-2060 for hours and information.

Open from dawn to dusk, 362 days a year, Snug Harbor hosts numerous outdoor events, including classical, pop, and jazz concerts in their south meadow and in the music hall. They also have an art lab with classes, workshops, and mini-camps at the Children's Museum.

The Snug Harbor gift shop sells jewelry, original art, posters, and books. Melville's Café serves sandwiches, entrees, and desserts. While touring the site is fun, seeing one of the numerous performances will really enhance your visit. Visiting Snug Harbor is a great way to sightsee, enjoy a concert, and even have a picnic. Also, it's not very expensive and is great for the whole family.

Alice Austen House Museum

The former home of photographer Alice Austen is a cozy little eighteenth-century Dutch cottage that has been restored and has become a landmark. Austen, who took more than eight thousand photos depicting life at the turn of the century, made her mark with the publication of her photos in *Life* magazine in the late 1940s. You can visit the cottage, known as Clear Comfort, for a $3 admission fee March through December from noon to 5 P.M. Many of Austen's marvelous photographs are on display in the house.

The site is open free to the public from dawn to dusk. The Newhouse Center for Contemporary Art is open Wednesday through Sunday from noon to 5 P.M. The suggested donation of $2. For information on events and hours, call the Snug Harbor Cultural Center at 718-448-2500.

Long Island

In 1524 an Italian explorer named Verrazano spotted the area now known as Long Island. The beaches were empty, and there were no gold coast mansions or shopping malls, but there were over 1,000 square miles of uncharted land. Not an island unto itself, Long Island is attached to Queens and Brooklyn.

Today, Long Island is "the suburbs" for Manhattanites. It is a place where many former city dwellers relocated in their quest for larger homes and backyards for patios and cookouts. Many city dwellers visit Long Island for the beaches, sporting activities, and other fun.

The Long Island Railroad is one route through Queens to "the Island," as it's known, and the Long Island Expressway is the most traveled major road. Often crowded, the LIE has earned the nickname "the world's biggest parking lot." Other major roads such as the Northern State and Southern State Parkways also transport visitors and Long Islanders around the many towns that make up Long Island.

Long Island consists of both Nassau and Suffolk Counties, home to some 2.7 million people. Many more people visit, especially on summer weekends when the beach is the best way to beat the city heat. Of the more than one hundred beaches, Jones Beach is the most popular. Built in the 1920s by developer Robert Moses, Jones has 6 miles of beaches, a boardwalk, a miniature golf course, old bath houses, a pitch and putt golf course, a public swimming pool, and an outdoor theater for big-name concerts. The beach

Staten Island Zoo

In Barrett Park (614 Broadway) in West New Brighton, you'll find the Staten Island Zoo; it houses an internationally acclaimed reptile exhibit complete with North American rattlesnakes. The zoo also features a South American tropical forest, a children's center, a New England farm setting, an African Savannah exhibit, and an aquarium with sharks! Admission is $3 for anyone over twelve and $2 for children two through eleven. Call 718-442-3100 for more information and hours.

draws large crowds during the summer months, so pack up your sunscreen and towels and set out early. From Memorial Day to Labor Day, there are parking fees. The west end and central sections are particular favorites, with long stretches of white sand. The waves are fun for playing, but this is not the place for surfing. Continuing past Jones Beach, you'll find Robert Moses State Park; because it's just that much farther from the city, it is usually a little less crowded

The Hamptons, consisting of four small towns, are a longer ride, but worthwhile if you want to see mansions, beautiful beaches, and perhaps even a celebrity or two. The shops are upscale, the prices can be high, parking is difficult, and you'll find an air of pretentiousness. But if you've planned well and know where you're heading, the area can be beautiful and the beaches delightful. With that in mind, many New Yorkers take shares in homes owned by the rich who rent them out to the "summer crowd" who want to *weekend in the Hamptons, darling.*"

Also for fun, sun, and sand, you might try Shelter Island or Fire Island. Shelter Island is a 12-mile island reachable by ferry only. For sunning or fishing, it's a marvelous departure from "civilization." Fire Island is also primarily accessible by ferry. The 32-mile-long seashore includes the only federally declared wilderness area in New York State.

Private homes, shops, and malls dominate the landscape on Long Island, which is sprawling with a wealth of very attractive neighborhoods including Oyster Bay, Kingspoint, Sands Point, Old Westbury, Roslyn Heights, Dix Hills, and numerous others. Numerous gold coast mansions line the island; some are noted on tours, and others you'll need to find for yourself. A few, in places like Sands Point Preserve, afford you the opportunity to step inside these spacious old homes.

There is a lot to see on Long Island, and because it's so very spread out, it's advantageous to plan a day trip carefully and to drive. Decide what you want to see, get directions from your hotel, and plan ahead.

First-Class Concert Venue

The most notable concert hall on Long Island is the Westbury Music Fair. The nearly three-thousand-seat theater-in-the-round has been around nearly 40 years and has played host to numerous major name performers running the gamut from Tommy Dorsey to the Vanilla Fudge. Tickets are available at the box office and at all Ticketmasters. For information on ordering tickets, call 516-334-0800. The Westbury Music Fair is just off the Long Island Expressway in Westbury at exit 40W, at 960 Brush Hollow Road. For more information, call 516-333-7228.

The Big Arena

From the roar of Islander fans during their reign of four Stanley Cups to Led Zeppelin concerts, the Nassau Veterans Memorial Coliseum has been home to all sorts of activities including the circus in the main arena and golf or computer shows in a 60,000-square-foot exhibition hall. The Coliseum is in Uniondale, which is 40 minutes by car from Manhattan. Often the same shows that are passing through Madison Square Garden will play the Nassau Coliseum, but tickets may be easier to come by here, and you may get better seats. For information and schedules, call 516-794-9300.

Old Bethpage Village Restoration

Round Swamp Road
Bethpage (Long Island Expressway exit 48 south)

Old Bethpage Village Restoration is a 200-acre open-air museum of sorts. It represents a historical Long Island village of the nineteenth century. The restoration project began in 1963 in an attempt to save and preserve landmark buildings. Plainview Long Island s historic Manetto Hill Methodist Church was the first building moved onto the sight and restored. The current village setting now has over fifty buildings that have been carefully transported onto the vast property and restored to a specific point in their history. Thus, all the buildings are not from the same years, allowing for a more detailed look at history over a wider range of time.

There is a reception center, where you can start your tour of the village. Roads then lead past the stores, an inn, a blacksmith shop, and on to several homes and farmhouses. Each building is complete with the details you would have found inside over a hundred years ago. Up the hill sits a one-room schoolhouse and a church. Down the road is a farm with horses, oxen, pigs, sheep, and other animals.

You can take a self-guided or guided tour of the grounds. There are also educational programs, crafts demonstrations, old brass band concerts, and other various special events including a spring festival, nineteenth-century baseball games, traditional dance and music weekends, and a Long Island fair in early October.

The village offers a fun look into the past in a very relaxing setting. It s Long Island s answer to stepping into a time machine and going back to pre Civil War days.

Old Bethpage is open Wednesday through Sunday 10 A.M. to 5 P.M., March through October, and closed at 4 P.M. in November and December. The village is closed on Monday and Tuesday and also for the months of January and February. They are open on some holidays; call first.

There is a cafeteria for a casual lunch. There is also a village shop with plenty of books, postcards, and gift items relating to the theme of yesteryear. Admission is $6 for adults, $4 for children 5 to 12 and seniors, and free for children under age 5. For more information, call 516-572-8400. Unlike Manhattan, parking is plentiful.

The Nassau County Museum of Art

One Museum Drive
Roslyn Harbor, off Glen Cove Road

One of the advantages of housing an art museum on Long Island, in a mansion, is that visitors can enjoy both the works of art inside and the beautifully landscaped grounds. Nassau County's Museum of Art is in a Georgian manor that was home to Henry Clay Frick, founder of U.S. Steel. In 1969, after Frick's death, Nassau County purchased the property and earmarked it for a museum.

Today the museum mounts four major exhibits every year from their massive collection that includes the works of Lichtenstein, Rauschenberg, Raphael, Moses, Daumier, and many other highly acclaimed international artists. Nearly a quarter of a million people visit the museum every year and stroll the 145-acre preserve featuring lawns, wooded areas, ponds, and a permanent display of outdoor sculptures. The indoor/outdoor pairing of culture and nature makes visiting this museum a unique experience.

The museum is also home to an international gift shop with a variety of items including scented candles, crafts, and jewelry. A bookstore/art gallery has a wide variety of books about art, gardening, and other crafts; the art selection includes original works by Long Island artists as well as prints, posters, and postcards.

The Nassau County Museum of Art is open Tuesday through Sunday from 11 A.M. to 5 P.M. Admission is $4 for adults, $3 for seniors, and $2 for children and students. Free tours are given every day (except Sunday) at 2 P.M. For more information, call 516-484-9338.

Wineries

If you like wine, Long Island has fourteen full-time wineries and over 1,400 acres of vineyards. The island produces over three million bottles of wine annually. A winery guide book can be yours by calling 800-441-4601. You can then visit or tour any of several wineries, mostly located in the town of Cutchogue, and enjoy a taste of Chardonnay, Merlot, Blanc, or other favorites.

Old Westbury Gardens

71 Old Westbury Road, Old Westbury
(Long Island Expressway, Exit 39S, Glen Cove Road)

Nearly 90 acres of formal gardens, tree-lined walkways, ponds, and superb landscaping feature a stunning variety of plants and flowers in this magnificent garden that surrounds a mansion built in 1906. Seven original historic buildings include Westbury House, with its grand eighteenth-century architectural features. It's furnished with English antiques and decorative arts collected by the Phipps family,

Fire Island National Seashore

Over half a million visitors every year come to Fire Island, just over one hour east of New York City. The area includes several points of interest, some with tours, such as Fire Island Light Station or Sailor's Haven, which also houses a visitors center, boathouses, and a marina. There is also the William Floyd Estate, which is a museum. But the lure of Fire Island are the ocean-washed beaches, dunes, and tranquillity. And finally, there is a wildlife preserve. Call 516-289-4810 for information on Fire Island and ferry schedules.

who lived in the stately mansion for over 50 years. Tours of the house start in the foyer area and are free. The beautifully landscaped gardens surrounding the house include the Walled Garden, the Rose Garden, the Lilac Walk, and the Vegetable Garden. There is also a greenhouse, as well as a gift shop and picnic area. A small restaurant, Café in the Woods, offers sandwiches, salads, and other light fare. You can also take a free garden tour.

Old Westbury Gardens is open every day (except Tuesday) from 10 A.M. to 5 P.M. (last visitors admitted at 4 P.M.), late April through October, with later hours on weekends in the summer (until 7 P.M.). There are some November dates and holiday dates in December. Admission for the house and garden is $10 for adults, $8 for seniors, and $6 for children 6 through 12.

You can also pay less and just visit the gardens. There are lower rates in November. Call 516-333-0048 for information on rates and schedules.

You should also inquire about the special events; they include the Scottish Games, complete with bagpipes, highland dancing, and various activities and events, a Picnic Pops concert, special talks and tours, and an annual Christmas celebration. Since its opening to the public in 1959, Old Westbury has gained a reputation as one of Long Island's most popular attractions, now hosting some eighty thousand visitors annually.

Sands Point Preserve

95 Middleneck Road
Port Washington

If you want to see mansions, you'll enjoy Sands Point; it features Hempstead House, Falise, and Castlegould. Hempstead House, built in 1912, is a spectacular gold coast mansion that features a walnut paneled library, billiard room with a gold leaf ceiling, stone gargoyles, and artwork that includes stained and leaded glass, velvet draperies, and paintings by Rembrandt and Rubens. Falise was built by Harry F. Guggenheim in 1923 and has French eclectic architecture based on a thirteenth century Norman manor house. There is a cobblestone courtyard and a round tower (which sets the medieval tone), along with Renaissance paintings. Castlegould, built in 1904, is a 100,000-square-foot castle-shaped complex that contained horse stalls, blacksmith shops, an equestrian arena, and housing for some two hundred workers.

All of this is part of the elegant past that make up Sands Point Preserve in Port Washington. Hempstead House offers self-guided tours and is open Friday, Saturday, and Sunday; Falise offers guided tours and is open Wednesday through Sunday from noon to 3 P.M. Children under 10 are not admitted. Castlegould's schedule depends on current exhibitions. A visitor center and museum shop are located within. Special events and a medieval festival also take place within the preserve.

Basically, Sands Point offers a look at the high life of the past. You can enjoy a scenic and historic visit. Falise House costs $5 for adults and $4 for seniors; Hempstead House costs $2. Hours, rates, and policies vary between the buildings, so call 516-571-7900 for information.

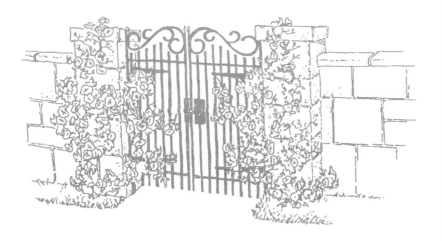

Chapter 9

A Year–Round Calendar of Events

You should have all bases covered when it comes to finding something to do in or around New York City. From sporting activities to theater, there are numerous activities and events for participants and spectators of all ages. While there is a great nightlife in the "city that never sleeps," there are also a tremendous number of activities for children and families.

Within the city itself is the greatest theater base in the country. Broadway offers over thirty shows, and there are over fifty more in off- and off-off-Broadway theaters. Culturally the city has everything you could ask for, from museums (see Chapter 5), opera, and ballet to jazz, dance, and comedy clubs. For sports fans, all major teams can be found for those who enjoy being a spectator, and players have their choice of activities from golf and bowling to space-age video and virtual reality arcades.

And then there are the annual events. New York always has something to go and see. Some of the most spectacular parades in the country march annually through the streets of Manhattan, from the Greenwich Village Halloween Parade, featuring a bizarre assortment of costumes, to the more "mainstream" leader of all New York parades—the Macy's Thanksgiving Day Parade.

Annual New York Events

There's always something going on in New York City. Here are just some of the city's fun events to watch for when in town:

JANUARY:	National Boat Show at the Jacob K. Javits Center
	Winter Antique Show at the Seventh Regiment Armory
FEBRUARY:	Chinese New Year Celebration in Chinatown
	Westminster Dog Show at Madison Square Garden
MARCH:	St. Patrick's Day Parade on Fifth Avenue (since 1762)
	Art Expo (pop art) at the Jacob K. Javits Center
	Greek Independence Day Parade on Fifth Avenue
APRIL:	Easter Parade along Fifth Avenue
	Mets baseball at Shea Stadium. (season begins)

Yankees baseball at Yankee Stadium (season begins)
Ringling Brothers & Barnum & Bailey Circus at
Madison Square Garden
Cherry Blossom Festival at Brooklyn Botanic Garden
Annual Macy's Flower Show
New York City Ballet (spring season begins)

MAY: Bike New York (a 42-mile bike tour of all five
boroughs)
Martin Luther King Jr. Parade on Fifth Avenue
Art Show in Washington Square Park, Greenwich
Village
Memorial Day Parade on Fifth Avenue

JUNE: National Puerto Rican Day Parade on Fifth Avenue
Annual AIDS Walk
The Belmont Stakes at Belmont Race Track (part
of horse racing's Triple Crown)
JVC Jazz Festival New York at Carnegie Hall,
Lincoln Center and other venues
Restaurant Week (featuring price-fixed meals in
over a hundred restaurants)
New York Philharmonic Concerts in the Park
(series begins)

JULY: Macy's Annual Fourth of July Fireworks Display
Midsummer Night Swing at Lincoln Center
(features outdoor dancing)
Summerstage Concerts in Central Park
(season begins)
Shakespeare in the Park at the Delacorte Theater
in Central Park (season begins)
American Crafts Festival in Lincoln Center

AUGUST: U.S. Open Tennis Championships at Flushing
Meadow Park in Queens
West Indian American Day Parade in Brooklyn
Harlem Week in Upper Manhattan

SEPTEMBER: Giants & Jets football across the river in
New Jersey at the Meadowlands (season begins)
The New York Philharmonic at Lincoln Center
(season begins)

If You're Planning to See a Parade

1. Arrive very early—especially for the Thanksgiving Parade and the Halloween Parade, which draw enormous crowds.
2. Take public transportation.
3. Keep a firm hold on children's hands.
4. Plan a central meeting place in case you and your group get separated.

The Metropolitan Opera at Lincoln Center (season begins)

San Gennaro Festival in Little Italy

Art Show in Washington Square Park, Greenwich Village

The New York Film Festival (season begins)

Caribbean Carnival on Eastern Parkway in Brooklyn

OCTOBER: Columbus Day Parade on Fifth Avenue

Rangers hockey at Madison Square Garden (season begins)

Islanders hockey at the Nassau Coliseum on Long Island (season begins)

The Devils hockey at the Meadowlands in New Jersey (season begins)

Halloween Parade in Greenwich Village

NOVEMBER: Veterans Day Parade down Fifth Avenue

The New York City Marathon (covers 26 miles through all five boroughs)

The Knicks basketball at Madison Square Garden (season begins)

The Nets basketball across the river at the Meadowlands in New Jersey (season begins)

Macy's Thanksgiving Day Parade

The Radio City Christmas Spectacular (season begins)

New York City Ballet (fall season begins)

DECEMBER: The lighting of the Rockefeller Center Christmas Tree

The lighting of the giant Hanukkah Menorah at Grand Army Plaza

The Nutcracker Suite at Lincoln Center

Midnight Run in Central Park on New Years Eve (sponsored by the New York Road Runners Club)

New Years Eve (ball dropping at Times Square)

As you can see, there are events galore. All major sports can be found in New York City, to watch or to play. Concert tours generally make a stop in the Big Apple, as does every circus. While Madison Square Garden is the leading Manhattan venue for big sporting events, expos and shows featuring every kind of merchandise from antiques to the latest in computers can also be found in the Big Apple. Some of these shows and exhibitions are at the Madison Square Garden exhibition area; others are at the Jacob K. Javits Convention Center. Lincoln Center (see Chapter 4) is the leading cultural center. And then there's Broadway, home to world-class theater, and off-Broadway, home to numerous other first-rate shows (more reasonably priced). There are several new off-Broadway theaters on the revamped 42nd Street between Ninth and Tenth Avenues.

For the more daring, there is even off-off-Broadway, with a host of more eclectic performances at small venues around the city. For more listings, see *Time Out New York, New York* magazine, the Arts and Leisure Section of the Sunday *New York Times* or the *Village Voice*.

In addition to all the theater in New York, you'll find clubs for music, dancing, and comedy, and there's a lot to choose from. And although they're not listed here, it's not hard to find a movie theater in New York City. Some show independent features, foreign films, or revivals of old classics; the majority show the latest box office hits (and misses). One of the more interesting movie theaters you will find is the massive SONY Theater complex on Broadway and 68th Street; it includes a 3-D IMAX theater with an eight-story screen!

Madison Square Garden

You can always check out what's going on at "the Garden"; it's very busy from fall to spring, with the Knicks and Rangers in action, and into the summer, when the New York Liberty (the great WNBA team) are in action. Depending on when you're in town, you might also catch an ice show, a concert, the circus, a dog show, a cat show, boxing, tennis matches, or any number of exciting events that take place at the Garden or in the neighboring Theater at Madison Square Garden.

See the Big Balloons

If you're not planning on braving the crowds and the cold to watch the Macy's Thanksgiving Parade (although it's worth it), you might want to get a close look at the giant balloons that will be paraded down the streets. The night prior to the parade, the balloons are inflated along Central Park West in the upper 70s. The practice of sneaking a peek at these giant balloons the night before has started to catch on in recent years—don't be surprised if crowds await.

The latest version of Madison *Square* is actually round. It is also the fourth version of the famed arena first built on 26th Street and Madison by P. T. Barnum. It was an outdoor arena that housed such events as chariot races and fire-eating exhibitions. Under a couple of other names, the arena was sold, and the name changed to Madison Square Garden in 1879.

In 1890, it was replaced by a new garden at the same location; it stood until 1925. Then came the third version of Madison Square Garden on Eighth Avenue. This marvelous arena stood for 43 years and saw the birth of the Knicks, bike races, track and field, Rangers hockey, concerts, and, of course, the celebrated visits of the circus, among other events.

Finally, in 1968, the Garden closed. "Long live the Garden!" was the cry as the new garden, number four, took its place. The giant round structure between Seventh and Eighth Avenues and bordering on 31st and 33rd Streets sits over Penn Station and sports the main rotunda, an office tower, and the Theater at Madison Square Garden, formerly known as the Felt Forum.

Just over 30 years old, the Garden has been home to some of the biggest boxing matches over the years, including the classic Frazier-Ali championship fight in '71. The Garden has been home to the *Wizard of Oz* on Ice, Disney on Ice, championship skaters, awards shows such as the Grammys, political conventions, and concerts by the Rolling Stones, Bruce Springsteen, Michael Jackson, Led Zeppelin, Frank Sinatra, Elvis Presley, and so on. In fact, the Grateful Dead hold the record, having played fifty-two shows at the Garden over a span of 15 years. Also worth noting is that the National Horse Show, the Westminster Kennel Club Dog Show, and Barnum's circus (now, of course, Ringling Brothers Barnum & Bailey) played in all four variations of Madison Square Garden over the more than one hundred years that it has been the leading home for events in New York City.

If you visit the Garden today, as over five million people do annually for events, as you enter from the Seventh Avenue side

you'll see a wall with names of famous people who've appeared at the Garden, along with a sporting goods store and entrances to Penn Station below. You'll also find a number of ticket scalpers for sold-out performances. Ticket scalping is illegal in New York City. Besides the possibility of being arrested, you also run the possibility of buying phony tickets. Ticket prices are high enough for most events without paying extra to scalpers (and for bail)!

Inside the main arena, you'll notice a wealth of luxury boxes overhead. The scoreboard hangs at center court, or center ice, depending on when you are there, and includes the latest in "Diamond Vision" features. There is plenty to eat from food courts and vendors; the prices are high!

For information including box office info, call 212-465-6741. For information on seating for people with disabilities, call 212-465-6034 (the Garden is wheelchair accessible). Most events also are sold through Ticketmaster at 212-307-4100. Along with the main arena, there is also the Theater at Madison Square Garden. The theater has been home to productions of the *Wizard of Oz*, *A Christmas Carol*, numerous concerts, and various other events.

You can also take a tour of Madison Square Garden. The All Access Tour takes an hour and features the behind-the-scenes inner workings of the twenty-thousand seat garden, including Knicks and Rangers locker rooms, luxury suites, the "walk of fame," and much more. Tours are given Monday through Saturday hourly from 10 A.M. to 3 p.m. and Sunday from 11 A.M. to 3 p.m. (Tour information is subject to change depending on what's going on at the garden.) Tours cost $14 for adults and $12 for children 12 and under. You can buy tickets at the Garden box office. You can also grab a bite at the Play by Play Restaurant. Billed as the "World's Most Famous Arena," the Garden is worth visiting, even if it's just a look from the outside.

Broadway: The Great White Way

A Broadway musical can set a family back a few hundred dollars, but it's one of those rare treats you'll always remember. The long running *Cats* is literally packed with "memories"; for story and pizzazz you can see the *Lion King*; for more great family fare, you

The Jacob K. Javits Convention Center

This massive, modern, glass-enclosed, 14-year-old complex stretches over 20 acres on the West Side of Manhattan and houses some 900,000 square feet of exhibit space. The building, which occupies five blocks of Manhattan's West Side (655 West 34th Street between Eleventh and Twelfth Avenues), houses trade shows and commercial shows of all kinds (such as the New York Boat Show). It is lit from within at night and practically glows. For more information, call 212-216-2000.

Half-Price Tickets For Broadway Shows

Between Broadway and Seventh Avenue at 47th Street, on Duffy Square, is the TKTS booth. It usually has a good selection of hit shows available.

Tickets for evening performances start selling at 3 P.M. and for matinees at 10 A.M., so you should get there early. However, close to curtain time, you might find last-minute tickets available. Also, weeknights are better than weekends, and Wednesday matinees are a good time to get better seats for more popular shows. TKTS does not accept credit cards.

There is a second TKTS booth at the World Trade Center at 2 World Trade Center Plaza on the mezzanine level. It is open weekdays from 11 A.M. to 5:30 P.M. and on Saturday from 11 A.M. to 3:30 P.M.

can see *Beauty & the Beast. New York* magazine, among other publications, will fill you in on the shows, as will the concierge in any good hotel. It's not hard to find out what shows are the talk of the town. Whether you enjoy musicals or dramas, there's always a selection of first-rate shows available. The theater in New York City is a captivating experience.

Recent years have seen few new ventures opening on Broadway. The great expense of putting on a production is more than most backers are willing to gamble on. Classics like *Annie Get Your Gun*, the *Sound of Music*, and *Cabaret* have returned, along with the marvelous dancing in the former Tony winner *Chicago* and the intense drama of the *Iceman Cometh* and *Death of a Salesman*. And then there's *Footloose* and, for those who didn't spend enough money in the discos in the late '70s, *Saturday Night Fever*. Meanwhile, *Les Miserables*, *Miss Saigon*, and Andrew Lloyd Webber's *Phantom of the Opera* continued to thrive. While *Les Mis* may be a bit heavy for kids, musicals in general are a wonderful entertainment experience for all ages.

Despite the high prices, Broadway has enjoyed a tremendous resurgence in recent years. Marketing on busses, TV, and even milk containers has promoted the idea of taking in a Broadway show to a much wider audience. No longer is "the theater" a pastime for only the well to do. Discount tickets can be obtained for many shows. For the most popular ones, you'll still need to plan ahead. If you can afford it, a Broadway show is something you should plan on.

To order tickets by phone, call Tele-charge at 212-239-6200 (800-432-7250 from outside New York City) or Ticketmaster at 212-307-4100. The theater shows are divided between the two ticket companies, so if tickets for the show you want to see are not sold at one, they will most likely be sold at the other. A surcharge is added per ticket. In some cases, you can call the theater box office. You can also go to the box office directly, but you would be better trying the TKTS booth when you get to the city.

Hotels and Tickets

The concierge in any major hotel should be able to help you buy tickets for a show or an event. While they do not sell tickets, they may know ticket brokers who do. There are legal brokers in the city, and although they charge higher prices, they can get tickets for hard-to-get shows and events. The largest broker in New York City is Golden Leblangs; call 212-944-8910. With booths in eight major hotels, Golden Leblangs features Broadway and off-Broadway shows, sporting events, and more. For some shows, you need to be a guest of the hotel, but in most cases, they'll get you tickets. Other hotels have ticket booths as well.

Besides the great shows, the ambiance of the theaters themselves is first rate. Plush seating, chandeliers, and ornate overhanging balconies are part of the architecture of these marvelous old structures that have been painstakingly remodeled. The theaters around Broadway have housed the greatest plays of the twentieth century. In addition to the shows mentioned already, there are others slated for the year 2000 that may run, depending on reviews. They include the Cole Porter musical *Kiss Me, Kate*, a new Broadway musical called *Martin Guerre*, the *Night They Raided Minsky's*, another production of *Oliver!*, Noel Coward's *Waiting in the Wings*, the old *Rainmaker*, and Stephen Sondheim's *Wise Guys*. Also, *Amadeus* has recently returned.

Broadway theaters include the following:

Ambassador Theater, built in 1921, is at 215 West 49th
Street. Call 212-735-0500 or Tele-charge.

Barrymore Theater opened in 1928 and was once home to
Streetcar Named Desire with Marlon Brando. It's at 243
West 47th Street. Call Tele-charge.

Bellasco Theater is at 111 West 44th Street. Call Tele-charge.

Booth Theater, built in 1913 with a stage door in Shubert
Alley, is at 222 West 45th Street. Call Tele-charge.

Broadhurst Theater, built in 1918, is at 235 West 44th Street.
Call Tele-charge.

Broadway Theatre, home of the long-running *Miss Saigon*, is
at 1681 Broadway. Call Tele-charge.

Brooks Atkinson Theater, built in 1926, is at 256 West 47th
Street. Call 212-719-4099.

Cort Theater is at 138 West 48th Street. Call Tele-charge.

Eugene O'Neill Theater opened in 1925 at 230 West 49th
Street. Call Tele-charge.

Ford Center for the Performing Arts is the marvelous
new theater built to resemble two great New York theaters,
the Lyric and the Apollo. It's currently home to the hit
show *Ragtime*. It's at 213-215 West 42nd Street.
Call 212-582-4100.

Gershwin Theater, most recent home to the flying *Peter
Pan*, is at 222 West 51st Street. Call 212-586-6510 or
Ticketmaster.

John Golden Theater, is at 252 West 54th Street.
Call Tele-charge.

Helen Hayes Theater was built in 1912 and named for
Helen Hayes in 1983. It's at 240 West 44th Street.
Call 212-944-9450.

Imperial Theater, longtime home to *Les Miserables*, is at
249 West 45th Street. Call Tele-charge.

Longacre Theater, built in 1913, is at 220 West 48th Street.
Call Tele-charge.

Lunt-Fontanne Theater, built in 1910, is at 205 West 46th
Street. Call 212-575-9200.

Majestic Theater, built in 1927, has been home to *Phantom of the Opera* for more than a decade at 247 West 44th Street. Call Tele-charge.

Marquis Theater is a large modern venue that sits in the Marriott Marquis Hotel and currently is home to *Annie Get Your Gun*. It's at 1535 Broadway between 45th and 46th Streets. Call Ticketmaster.

Martin Beck Theater, built in 1924, saw the recent return of the *Sound of Music*. It's at 302 West 45th Street. Call Tele-charge.

Minskoff Theater, a modern technically innovative theater, has most recently become home to *Saturday Night Fever*. It's at 200 West 45th Street. Call 212-869-0550.

Music Box was built by Irving Berlin and opened in 1921. It's at 239 West 45th Street. Call Tele-charge.

Nederlander Theater has been home to one of the '90s hits, *Rent*, for several years. It's at 208 East 41st Street. Call Tele-charge.

Neil Simon Theater was built in 1927 and renamed for one of Broadway's legendary playwrights. It's at 250 West 52nd Street. Call Ticketmaster.

New Amsterdam Theater, a grand theater built in 1903, with an elaborate interior, was refurbished by Disney and is now home to *Lion King*. It's at 214 West 42nd Street. Call Ticketmaster.

Palace Theater, a vaudeville institution in the '20s and modern home to musicals, is at 1564 Broadway. Call 212-730-8200 or Ticketmaster.

Plymouth Theater, is at 236 West 45th Street. Call Tele-charge.

Richard Rogers Theater, built in 1925, was renamed for the legendary Rogers in 1990 and is home to *Footloose*. It's at 226 West 46th Street. Call 212-221-1211.

Royale Theater is probably best remembered as the longtime home of the hit show *Grease* (no longer playing). It's at 242 West 45th Street. Call Tele-charge.

St. James Theater was the home to the original *King and I*. It's at 246 West 44th Street. Call 212-239-6200.

Original Cast CDs at Tele-charge

Believe it or not, Tele-charge not only sells tickets for shows but also sells the original soundtrack CDs. They even offer discounts on hotel rooms! Call 212-239-6000.

Shubert Theater, just off the famous theater stomping ground Shubert Alley, was built in 1913 at 225 West 45th Street. Call Tele-charge.

Studio 54, on 54th Street, most recently home to *Cabaret*, is less known as a Broadway Theater than as the famed disco of the late '70s and early '80s. It's at 254 West 54th Street. Call Tele-Charge.

Virginia Theater can be found at 245 West 52nd Street. Call Tele-charge.

Walter Kerr Theater, sporting beautiful architecture, opened in 1921 and was restored in the '80s. It's at 219 West 48th Street. Call Tele-charge.

Winter Garden, built in 1911, has run the gamut from Al Jolson to the long-running *Cats*. It's at 1634 Broadway. Call 212-239-6200 or Tele-charge.

Off-Broadway theaters include the following:

Actor's Playhouse is at 100 Seventh Avenue. Call 212-239-6200.

Astor Place Theater is at 434 Lafayette Street. Call 212-254-4370.

Atlantic Theater is at 336 West 20th Street. Call Tele-charge.

Castillo Theater is at 500 Greenwich Street. Call 212-941-1234.

Century Center Theater is at 111 East 15th Street. Call Tele-charge.

Cherry Lane Theater is at 38 Commerce Street. Call 212-727-3673 or Tele-charge.

Chicago City Limits Theater is at 1105 First Avenue. Call 212-888-LAFF, for improv comedy at its best.

Circle in the Square is at 1633 Broadway. Call Tele-charge.

Classic Stage Company is at 136 East 13th Street. Call 212-677-4210.

Daryl Roth Theater is at 20 Union Square. Call Tele-charge.

Douglas Fairbanks Theater is at 432 West 42nd Street. Call 212-239-4321 or Tele-charge.

Duffy Theater is at 1553 Broadway. Call Ticketmaster.

Ensemble Studio Theater is at 549 West 52nd Street. It features one-act plays by new writers. Call 212-247-4982.

Gramercy Theater is at 127 East 23rd Street.
Call 212-719-1300.

Here Arts Center is at 145 Sixth Avenue.
Call 212-647-0202.

Ibis Supper Club is at 321 West 44th Street.
Call Tele-charge.

Irish Repertory Theater is at 132 West
22nd Street. Call 212-727-2732.

Kit Kat Klub is at 124 West 43rd Street.
Call Tele-charge.

Jane Street Theater is at 113 Jane Street, Hotel
Riverview. Call Tele-charge.

**Joseph Papp Public Theater/New York Shakespeare
Festival** is at 425 Lafayette Street. Call 212-260-2400.

Joyce Theater is at 175 Eighth Avenue. Call 212-242-0800.

The Loft Theater is at 136 Duane Street. Call 212-732-9908.

Lucille Lortel Theater is at 121 Christopher Street.
Call Tele-charge.

Manhattan Playhouse is at 439 West 49th Street.
Call 212-245-7798.

Manhattan Theater Club, City Center is at 131-55th Street.
Call 212-581-1212.

MCC Theater is at 120 West 28th Street. Call 212-727-7765.

Nada 45 is at 445 West 45th Street. Call 212-502-0868.

New Dramatists is at 424 West 44th Street. It features one-act
plays. Call 212-757-6960.

Orpheum Theater, longtime home of the dance show
Stomp, is at 126 Second Avenue. Call 212-477-2477 or
Ticketmaster.

Playhouse 91, developed by the 92nd Street "Y," featuring
Jewish-related plays by the Jewish Repertory Theater, is at
316 East 91st Street. Call 212-996-1100.

Performing Garage is at 33 Wooster Street. Call 212-966-3651.

Phil Bosakowski Theater is at 354 West 45th Street.
Call 212-279-4200.

Playwrights Horizons, home of the annual Young
Playwrights series, featuring great works by kids, is at 416
West 42nd Street. Call 212-279-4200.

Promenade Theater is at 2162 Broadway. Call 212-580-1313.

P.S. 122, featuring performance art and more, is at 150 First Avenue. Call 212-477-5288.

Riant Theater is at 161 Hudson Street. Call 212-925-8353.

Rio's Supper Club, featuring murder mysteries, is at 393 Eight Avenue. Call 800-MURDER-INC.

Roundabout Theater Company is at 1530 Broadway. Call 212-869-8400.

Second Stage Theater is at 307 West 43rd Street. Call 212-246-4422.

SoHo Playhouse is at 15 Vandam Street. Call 212-921-9341.

Stardust Theater, featuring "Forbidden Broadway," is at 51st Street and Broadway. Call Tele-charge.

Sullivan Street Playhouse, home to the *Fantasticks*, the longest running musical in the city, and probably the world, is at 181 Sullivan Street. Call 212-674-3838.

Theater Four is at 424 West 55th Street. Call Tele-charge.

13th Street Repertory Company is at 50 West 13th Street. Call 212-675-6677.

Triad Theater is at 158 West 72nd Street. Call 212-799-4599.

Ubu Repertory Theater, Florence Gould Hall, is at 55 East 59th Street. Call 212-355-6160.

Union Square Theater is at 100 East 17th Street. Call Ticketmaster.

Vivian Beaumont Theater is at 150 West 65th Street in Lincoln Center. Call Tele-charge.

Westside Theater is at 407 West 43rd Street. Call Tele-charge.

Television Shows in New York!

TV Shows are free if you want to watch a taping. The problem is that tickets are **very** hard to get for most shows. Below are some phone numbers that will provide the information on tickets. Most shows do not allow children under 18, so, if you get a real person on the phone, ask what the cutoff is. Shows also have standby policies whereby you can spend a great portion of your

day on-line in hopes of getting one of the few tickets that become available prior to taping. Or you could do something more productive with your day and then watch the show on TV that night or the following night.

Among the growing number of shows taped in New York City are the following:

Cosby, one of New York's only sitcoms, is taped in Queens. Call 718-706-5389.

Spin City is essentially the only other current New York-based sitcom that has lasted. Call 212-336-6993.

The Daily Show stars Jon Stewart and includes pre-taped segments. Call 212-468-1700.

The Late Show with David Letterman, which tapes at the famous old Ed Sullivan Theater on Broadway and 53rd, is the best TV taping in the city and hardest to get tickets for. Send a postcard at least six months ahead. Call 212-975-1003 or try the Web site at www.cbs.com.

Late Night with Conan O'Brien tapes at 30 Rockefeller Plaza. Send a postcard many months in advance; this show is also a very hot item. Call 212-664-3056.

Saturday Night Live will accept postcard ticket requests. Write to the show care of NBC Studios, 30 Rockefeller Plaza, New York, N.Y. 10112. The card must be postmarked in August. Tickets are given out by a lottery system.

Other shows taping with a studio audience include MTV's Tom Greene Show, the Rosie O'Donnell Show, and Live with Regis and Kathy Lee.

If you don't feel like chasing after tickets to New York's few hot TV tapings, you can always stroll by the Good Morning America studios on the corner of 44th and Broadway, the Today Show across from 30 Rock on 49th Street, or The Early Show on 59th and Fifth Avenue. The glass-enclosed studios let you watch while they do the show, and when you've had enough, you can simply stroll away.

New York but Not New York

Although *The Honeymooners* and *The Cosby Show* were taped in New York, many other shows have made it look like they were based in New York. Among the most popular pseudo New York City sitcoms have been:

- *Seinfeld*
- *Friends*
- *Taxi*
- *All in the Family*
- *The Nanny*
- *The Jeffersons*
- *Maude*
- *Barney Miller*

Family Fun: 50 Places to Go with Kids in the City

You've probably already thought of the Statue of Liberty, the Empire State Building, Central Park, FAO Schwarz, and some of the city's other sights for the whole family. Following is a list of places you may not have considered.

Adventureland Amusement Park and Arcade. Okay, it's not in the city, but it's a fun amusement park, without all the hoopla and long lines of massive places like Great Adventure. Plenty of standard fun rides for kids of all ages including a roller coaster, bumper cars, and bumper boats, as well as many choices for the little ones. There are also over 200 games and attractions in the arcade. Also featured are a restaurant and miniature golf course. Long Island's favorite amusement park is at 2245 Route 110, East Farmingdale, New York (Long Island Expressway, exit 49). Call 516-694-6868.

American Museum of Natural History features something for all ages. It is truly an exciting experience and worth the admission to watch the expression on your youngster's face when he or she looks up at the giant dinosaurs. It's in Central Park at West 79th Street (you can't miss it). Call 212-769-5100. (See Chapter 5.)

American Museum of the Moving Image features the history of film and TV, with a wide range of exhibits that even include video games! The museum is at 36-01 35th Avenue in Astoria Queens. Call 718-784-4777. (See Chapter 8.)

Aquarium for Wildlife Conservation is New York City's only aquarium. It is in Brooklyn, on Surf Avenue in Coney Island, and offers a marvelous look at sharks, whales, sea lions, penguins, and anything else that lives in or around water. There's a Discovery Cove for kids to pet sea creatures (no not sharks!). Call 718-265-3400. (See Chapter 8.)

Asphalt Green is a former asphalt storage facility that some forward thinking entrepreneur turned into a major play location featuring 74,000 square feet of aquatics, sports, and fitness facilities. There's a large pool, running track, gym, and much more, for children and adults! It's at 555 East 90th Street at East End Drive, further east than York Avenue. Call 212-369-8890.

Barnes & Noble has several super-stores scattered around Manhattan, including one on the Upper West Side at Broadway and 82nd Street, another on West 66th and Broadway, one on East 86th Street, one in the Citicorp Building on 51st and Third, and one in the Village. These are marvelous super-stores for all ages. They are terrific places to interest youngsters in books; you can read to them there (and sometimes there are readings and activities for children offered). They can also select from an incredible array of children's books. It's a fun place for families to browse or simply sit and read for a while.

The Beach! New York City has several, although none are in Manhattan. The Bronx has Orchard Beach and Boardwalk (718-885-2275). Brooklyn has Brighton Beach/Coney Island (718-946-1350) and Manhattan Beach (718-946-1373). Queens is home to Rockaway Beach and Boardwalk (718-318-4000). Staten Island is home to South and Midland Beaches (718-987-1709) and Wolfe's Pond Beach (718-984-8266). And there are the many Long Island beaches, including Jones, Fire Island, and Robert Moses State Park. (See Chapter 8.)

Beauty & the Beast, is now featured at the Lunt Fontanne Theater on West 46t Street. It's one of the best family shows of all time. Call 212-575-9200.

Big Apple Circus is dedicated to classical circus acts. It is a one-ring circus under a big-top tent, featuring world renowned acrobats, clowns, aerialists, tightrope walkers, jugglers, hoop divers, and more. Also in the lineup are some dogs, birds, horses, and elephants. The international circus rolls into town in May and can be found in Queens at Cunningham Park and, later in the month, on Long Island at Long Island University's C.W. Post Campus. The extravaganza hits Manhattan in October at Damrosch Park, behind Lincoln Center on West 65th Street. On a smaller, more personal scale than Ringling Brothers, Big Apple Circus lets you get closer to the action. Call 212-268-2500.

Big City Kites is a shop at Lexington Avenue and 82nd Street that sells a couple hundred varieties of kites. They'll show you how to make kites and tell you how to fly them. It's a fun store to drop by. And if you do buy one, there's a place called Central Park just three blocks away. Call 212-472-2623.

Brooklyn Botanic Gardens includes a beautiful, fun-for-all-ages children's garden and much more. It's located at 1000 Washington Avenue. Call 718-623-7200. (See Chapter 8.)

Brooklyn Children's Museum has a unique water tunnel, multicultural artifacts, ethno-musical instruments, and much more. It's at 145 Brooklyn Avenue. Call 718-735-4407. (See Chapter 8.)

Bronx Zoo, Wildlife Conservatory, one of the most spectacular zoos in the world, features thousands of animals on over 265 acres. (See Chapter 8.)

Chelsea Piers features a host of activities on the 30-acre piers, including skating, batting cages, basketball, and golf. It's at 23rd Street and Hudson River. Call 212-236-6666.

Children's Museum of the Arts in SoHo, 182 Lafayette Street, has a ball pond, "Magnetic Masterpieces." and many activities for children under ten. Call 212-274-0986.

The Children's Museum of Manhattan has several floors of hands-on exhibits and fun/learning activities including a children's TV studio, story reading, and more. It's at 212 West 83rd Street. Call 212-721-1223. (See Chapter 5.)

A Christmas Carol, at the Theater at Madison Square Garden, starts late in November. It's an entertaining version of the old favorite. Call 212-465-6741.

The Columbus Day Parade is an annual Columbus Day event and has been for over 50 years. It begins on 44th Street and goes to 79th on Fifth Avenue. Get there early!

Coney Island, in Brooklyn, is a great place to visit. Walk the boardwalk, enjoy the beach, visit Astroland amusement park, and have lunch at Nathans. (See Chapter 8.)

The Disney Store, on 42nd Street and Seventh Avenue, is New York's home base for Mickey, Minnie, Hercules, Belle, and all your favorites on everything from clothing to dishes, notebooks, and everything else, including stuffed animals, books, and more. Call 212-221-0430. Disney stores are also on Columbus and 66th Street and 55th and Fifth.

Forbes Magazine Galleries, with toy soldiers, games, and model boats on display, is an enjoyable place for kids (and their parents) to browse. It's at 62 Fifth Avenue at 12th Street. Call 212-206-5548. (See Chapter 7.)

Fun Station USA is an indoor amusement park and arcade in Staten Island that includes everything from batting cages and basketball courts to a soft play area and kiddie rides for the smaller ones. It's at 3555 Victory Boulevard on Staten Island. Call 718-370-0077.

Green Meadows Children's Farm in Floral Park (just over the Queens border) has a farm with a guided tour and allows animal petting. It's also a place for a hay ride, a pony ride, and an opportunity to milk a cow (something not often found in New York City). It's located at 73-50 Little Neck Parkway (Long Island Expressway, exit 32). Call 718-470-0224.

Hackers, Hitters, and Hoops, at 123 West 18th Street, has space-age basketball, wall climbing, batting cages, and even video games for you couch potatoes. It's not inexpensive, but there's plenty to do. Call 212-929-7482.

Intrepid Sea-Air-Space Museum, in the Hudson River off Pier 86, lets you walk along and inside a modern aircraft carrier and other boats, including a submarine. It's at Pier 86 and 12th Avenue. Call 212-245-0072. (See Chapter 5.)

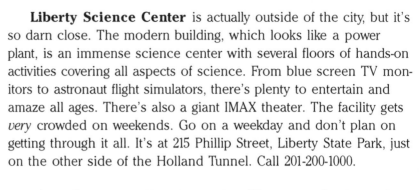

Liberty Science Center is actually outside of the city, but it's so darn close. The modern building, which looks like a power plant, is an immense science center with several floors of hands-on activities covering all aspects of science. From blue screen TV monitors to astronaut flight simulators, there's plenty to entertain and amaze all ages. There's also a giant IMAX theater. The facility gets *very* crowded on weekends. Go on a weekday and don't plan on getting through it all. It's at 215 Phillip Street, Liberty State Park, just on the other side of the Holland Tunnel. Call 201-200-1000.

Lion King, at the New Amsterdam Theater, on 214 West 42nd Street, is a fabulous show. But it's hard to get tickets! Call Ticketmaster or, better yet, try a ticket broker.

Little Shop of Plaster is a fun-filled activity center where you can buy a plaster item, paint it, and have it baked—for a fabulous finish. You can also design T-shirts. Two locations are at 431 East 73rd Street between York and First and on the West Side at 106 West 90th between Columbus and Amsterdam. Call (East Side) 212-717-6636 or (West Side) 212-877-9771.

Macy's Thanksgiving Day Parade is one of the city's most spectacular annual parades. It begins at Central Park West at 77th Street, goes down Broadway to Macy's Herald Square, and finishes at Seventh Avenue. Where else can you find the Rockettes, Santa, giant balloons, marching bands, name performers, and more? Get there very early. Call 212-494-4495.

Nellie Bly Amusement Park, in Brooklyn, features many rides, including a roller coaster, giant water ride, bumper cars, and more, plus a petting farms, arcade, miniature golf, and plenty of other fun things for kids of all ages. It's at 1824 Shore Parkway at 26th Avenue. Call 718-996-4002.

New Victory Theater, built in 1900, was among the first of the revitalization projects of 42nd Street in 1995. Now it features a wide variety of shows for children, from a flying circus to presentations by the Children's Television Workshop to various theatrical productions. It's at 209 West 42nd Street. Call Tele-charge.

New York City Fire Museum features exhibits on everything to do with fire fighting, from classic old fire engines to toys. It's fun for kids and interesting for adults. The museum is located at 278 Spring Street. Call 212-691-1303. (See Chapter 5.)

New York Hall of Science, in Flushing Meadow Park at 111th Street, in Queens, has plenty of hands-on exhibits and a science playground, and it's less crowded than the Liberty Science Center in New Jersey. Call 718-699-0005. (See Chapter 8.)

The Nutcracker Suite visits Lincoln Center every holiday season. It's a marvelous performance for all ages. Call 212-875-5000. (See Chapter 4.)

Our Name Is Mud is a hands-on store where kids of all ages can paint handmade ceramics at a paint bar. It's a fun store and has three locations: 59 Greenwich Street at Seventh Avenue (212-647-7899), 1566 Second Avenue by 81st Street (212-570-6868) and 506 Amsterdam Avenue between 84th and 85th Streets (212-579-5575).

Playspace, on Broadway and 92nd Street, offers a fun-filled and safe indoor playground environment with a wealth of things to do for kids under six. It's well run and marvelous on a rainy day, although it can get crowded. It's pay to play. There are snack foods available. Call 212-769-2300.

Prospect Park Wildlife Center is a fun zoo in Brooklyn. There are over 150 animals—including a large exhibit of hamadryas baboons—in three main exhibit areas. It's located at Flatbush Avenue and Empire Boulevard. (See Chapter 8.)

Queens Wildlife Center, in Flushing Meadow Park, is a fun zoo with 250 animals in natural habitats. Along with the big animals, there are some smaller, gentler ones in a petting section. It's at 53-51 111th Street at 54th Avenue. Call 718-271-1500. (See Chapter 8.)

The Radio City Christmas Spectacular has been going strong for over 65 years. Complete with the "Parade of the Wooden Soldiers" and the "Living Nativity," it's an exciting seasonal spectacle. If you're in town between November and early January, it's worth seeing. Call 212-247-4777.

Ringling Brothers & Barnum & Bailey Circus hits Madison Square Garden every spring. After well over one hundred years, it's still "the Greatest Show on Earth." It features a full-fledged extravaganza with three rings of animals, clowns, and jugglers, plus acrobats swinging overhead. Stuff your face with cotton candy and enjoy. Call the Madison Square Garden box office at 212-465-6741 for information—as the spring approaches.

Rockefeller Center ice skating, below the fabulous tree in December and in the shadow of 30 Rock, is fun all winter long. Call 212-332-7654.

Roosevelt Island Aerial Tram is actually a mode of transportation from Manhattan to the tiny island in the East River. Besides transporting commuters at rush hour, it also serves as a fun 5-minute ride high over the river for $3 per person (round trip). The tram is at 59th Street and Second Avenue, and it runs on a regular schedule. Call 212-832-4555.

Shea Stadium, home to the Mets, is located just north of Flushing Meadow Park in Queens. There's nothing like taking in a baseball game. Besides, baseball games are still much easier to get tickets to than the winter sports, football, hockey, and basketball, and less expensive and fun for the whole family. Call 718-507-TIXX for tickets.

South Street Seaport has a variety of old sailing vessels, some of which you can take a ride on. From the Maritime Museum to the stores, restaurants, cobblestone streets, and outdoor entertainment, there's something for everyone at the Seaport. (See Chapter 4.)

The Staten Island Ferry, like the Roosevelt Island Tram, provides a means of transportation for millions of riders every year. It is also a fun, free way to see the Statue of Liberty and New York Harbor while relaxing and enjoying the 20-minute ride. You can then either take in Snug Harbor, Historic Richmond Town, or one of the other sights on Staten Island. Call 718-390-5253.

Staten Island Zoo is home to a South American tropical forest, a children's center, a New England farm setting, an African Savannah exhibit, and an aquarium with sharks. It's all at 614 Broadway in Barrat Park in West Brighton. Call 718-442-3100. (See Chapter 8.)

Snug Harbor Cultural Center features historic buildings, concerts, a botanical garden, and the Staten Island Children's Museum, which is on the premises and features numerous interactive exhibits. It's at 1000 Richmond Terrace. Call 718-273-8200. (See Chapter 8.)

TADA! Theater, with just under a hundred seats, features performances for kids and their families, presented by kids ages 6 through 17. The theater is at 120 West 28th Street between Sixth and Seventh Avenues. Call 212-627-1732.

XS New York is an interactive event center located on Seventh Avenue between 41st and 42nd Streets. It's for older kids, and their parents, with three floors of virtual simulation and hi-tech video games, plus a cyber bar and café. There's a laser tag team area, hydraulic lift, and DJ booth. If you're in the Times Square area, it's a fun stop. Just walk in and play. Games range from $1 to $5. XS New York is open Sunday to Thursday from 11 A.M. to midnight and Friday and Saturday until 2 A.M. It does get crowded. Call 212-398-5467.

Yankee Stadium is home to baseball's most historically successful franchise. While many games sell out, you can often get tickets on weeknights throughout the summer (depending on what team is visiting) and more likely on a weekday afternoon. Just being in the classic stadium is exciting, no matter whether you're a fan or not. For ticket information, call 212-307-1212 or 212-293-6000. (See Chapter 8.)

Chelsea Piers: Infamous in History

The piers are also noted in history books as being associated with two of the most famous ship-based disasters. The *Titanic* was scheduled to arrive on April 16, 1912. On April 20, 1912, those passengers who survived the shipwreck arrived at Chelsea Piers. In May of 1915, the *Lusitania* departed from Chelsea Piers. It was later torpedoed by a German U-boat, killing nearly two thousand people.

Chelsea Piers

Today Chelsea Piers is one of Manhattan's few indoor facilities for sports enthusiasts. It was designed by the architectural firm of Warren and Westmore, who were also busy designing Grand Central Terminal at the same time. Originally opened in 1910, after 8 years of construction, it would serve as an active port for some 50 years. In fact, it was the city's premier passenger ship terminal. During World Wars I and II, it was an embarkation point for soldiers, and during the 1950s and 1960s, it served as a cargo terminal.

Unfortunately, after the 1960s, the piers were neglected and forgotten, as was much of Manhattan's waterfront. The Piers were scheduled for demolition to make way for the Westway Plan, a major highway project that never materialized. In May of 1992, a newly formed company, Chelsea Piers Management, submitted a bid and proposal to the state Department of Transportation to develop and operate a sports and entertainment facilities on the premises. In May of 1994, the final building permits were granted. Thus, the foundation was set for what is now New York City's biggest and most popular sports facility. You can find the action on the piers at 23rd Street and the Hudson River. Call 212 336-6200.

Here are some of the many activities available at the Piers:

Pier 59: Golf Club (212-336-6400); Golf Academy—schools, clinics, and lessons (212-336-6444)
Between Piers 59 and 60: AMF Bowl (212-835-2695)
Pier 61: Sky Rink—ice skating and skate rental (212-336-6100)
Pier 62: Field House—batting cages, open gym, rock climbing, basketball courts, playing fields, open toddler gym (212-336-6500)
Pier 62: Roller Rink, skate boarding, including rentals; private instruction available

Sports for All Ages

While the Chelsea Piers offers skating, a driving range, and much more, there are also a number of other places to play in the city. Below are a just a few places where you can find some popular sporting activities in Manhattan.

Basketball City is New York's premier indoor basketball facility, with six full-sized courts in an air conditioned environment. You can come and play on weekdays and sign up for session play on weekends (group play). While numerous playgrounds all over the city have courts, it's fun to play indoors on a first-rate court, particularly in the cold of winter or during the humid 90 degree summer days. Call 212-924-4040.

Bicycles can be rented in Central Park at the Loeb Boathouse. Call 212-861-4137. Metro Bicycle Stores rent bikes at several locations including these:

- Lexington Avenue and 88th Street (212-427-4450)
- 360 West 47th Street at Ninth Avenue (212-581-4500)
- 96th Street and Broadway (212-663-7531)
- 14th Street between First and Second Avenues (212-228-4344)
- Sixth Avenue and 15th Street (212-255-5100)
- Sixth Avenue between Canal and Grand (212-334-8000)

You can also rent bikes at these places:

- Pedal Pusher, Second Avenue between 68th and 69th Streets (212-722-2201)
- Larry & Jeff's Bicycles Plus, Second Avenue between 87th and 88th Streets (212-722-2201)
- Toga Bike Shop, West End Avenue and 64th Street (212-799-9625)
- Gotham Bikes, 116 West Broadway (212-732-2453)

Bowling in Manhattan can be found at Leisure Time Bowling & Recreation Center at Port Authority on 42nd Street and Eighth Avenue and at Bowlmor at 110 University Place—which features a 42-lane bi-level facility. Other alleys can be found throughout the boroughs.

Horseback riding in Central Park is possible thanks to Claremont Stables on West 89th Street. Call 212-724-5100.

Ice skating can be found at Lasker Rink and Wollman Rink in Central Park and the other Wollman Rink in Prospect Park in

Golf on Another Island

Randalls Island, just off the Bronx, near Manhattan, tucked away under the Triborough Bridge, is home to Family Golf. It includes a golf range, miniature golf, golf shop, batting cages, and more. Call 212-427-5689 for information.

Brooklyn. And don't forget the rinks at Rockefeller Center and Chelsea Piers.

In-line skating and rollerblading is most popular in Central Park and at the Chelsea Piers.

Indoor rock climbing can be found at the Extra Vertical Climbing Club at 61 West 62nd Street. You can scale 30- to 50-foot walls! Call 212-586-5718.

Tennis courts are available in Central Park near 94th Street. Call 212-280-0206. The rates are $5 per hour per person. There are also a number of tennis facilities that are more costly. Many cater only to members. A couple that are available to nonmembers are Crosstown Tennis at 14 West 31st Street (212-947-5780) and Midtown Tennis Club at 341 Eighth Avenue (212-989-8572).

Golf is not available in Manhattan, but there are some fourteen courses for public play in the boroughs. Call in advance, prepare to use a handcart on most courses, and prepare to wait—these city courses get crowded. Hint: Go in the afternoon and play at 2 or 2:30. It's less crowded. Most courses are well kept, though not overly challenging.

The city courses in the boroughs include the following:

- **Clearview Golf Course**, on Willets Point Boulevard in Bayside, Queens, is a flat wide-open course—your basic walk in the park. It's a pleasant, if not very challenging, course for the better golfers. Call 718-229-2570.
- **Douglaston Golf Course**, on Marathon Parkway in Douglaston, Queens, is situated just off the Long Island Expressway. It provides some nice views of Manhattan in the distance. The hilly course is short, with lots of par threes, but it's entertaining. Call 718-224-6566.
- **Dyker Beach Golf Course,** on 86th Street and Seventh Avenue in Brooklyn, is a short but fun course with tree-lined fairways. Nothing fancy, but pleasant. Call 718-836-9722.

- **Forest Park Golf Course**, on Park Lane in Forest Park, Queens, is appropriately named; the surrounding foliage more than "creeps" onto the course. You can lose your ball on the fairway! It's a fun course between the trees. Call 718-296-0999.
- **La Tourette Golf Course**, at 1001 Richmond Hill Road in Staten Island, is a par 72 course that is wide open and walkable. Call 718-351-1889.
- **Pelham Split Rock Golf Course**, at 870 Shore Parkway in the Bronx, is actually home to two courses, each par 71. The "split" course is perhaps the city's most challenging. The 70-year-old facility is kept in good shape. Call 718-885-1258.
- **Van Cortlandt Park Golf Course**, at Van Cortlandt Park South in the Bronx, is a one-hundred-year-old course. It's the city's first public course and even saw Babe Ruth play in the 1920s. Call 718-543-4595.

Note: Flushing Meadow Park has a fun little par 3 pitch and putt course on the far northeast corner near College Point Boulevard.

Note: Chelsea Piers and Family Golf at the Port Authority bus terminal both have driving ranges.

Sports: For Spectators

If you want to see a game, there are plenty of pro teams to choose from. Tickets for most are not easy to get, so call in advance.

At Madison Square Garden you'll find NBA basketball with the New York Knicks, WNBA basketball with the New York Liberty, NHL hockey with the New York Rangers, and Arena football with the New York CityHawks, plus tennis tournament and boxing, among other sports. Call the box office at 212-465-6741. You can also check in with Ticketmaster at 212-307-7171.

You can also find NHL hockey and NBA basketball across the river at the Meadowlands in New Jersey. The Nets and Devils play there. Call 201-935-3900 for tickets. *Hint: Call in advance to find out when the Knicks are coming to town.* More NHL hockey can be

For Real Golf Lovers

The finest courses in the New York City area, open to the public, are in Farmingdale. The Bethpage State Park Golf Courses, 18 miles east of Manhattan (about 40 minutes) include the famed Black Course, which has been rated one of the best in the country by the leading golf magazines. The 7,000 plus yard, par 71 course has been home to tournaments since its opening some 65 years ago. It's a marvelous test of your abilities. There are three other excellent courses also available. Call 516-293-8899.

Not the Real Yankees, but a Cheap Imitation!

For some fun (plus low prices and small crowds), you can see a minor league baseball game with a class A team called the Staten Island Yankees. They play at the College of Staten Island. It's not the big league stuff, but it's a great novelty! Call 718-982 3589 for the box office.

found on Long Island at the Nassau Veterans Memorial Coliseum in Uniondale Long Island. Call 516-888-9000 for Ticketmaster tickets.

Baseball tickets are also available. For Yankee Stadium, call 718-293-6000 or 212-307-1212; for Shea Stadium and the Mets, call 718-507-8499.

If you want to see a football game, you'd better know someone with season tickets. Nonetheless, you can call the Giants Stadium at the Meadowlands in New Jersey (just 15 minutes from Manhattan). For the Giants, call 201-935-8222; for the Jets, call 201-935-3900. Good luck.

The NY/NJ Metro Stars professional soccer can also be seen at the Meadowlands. Call 201-583-7000.

The U.S. Open tennis tournament at the Arthur Ashe Tennis Center in Flushing Meadow Park in Queens takes place starting the week preceding Labor Day and runs for 2 weeks. Call 718-760-6200; tickets are scarce, so call way in advance.

If you like betting on the horses, there's Aqueduct Racetrack (718-641-4700) and Belmont Racetrack (718-641-4700), both in Queens. And there's offtrack betting (OTB) all over the city.

New York after Dark

It's the city that never sleeps, remember? Music is always playing in New York nightspots. Here are some of the many music clubs to hear it live while either dancing or having a drink to unwind:

Acme Underground
9 Great Jones Street (at Lafayette Street)
212-677-6963
Enjoy alternative rock with comparable drinks and decent sound. It's a bit of an off-the-beaten-path club.

Arlene Grocery
95 Stanton Street (between Ludlow and Orchard Streets)
212-358-1633
Money tight? No problem here: There's no cover charge and reasonable drink prices. Enjoy music every night in a tiny comfortable space.

Baby Jupiter
170 Orchard Street (at Stanton Street)
212-982-2229
There's a bar and restaurant on one side with a back room
for live music—and a small area for bands. Fun atmosphere!

Birdland
315 West 44th Street
212-581-3080
Some call it the nicest jazz room in New York—comfortable and
great talent.

Blue Note
131 West 3rd Street
212-475-8592
This is a popular tourist destination—host
to the biggest name jazz acts.

The Bottom Line
15 West 4th Street (at Mercer Street)
212-228-7880
This Village institution is the starting ground for top
acts including folk, pop, rock, and jazz.

Bowery Ballroom
6 Delancey Street (between Bowery and Chrystie Streets)
212-533-2111
Enjoy this large space with balconies, excellent sound, and popular bands. There's a separate bar in the basement that lets you
escape the crowd.

Brownies
169 Avenue A (between 10th and 11th Streets)
212-420-8392
The mix of local music and national acts in a small club with
good sound offers rock and alternative styles. It's a type of
industry hangout.

CBGB
315 Bowery (at Bleecker Street)
212-982-4052
CBGB is a legendary club that spawned the Talking Heads, Ramones, and others. Enjoy the good atmosphere and decent sound system.

Cleopatra's Needle
2485 Broadway at 92nd Street
212-769-6969
Here's an Upper West Side jaunt with some first-rate performers.

Continental
25 Third Avenue (at St. Mark's Place)
212-529-6924
Continental offers good space and a stage with a respectable sound system that targets mostly rock and punk bands and crowds from St. Mark's Place.

Don Hill's
511 Greenwich Street (at Spring Street)
212-334-1390
Enjoy mostly glitter bands with an excellent stage and good sound. It's a bit out of the way but worth checking out.

Downtime
251 West 30th Street (between Seventh and Eighth Avenues)
212-695-2747
Here's an intimate setting with a nice stage and sound. Dark room with tables provides a good place to see a performance and hang out afterward.

Fez
380 Lafayette Street (at Great Jones Street)
212-533-2680
Fez offers good food with a Moroccan/Mediterranean flavor and music in a small setting downstairs. It's also home to the Mingus Big Band.

Hammerstein Ballroom

311 West 34th Street (between Eighth and Ninth Avenues)
212-279-7740
Enjoy the large venue that caters to national acts.

Iridium Restaurant & Jazz Club

48 West 63rd Street
212-582-2121
This nice room near Lincoln Center showcases top jazz talent
beyond the play list.

Irving Plaza

17 Irving Plaza (at 15th Street)
212-777-6800
Showcasing major bands, this is one of the prime locations to
play in the city. It's smaller than Roseland but bigger than most
other venues and has a good sound system and stage.

Jazz Standard

116 East 27th Street (between Park Avenue South and
Lexington Avenue)
212-576-2232
Bebop on tap!

Kenny's Castaways

157 Bleecker Street (between Thompson and Sullivan Streets)
212-473-9870
It's full of the usual Bleecker Street characters: college students,
tourists, and bridge and tunnel people. This place has average
bands and cheap beer.

Knickerbocker

33 University Place
212-228-8490
Enjoy this intimate jazz-flavored room that hosts some surprising
talents.

Just Good Tennis

If you simply want to see some good tennis, stop by a week before the U.S. Open begins and watch as the last group of hopefuls play for the qualifying spots. You won't see Sampras or Agassi, but you'll see some great up and comers playing top-notch tennis for free.

Knitting Factory
74 Leonard Street (between Broadway and Church Street)
212-219-3055
Enjoy eclectic music in this venerable institution; it's a New York musical sanctuary and offers multiple stages with a variety of bands.

Lenox Lounge
288 Lenox Avenue
212-427-0253
The Lenox Lounge pays homage to Harlem as the center of jazz.

Lion's Den
214 Sullivan Street (between Bleecker and West 3rd Streets)
212-477-2782
In the heart of Greenwich Village, this medium-sized club provides a good atmosphere to catch a show. The musical styles vary.

Luna Lounge
171 Ludlow Street (between Houston and Stanton Streets)
212-260-2323
Enjoy the bar with music in a dark back room in the middle of Ludlow Street. It also has "alternative comedy" nights.

Mercury Lounge
217 Houston Street (at Essex Street)
212-260-4700
This medium-sized club has a separate bar area and one of the best sound systems in the city. It gets some popular acts, and the location in the East Village couldn't be better.

Metronome Jazz Lounge
Broadway and 21st Street
212-505-7400
This club is polished and a little more expensive; it draws the "professional" crowd for good jazz.

9C

700 East 9th Street (at Avenue C)

212-358-0048

9C offers a small venue with different types of music each night. Check out the Monday honky-tonk night while knocking back a few Dixie beers.

Roseland

239 West 52nd Street (between Eighth Avenue and Broadway)

212-249-8870

A huge old place, Roseland attracts acts that aren't quite big enough for Madison Square Garden but can draw big numbers.

Savoy

355 West 41st Street

212-947-5255

Savoy's well known for its late-night jazz sessions.

Sidewalk

94 Avenue A (at 6th Street)

212-473-7373

Here's a bar that serves food—with some tables outside and music inside. There's no cover charge.

Smalls

183 West 10th Street

212-929-7565

This unique spot serves as a training ground for young jazz talent. And these guys can blow!

S.O.B.'s

204 Varick Street (corner of West Houston)

212-242-1785

S.O.B.'s is the city's number one spot for Latin jazz.

Spiral Lounge

244 Houston Street (at Avenue A)

212-353-1740

Enjoy varied musical acts in small, grungy and dark room—like all rock clubs should be.

Chaos on Stage

The self-billed purveyors of Chaos, The Upright Citizens Brigade (UCB) who thrive on being outrageous and edgy in their sketches and improvisational shows, have found a home on 161 West 22nd Street, where they have opened their own theater for seven nights of performances (not for the kids). Shows are $5 or less. For more information call 212-366-9176.

Swing 46

349 West 46th Street (between Eighth and Ninth Avenues)

212-262-9554

Bring your dancing shoes to this club. Enjoy swing and big band music every night.

Tonic

107 Norfolk Street

212-358-7503

This home to a new jazz sound is in the heart of a hot part of town and offers musicians who take risks.

Village Vanguard

178 Seventh Avenue South

212-255-7037

Village Vanguard, a venerable jazz club, still echoes with sounds of Coltrane, Monk, Miles, and the other legends of jazz history.

Webster Hall

125 East 11th Street (between Third and Fourth Avenues)

212-353-1600

Webster Hall is primarily a dance club that has a separate bar with music upstairs. The whole place is a spectacle. It's worth checking out at least once. But be prepared to wait in line and pay a hefty cover.

Wetlands Preserve

161 Hudson Street (at Laight Street)

212-966-4225

Wetlands Preserve specializes in jam bands, funk, and R&B, with a nice stage and large, open bar area.

Zinc Bar

90 West Houston Street

212-477-8337

The Zinc Bar is a great downtown spot for live jazz, Latin, and Brazilian music. It's a musicians' hangout.

While you can dance at some of the clubs listed above, here are a few other dance clubs with DJs playing music all night long—or most of it:

The China Club
268 West 47th Street
212-398-3800
This massive high-tech dance club is very popular, very trendy, and crowded.

Cream
246 Columbus Avenue (between 71st and 72nd Streets)
212-712-1666
Cream is a large, trendy five-room dance club on the Upper West Side.

Decade
1117 First Avenue (at 61st Street)
212-835-5979
This Upper East club features the sounds of '59 through '79, with Disco Tuesdays and lots of cigars.

Life
158 Bleecker Street
212-420-1999
Life is a popular Village nightclub.
And here are a few of the city's comedy clubs:

Caroline's Comedy Club
1626 Broadway (between 49th and 50th Streets)
212-757-4100
This first-rate club features headliner and stand-up comics including Rich Jeni, Margaret Cho, and other frequent late-night TV guests. It's a top comedy room. Call for reservations on weekends.

Nightlife Tips

If you're not familiar with the city, you may not be comfortable exploring after dark. It is important that you know where you are going and how to get back to your hotel at a late hour. Busses and trains run 24 hours a day, although you have longer waits after 11 P.M. You can get a taxi in New York City at all hours, but this does not mean in all areas. It's advantageous to have your cellular phone and a phone number for a car service if you are going to be out past midnight. It's not advisable to ride subways late at night unless you are with at least one other person. Remember, if a neighborhood makes you feel uncomfortable at 8 P.M., it's going to make you more uncomfortable at 1 A.M. Exercise common sense and good judgment.

Comedy Club Etiquette

In the comedy rooms of the '90s, acts work long and hard to hone their material; heckling is not advised unless the comic invites it. If you don't want to be talked to by the MC, then don't sit in the front. Along with the cover charge, there is often a two-drink minimum, and food, which is pricey, doesn't fulfill a drink requirement. If you visit the restrooms, head in or out between acts or while the MC is on, particularly if you're sitting near the stage.

The Comic Strip

1568 Broadway
212-861-9386
This longtime club and starting ground for Eddie Murphy and others features a solid array of hot new comics, some seen on Letterman and Conan. Weeknights feature numerous performers. Call for reservations on weekends.

Gotham Comedy Club

34 West 22nd Street (Between Fifth and Sixth Avenues)
212-367-9000
The Gotham Comedy Club is one of the newer rising clubs, with good up-and-coming comics and a monthly Wednesday night Baby Boomer Humor (political comedy) Show. Call for reservations on weekends.

Pips

2005 Emmons Avenue
718-646-9433
Pips is a longtime Brooklyn comedy club in Sheepshead Bay, where people such as David Brenner and many others started out. Call for reservations on weekends.

Stand Up New York

236 West 78th Street (just off Broadway)
212-595-0850
This attractive Upper West Side club has nightly shows featuring working comics, plus amateur "occupation" contests, such as Funniest Accountant, Funniest Lawyer, and other such gimmicks.

Index

A

airlines, 26 27
airports
    JFK International
        Airport, 27 28
    LaGuardia Airport, 29
    Newark International
        Airport, 30
attractions, 110 37. *See also*
    family fun; museums;
    sights; zoos
avenues, 70 71
    maps of, 103 7

B

Barnes & Noble, 111, 247
baseball, 7, 9, 12, 13
    Yankee Stadium, 219 20,
        258
beaches, 204, 228, 247
Big Apple Greeters, 80, 199
boroughs, 71, 201 24. *See
    also* Bronx; Brooklyn;
    Long Island; Queens;
    Staten Island
    maps, 103 7
    parking in, 203
    reaching, 71
    transportation, 203
    traveling through, 202 3
bridges
    Alexander Hamilton
        Bridge, 24
    Brooklyn Bridge, 26, 110
    George Washington
        Bridge, 13, 24
    Henry Hudson
        Bridge, 25
    Macombs Dam
        Bridge, 25

Madison Avenue
    Bridge, 25
Manhattan Bridge, 26
maps of, 103 7
Queensboro Bridge, 25
Third Avenue Bridge, 25
Throggs Neck Bridge, 13
Triborough Bridge,
    25, 255
Verrazano-Narrows
    Bridge, 13
Williamsburg Bridge, 26
Willis Avenue Bridge, 25
Broadway, 16, 19, 237 38
    hotels, 239
    shows, 237 39
    soundtracks, 241
    theaters, 240 42
    tickets, 238, 239
Bronx, 214 15
    Bronx River Art Center
        and Gallery, 218
    Bronx Zoo, 216 18
    City Island, 218 19
    International Wildlife
        Conservation Center,
        216 18
    New York Botanical
        Garden, 215 16
    Van Cortlandt Park, 215
    Yankee Stadium,
        219 20, 258
Brooklyn, 203 4
    Brooklyn Botanic
        Gardens, 208 9
    Brooklyn Children s
        Museum, 203
    Brooklyn Museum of
        Art, 210
    Brooklyn s History
        Museum, 204

Coney Island, 204,
    206 7
Manhattan Beach, 204
New York Aquarium,
    205 6
New York City Transit
    Museum, 204 5
Prospect Park, 204, 207
Prospect Park Wildlife
    Center, 205
Brooklyn Dodgers, 12, 13
buildings
    Barnes & Noble, 111, 247
    Chrysler Building, 127
    Citicorp Building, 111
    Empire State Building, 9,
        10, 15, 114, 115 16
    Flatiron Building, 127
    Forbes Building, 192
    GE Building, 124, 125
    Rockefeller Center, 9 10,
        123 25, 126, 252
    Times Square Studio, 196
    UNICEF House, 133
    United Nations, 11,
        130 32
    World Financial Center,
        132 33
    World Trade Center, 15,
        35, 112, 134 35

C

calendar of events, 232 35
car rental, 28, 72 74,
    76 78. *See also*
    transportation
Carnegie Hall, 6, 112 13
Central Park, 35,
    166 67, 181
    activities, 166 74
    The Arsenal, 172 73

Belvedere Castle, 174
Bethesda Terrace, 173
The Boathouse CafØ, 178
carousel, 170 71
Central Park Zoo,
    167 68
Conservatory Garden,
    169, 176, 177
The Dairy, 173
Dana Discovery
    Center, 171
Delacorte Theater, 174
eateries, 178
family fun, 166 74
Great Lawn, 169, 175
hansom cabs, 172
Harlem Meer, 173 74
Loeb Boathouse and
    Lake, 171
The Mall, 169
maps, 181
movies filmed in, 167
music, 178
playgrounds, 170
plays, 174
The Pond, 169
The Ramble, 175
Reservoir, 174 75
Shakespeare Garden, 176
Sheep Meadow, 169, 175
sights, 169, 172 75
Strawberry Fields,
    169, 176
Swedish Cottage
    Marionette
    Theater, 171
Tavern on the Green,
    169, 177 78
tennis, 171 72
Tisch Children s
    Zoo, 168
Wildlife Center, 167 68

Wollman Memorial Rink, 168 70
Central Park map, 181
Chinatown, 151, 187 88, 189
    restaurants, 187 88
    shops, 187
churches
    Cathedral of St. John
        the Divine, 127
    Elderage Street
        Synagogue, 186
    Saint Patrick s
        Cathedral, 126
    Temple Emanu-El, 126
    Trinity Church, 113
City Island, 218 19
City Pass, 112
clubs
    comedy, 265 66
    dance, 265 66
    music, 258 64
    nightlife tips, 265
Columbus Circle, 122
comedy clubs, 265 66
Coney Island, 204, 206 7

D

dance clubs, 265 66
dining, 87 102. *See also*
    clubs; restaurants
directions, asking, 85
disabled persons, 80 81
    Access Project, 80
    hotlines, 81
drinking establishments, 87,
    186. *See also* clubs;
    restaurants

E

East Side, Lower, 185 87
Ellis Island, 6, 35, 113 14
Empire State Building, 9,
    10, 15, 114, 115 16
events, calendar of, 232 35

F

family fun, 246 58. *See also*
    museums; parks; zoos
Film Society of Lincoln
    Center, 117, 119
finding restaurants, 88 90
Fire Island, 225
Fire Island National
    Seashore, 228
fitting in, 37
food. *See also* restaurants
    burgers, 101
    ethnic, 95
    pizza, 102
    sandwiches, 99
    seafood, 93
    soups, 97
Forbes Building, 192
Forbes Magazine Galleries,
    192, 249

G

gardens. *See also* Central
    Park
    Brooklyn Botanic
        Gardens, 208 9
    Celebrity Path, 208, 209
    Children s Garden, 208
    Conservatory Garden,
        176, 177
    Cranford Rose
        Garden, 208
    C.V. Bonsai
        Museum, 208
    Fragrance Garden,
        208, 209
    Hunan Garden, 187
    Japanese Garden,
        208, 209
    New York Botanical
        Garden, 215 16
    Old Westbury Gardens,
        227 28
    Osbourne Garden,
        208, 209
    sculpture gardens, 213

Shakespeare Garden,
    176, 208, 209
Staten Island Botanical
    Garden, 223
Steinhardt Conservatory,
    208, 209
Strawberry Fields,
    176 77
Winter Garden, 133
getting around, 70 72. *See
    also* transportation
Giants Stadium, 258
golf, 255, 256 57
Good Morning, America,
    196, 245
Greenwich Village, 189 93
    concerts, 192
    cultural diversity, 190 91
    East Village, 191
    maps, 103 7
    restaurants, 193
    shops, 191
    theaters, 192
    Washington Square Park,
        191

H

Hamptons, 225
Hanks, Tom, 115, 116
hansom cabs, 172
Harlem, 197 99
    Cotton Club, 198, 199
    museums, 199
    music, 199
    theaters, 199
history of New York City,
    1 19
hospitals, 83
hotels, 34 38, 39 67
    amenities, 34, 36, 37, 38
    booking rooms, 55
    complimentary
        breakfast, 45
    downtown, 59 63
    free parking, 48
    kid-friendly, 51, 67

list of hotels, 39 67
location, 34 36
Midtown (east side),
    39 47
Midtown (west side),
    48 58
pet-friendly, 47
rates, 37 38
reservations, 38, 55
swimming pools, 49, 50
uptown, 64 67
Hudson, Henry, 2 3
Hudson River, 3, 24

I

ice skating, 124, 168 70,
    255 56
information
    United Nations, 132
    visitors, 73, 114, 220
International Center of
    Photography, 127
itinerary, 110

J

Jacob K. Javits Convention
    Center, 237
Japan Society, 127
Jazz at Lincoln Center,
    117, 118
JFK International Airport,
    27 28
JVC Jazz Festival, 117

K

kid-friendly activities,
    246 53. *See also*
    family fun
kid-friendly hotels, 51, 67.
    See also hotels

L

LaGuardia Airport, 10, 29
Lennon, John, 16, 176

Letterman, David, 12, 124
limousines, 73 74
Lincoln Center, 13, 19, 113,
    117 19
Little Italy, 187, 188 89
    restaurants, 189
    shops, 188
Long Island, 201 3, 224 25
    Fire Island, 225
    Fire Island National
        Seashore, 228
    Nassau County Museum
        of Art, 227
    Nassau Veterans
        Memorial
        Coliseum, 226
    Old Bethpage Village
        Restoration, 226
    Old Westbury Gardens,
        227 28
    parking, 225
    reaching, 224
    Sands Point Preserve,
        228 29
    Shelter Island, 225
    shops, 225
    traveling through, 224 25
    Westbury Music Fair, 225
    wineries, 227
Lower East Side, 185 87
Lower East Side Tenement
    Museum, 186
luggage
    lost, 30
    packing, 32 33

M

Macy s Thanksgiving Day
    Parade, 235, 250
Madison Square Garden,
    235 37, 257
Manhattan, 184 85, 202
    42nd Street, 193, 194 97
    Chinatown, 187 88, 189
    Greenwich Village,
        189 93

Harlem, 197 99
Little Italy, 187, 188 89
Lower East Side, 185 87
maps, 103 7
neighborhoods of,
    183 99
reaching, 24 26
Times Square, 193 97
maps, 103 7
    Central Park, 103 7, 181
    Greater New York
        City, 103
    Greenwich Village and
        Lower Manhattan, 107
    Manhattan: 96th to 14th
        Street, 105
mass transit, 74. *See also*
    transportation
    MetroCard, 80
mayors
    Beame, Abraham, 15
    Dinkins, David, 17
    Gaynor, William Jay, 5
    Giuliani, Rudolph, 8, 10,
        17, 18, 19
    Hylan, John, 6
    Impellitteri, Vincent
        Richard, 12
    Koch, Edward, 3, 16
    LaGuardia, Fiorello, 9,
        10, 11, 17
    Lindsay, John, 14
    Low, Seth, 3
    McClellan, George, 4, 7
    Mitchel, John, 6
    O Brien, John P., 8
    O Dwyer, William, 11
    Van Wyck, Robert, 2
    Wagner, Robert, 12
    Walker, James Jimmy ,
        7, 9, 10
Metropolitan Opera House,
    117, 118, 119
Midtown (east side), 39 47
Midtown (west side),
    48 58
Minuit, Peter, 3

monuments
    Ellis Island National
        Monument, 6, 35,
        113 14
    Grant s Tomb, 127
    Statue of Columbus, 122
    Statue of Liberty, 35, 114,
        129 30, 132
    Vietnam Veterans
        Memorial, 127
Moses, Robert, 11
museums, 140 64
    Abigail Adams Smith
        House Museum,
        142 43
    admissions, 141
    Alice Austen House
        Museum, 223
    American Craft
        Museum, 143
    American Museum of
        Natural History,
        143 45
    American Museum of
        the Moving Image,
        212 13
    American Numismatic
        Society, 161
    The Americas
        Society, 161
    Bronx River Art Center
        and Gallery, 218
    Brooklyn Children s
        Museum, 203, 248
    Brooklyn History
        Museum, 204
    Brooklyn Museum of
        Art, 210
    Children s Museum of
        Arts, 161
    Children s Museum
        of Manhattan,
        145 46, 248
    The Cloisters Museum,
        146 47

Cooper-Hewitt National
    Design Museum,
    147 48
The Dahesh
    Museum, 161
The Dykman Farmhouse
    Museum, 161
El Museo Del Barrio, 161
The Frick Collection,
    148 49
The Guggenheim
    Museum, 149 50
The Guggenheim SoHo
    Branch, 150
Intrepid Sea-Air-Space
    Museum, 150 51, 249
Jewish Museum, 152 53
Lower East Side
    Tenement Museum,
    153, 186
Mercantile Museum, 133
Metropolitan Museum of
    Art, 154 56
The Morris-Jumel
    Mansion Museum, 161
Museum of American
    Financial History, 161
Museum of American
    Folk Art, 155
Museum of Chinese in
    the Americas, 151, 187
Museum of Jewish
    Heritage, 161
Museum of Modern Art,
    9, 156 58
Museum of Natural
    History, 141
Museum of Television
    and Radio, 158 60
Museum of the
    American Piano, 161
Museum of the City of
    New York, 153, 159
Museum Row, 140 41
Nassau County Museum
    of Art, 227

The National Museum
of the American
Indian, 161
New Century Artists
Gallery, 149
New Museum of
Contemporary
Art, 147
New York City Fire
Museum, 160, 162, 251
New York City Transit
Museum, 204 5
New York Hall of
Science, 213, 251
New-York Historical
Society, 162 63
Old Bethpage Village
Restoration, 226
Old Merchant s House
Museum, 161
The Police Academy
Museum, 161
Queens Museum of
Art, 214
Rose Museum, 113
Staten Island Children s
Museum, 223
The Studio Museum in
Harlem, 163
Whitney Museum of
American Art, 163 64
music clubs, 258 64

N

New York City Ballet, 117
New York City history, 1 19
New York City maps, 103 7
New York City Marathon,
202, 221
New York City Municipal
Airport, 10
New York City Opera, 117
New York Evening Post, 6
New York Giants, 13
New York Hospital, 4
New York Jets, 14

New York Mets, 13
New York Philharmonic,
117 18
New York Public Library, 7,
119 20
New York Public Library for
the Performing Arts, 117
New York Stock Exchange,
121 22
New York Times, 6, 7, 195
New York Tribune, 6
New York Yankees, 9, 11,
13, 16. *See also* Yankee
Stadium
Newark International
Airport, 30
newspapers, 82

O

off-Broadway theaters,
242 44
Ono, Yoko, 176

P

packing for trip, 32 33
parades, 233, 235, 250
parking, 23, 34, 48, 203, 225
parking tax, 88
parks. *See also* Central
Park
Barrett Park, 224
Battery Park, 178
Borough Park, 204
Bowling Green, 128
Bryant Park, 197
Carl Schurz Park, 179
Central Park, 166 81
Flushing Meadow
Park, 211
Fort Tyron Park, 179
Fort Wadsworth, 222
Paley Park, 125
Prospect Park, 207
Riverside Park, 178
Snug Harbor Park,
222 23

Union Square Park, 180
Van Cortlandt Park, 215
Washington Square Park,
180, 191
Willowbrook Park, 222
Penn Station, 7, 31
performing arts halls. *See
also* theaters
Carnegie Hall, 6, 112 13
Lincoln Center, 13, 19,
113, 117 19
Radio City Music Hall,
19, 122 23
pet-friendly hotels, 47

Q

Queens, 211 12
American Museum of
the Moving Image,
212 13
Flushing Meadow Park,
211, 212
New York Hall of
Science, 213
Queens Museum of Art,
214
Queens Wildlife Center,
212
Shea Stadium, 14, 210,
215, 252, 258

R

Radio City Music Hall, 19,
122 23
radio stations, 23, 89
reservations
plane, 26
restaurant, 90
restaurants. *See also*
restaurants, list of
burgers, 101
costs, 90
dress codes, 90
ethnic, 95
finding, 88 90
pizza, 102

sandwiches, 99
soups, 97
restaurants, list of, 90 102
Bronx, 101
Brooklyn, 100 101
Downtown, 92 93
Lower Manhattan, 91 92
Midtown, 94 97
Queens, 101 2
Staten Island, 102
Upper East Side, 97 98
Uptown, 100
West Side, 99 100
Rockefeller Center, 9 10,
22, 123 25, 126, 252
roller-skating, 168 70, 256

S

safety tips, 43, 63, 72. *See
also* tips
airports, 33
fitting in, 37
money, 41
nightlife, 265
parking, 34
taxi, 31
walking, 37, 76
Saint Patrick s
Cathedral, 126
sales tax, 88
Schomburg Center, 136
Seinfeld, 97, 124, 212
Shea Stadium, 14, 210, 215,
252, 258
shopping, 135 37
Barney s New York, 135
Bloomingdale s, 135
Disney, 116
F.A.O. Schwarz, 116 17
Fortunoff, 121
Henri Bendel, 137
Macy s Herald
Square, 136
NBA Store, 116
Saks Fifth Avenue,
35, 136

Takashimaya, 137
Tiffany & Company, 35, 137
Warner Brothers Studio Store, 116
sights, 110 37. *See also* buildings; gardens; monuments; museums
admissions, 110 11
City Pass, 112
hours, 110
preparing for, 110 11
special, 127
Snug Harbor Cultural Center, 222 24
South Street Seaport, 35, 126 29
sports, 254 58
all ages, 254 57
Chelsea Piers, 254
golf courses, 255, 256 57
spectator, 257 58
stadiums, 257 58
tennis courts, 171 72, 215, 256, 261
Staten Island, 220 21
Alice Austen House Museum, 223
Barrett Park, 224
Botanical Garden, 223
Children s Museum, 223
Fort Wadsworth, 222
Historic Richmond Town, 221 22
information center, 220
Snug Harbor Cultural Center, 222 23, 253
Staten Island Ferry, 24, 115, 220, 253
Staten Island Zoo, 224, 253
Willowbrook Park, 222
Statue of Liberty, 35, 114, 129 30, 132
street vendors, 86
streets, 70 72

maps of, 103 7
Stuyvesant, Peter, 3 4
subway, 7, 19, 75, 77, 78. *See also* transportation
Sullivan, Ed, 12, 14

T

taxes, 88
taxis, 28, 30, 31, 40, 76 78
fares, 78
telephone calls, 76
television
NBC studios tour, 124
stations, 90
taped shows, 244 45
temperatures, 22
tennis, 171 72, 215, 256, 261
theaters, 6, 110, 237 38. *See also* performing arts halls
Apollo Theater, 111 12
Broadway theaters, 240 42
Cherry Lane Theater, 192
off-Broadway theaters, 242 44
Radio City Music Hall, 19, 122 23
Swedish Cottage Marionette Theater, 171
Times Square, 7, 19, 22, 34 35, 193 97
Bryant Park, 197
One Times Square Plaza, 195 96
restaurants, 195, 197
shops, 197
theaters, 196
visiting, 195 97
tipping, 28, 29, 39
tips. *See also* safety tips
asking directions, 85
City Pass, 112
clothing, 32 33, 110
nightlife, 265

packing, 32 33
phone calls, 76
subway, 78
taxis, 31, 77 78
travel, 33, 56
walking, 37, 76, 110
Today Show, 124, 245
tolls, 23, 24, 25, 28, 29, 30
tours, 81 87
boat, 83 85
bus, 82 83
helicopter, 85
NBC studios, 124
other, 86 87
questions to ask, 81 82
walking, 85 86
trade shows, 237
transportation, 23 32
air, 26 30
Amtrak, 31
bicycling, 81, 255
bus, 28, 30 31
car, 23, 24, 64
car rental, 28, 72 73, 76 78
and disabilities, 80 81
getting around, 70 72
ground, 23 26, 28, 29, 30
hansom cabs, 172
limousines, 73 74
mass transit, 74
Penn Station, 7, 31
Port Authority Bus Terminal, 30 31
Port Authority Ground Transportation, 27
subway, 7, 19, 75, 77, 78
taxi, 28, 30, 31, 40, 76 78
tips, 78
train, 31 32
walking, 37, 76, 85 86, 110
travel agents, 32, 35
travel tips, 33, 56. *See also* safety tips
tunnels

Brooklyn Battery Tunnel, 26
Holland Tunnel, 24
Lincoln Tunnel, 24
Queens Midtown Tunnel, 25

U

United Nations, 11, 130 32

V

visiting, best time, 22 23
visitor information, 73, 114, 220

W

walking, 37, 76, 85 86, 110
Wall Street, 7, 9, 121
weather, 22
Wollman Memorial Rink, 168
World s Fair, 11, 14

Y

Yankee Stadium, 219 20, 258

Z

zoos
Bronx Zoo, 216 18
Central Park Zoo, 167 68
International Wildlife Conservation Center, 216 18
Prospect Park Wildlife Center, 205
Queens Wildlife Center, 212
Staten Island Zoo, 224, 253
Tisch Children s Zoo, 168

We Have

EVERYTHING!

Available wherever books are sold!

Everything® **After College Book**
$12.95, 1-55850-847-3

Everything® **Astrology Book**
$12.95, 1-58062-062-0

Everything® **Baby Names Book**
$12.95, 1-55850-655-1

Everything® **Baby Shower Book**
$12.95, 1-58062-305-0

Everything® **Barbeque Cookbook**
$12.95, 1-58062-316-6

Everything® **Bartender's Book**
$9.95, 1-55850-536-9

Everything® **Bedtime Story Book**
$12.95, 1-58062-147-3

Everything® **Beer Book**
$12.95, 1-55850-843-0

Everything® **Bicycle Book**
$12.95, 1-55850-706-X

Everything® **Build Your Own Home Page**
$12.95, 1-58062-339-5

Everything® **Casino Gambling Book**
$12.95, 1-55850-762-0

Everything® **Cat Book**
$12.95, 1-55850-710-8

Everything® **Christmas Book**
$15.00, 1-55850-697-7

Everything® **College Survival Book**
$12.95, 1-55850-720-5

Everything® **Cover Letter Book**
$12.95, 1-58062-312-3

Everything® **Crossword and Puzzle B**
$12.95, 1-55850-764-7

Everything® **Dating Book**
$12.95, 1-58062-185-6

Everything® **Dessert Book**
$12.95, 1-55850-717-5

Everything® **Dog Book**
$12.95, 1-58062-144-9

Everything® **Dreams Book**
$12.95, 1-55850-806-6

Everything® **Etiquette Book**
$12.95, 1-55850-807-4

Everything® **Family Tree Book**
$12.95, 1-55850-763-9

Everything® **Fly-Fishing Book**
$12.95, 1-58062-148-1

Everything® **Games Book**
$12.95, 1-55850-643-8

Everything® **Get-a-Job Book**
$12.95, 1-58062-223-2

The ultimate reference for couples planning their wedding!

- Scheduling, budgeting, etiquette, hiring caterers, florists, and photographers
- Ceremony & reception ideas
- Over 100 forms and checklists
- And much, much more!

$12.95, 384 pages, 8" x 9¼"

Personal finance made easy—and fun!

- Create a budget you can live with
- Manage your credit cards
- Set up investment plans
- Money-saving tax strategies
- And much, much more!

$12.95, 288 pages, 8" x 9¼"

For more information, or to order, call 800-872-5627
or visit www.adamsmedia.com/everything
Adams Media Corporation, 260 Center Street, Holbrook, MA 02343